Victorian Fictions of
Middle-Class Status

Edinburgh Critical Studies in Victorian Culture

Recent books in the series:

Home and Identity in Nineteenth-Century Literary London
Lisa C. Robertson

Writing the Sphinx: Literature, Culture and Egyptology
Eleanor Dobson

Oscar Wilde and the Radical Politics of the Fin de Siècle
Deaglán Ó Donghaile

The Sculptural Body in Victorian Literature: Encrypted Sexualities
Patricia Pulham

New Media and the Rise of the Popular Woman Writer, 1832–1860
Alexis Easley

Elizabeth Robins Pennell: Critical Essays
Dave Buchanan and Kimberly Morse-Jones

Plotting the News in the Victorian Novel
Jessica Valdez

Reading Bodies in Victorian Fiction: Associationism, Empathy and Literary Authority
Peter Katz

The Alternative Modernity of the Bicycle in British and French Literature, 1880 – 1920
Una Brogan

The Gothic Forms of Victorian Poetry
Olivia Loksing Moy

Victorian Fictions of Middle-Class Status: Forms of Absence in the Age of Reform
Albert D. Pionke

For a complete list of titles published visit the Edinburgh Critical Studies in Victorian Culture web page at www.edinburghuniversitypress.com/series/ECVC

Also available:
Victoriographies – A Journal of Nineteenth-Century Writing, 1790–1914, edited by Diane Piccitto and Patricia Pulham
ISSN: 2044-2416
www.eupjournals.com/vic

Victorian Fictions of Middle-Class Status

Forms of Absence in the Age of Reform

Albert D. Pionke

EDINBURGH
University Press

Edinburgh University Press is one of the leading university presses in the UK. We publish academic books and journals in our selected subject areas across the humanities and social sciences, combining cutting-edge scholarship with high editorial and production values to produce academic works of lasting importance. For more information visit our website: edinburghuniversitypress.com

© Albert Pionke 2023, 2024

Edinburgh University Press Ltd
The Tun – Holyrood Road
12(2f) Jackson's Entry
Edinburgh EH8 8PJ

First published in hardback by Edinburgh University Press 2023

Typeset in 11/13 Adobe Sabon
by Manila Typesetting Company

A CIP record for this book is available from the British Library

ISBN 978 1 3995 0770 7 (hardback)
ISBN 978 1 3995 0771 4 (paperback)
ISBN 978 1 3995 0772 1 (webready PDF)
ISBN 978 1 3995 0773 8 (epub)

The right of Albert Pionke to be identified as the author of this work has been asserted in accordance with the Copyright, Designs and Patents Act 1988, and the Copyright and Related Rights Regulations 2003 (SI No. 2498).

Contents

Acknowledgements		vi
Introduction: Victorian Middle-Class Status and the Negative Assertion of Value		1
1.	The Orphan Narratives of a Class Lacking Antecedents	26
2.	Repudiations of Wealth in Victorian Financial Fiction	61
3.	The Violence at the Heart of the Social Problem Novel	99
4.	Social Domination, Social Scientific Empiricism, and Novelistic Distrust of the Modern Fact	136
5.	Legitimizing the Subjection of Middle-Class Women in Mid-Victorian Fiction	173
Afterword		209
Bibliography		214
Index		230

Acknowledgements

I am grateful for all those who, knowingly or not, helped me to understand the interanimating complexity of Victorian literature and middle-class status. Among those who did so self-consciously were the presenters at the 2015 University of Alabama English Department Symposium on The Literature of Status/The Status of Literature, including Maria K. Bachman, Samantha S. Caddis, Amy Chen, Cameron Dodworth, Frank Emmett, Michelle Golden, Shelby Heathcote, Amy Elizabeth Holley, Megan Holt, Russ McConnell, Claudie Massicotte, Deirdre Mikolajcik, Adam Parkes, Anne Reef, Matt Seybold, Susie Warley, Eloise A. Whisenhunt, Robert White, and Jen Zellner. At this same event, Marshall Brown was an incisive and generous keynote speaker, representative of the editors of learned journals, and indefatigable mentor to the students and junior scholars in attendance.

Some years later, co-editing *The Socio-Literary Imaginary in 19th and 20th Century Britain: Victorian and Edwardian Inflections* with Maria K. Bachman pushed me to refine my sociological method and consider further objects for its application in response to contributions from Carol Davison, Audrey Jaffe, Deborah Logan, Adam Parkes, Kristen H. Starkowski, Rachel Stern, Scott C. Thompson, and Rosetta Young.

Additionally, the students in both my spring 2015 undergraduate honors seminar on literature and status (Kelly Bullard, Amy Carlson, Anna Davis-Abel, Alyx Eva, Hannah Fulmer, Halley Lamkin, Sarah Potts, Jared Powell, Carissa Schreiber, Laura Tolbert, and Emily Warwick) and my fall 2019 graduate seminar on Victorian fictions of (il)legitimacy (Saul Alpert-Adams, Aubree Bailey, Charlie Bell, Lily Davenport, Cheryl Garrett, Vic Kjoss, Micky Mitchell, and Abbey Perschall) asked perceptive questions and offered intelligent arguments that helped me to formulate my own.

I also received advice, encouragement, text suggestions, and timely feedback on the manuscript of this book from Steve Arata,

Marshall Brown, Pamela K. Gilbert, John Plotz, David Latané, Steve Tedeschi, William Ulmer, Tamara S. Wagner, Heather White, and Fred Whiting. My editor, Michelle Houston, and the entire editorial team at Edinburgh University Press remained enthusiastic and supportive despite a global pandemic, to which my external reviewers remained similarly immune. Any errors that remain are, of course, my own, but there are fewer because of their collective interventions.

Portions of this book have appeared, in somewhat different forms, in *Dickens Studies Annual*, *Philosophy and Literature*, and *Studies in the Novel*. I am thankful to the editors and publishers for their permission to reprint.

Introduction: Victorian Middle-Class Status and the Negative Assertion of Value

Victorian England experienced a crisis over social stratification that might once have been dismissed as mere semantics, but that the affordances of more recent criticism now allow us to recognize as a collision of form.[1] Two overlapping explanations for collective inequality – the first a time-honored subdivision of society into numerous historically if not divinely ordained stations, each dependent upon those above it and responsible to those below, with the borders between them recorded in sumptuary law; and the second a much simpler and more confrontational separation between the privileged and the people intensified by industrialization, post-war economic depression, and Regency-era repressive legislation – were being challenged by a newer model made up of three primary strata.[2] The most problematic element of this recent schema was its intermediate layer, whose overwhelmingly urban members had been increasing rapidly in numbers, wealth, and desire for influence since the 1780s.

Even what to call these social in-betweeners was a matter of some debate, quite literally so during the 1831 session of Parliament. For instance, future historian Thomas Babington Macaulay, speaking in favor of what we now know as the First Reform Bill in his capacity as MP for the doomed pocket borough of Calne, peppered what was certainly one of the most powerful speeches of the session, on 2 March 1831, with three different referents for the same constituency: middle "class"; "middle classes"; and "middle order."[3] Speaking two days later, Francis Jeffrey advocated in favor of enfranchising "the great number of persons of wealth, respectability, intelligence, and loyalty, belonging to the middle ranks"[4]; and three days after that Lord Dudley Stuart fulsomely praised "the middling classes; the most virtuous, and generally the most influential, in all countries; and particularly the pride and flower of England."[5] Opponents of reform were similarly uncertain of how to label those whom they wished to remain without a vote, with Sir Robert Peel referring repeatedly to "the middle classes" on 3 March 1831; Colonel Edward Michael Conolly on 24 August 1831 lamenting a foreseeable decline in "the middle orders" as a result of the bill; and the Duke of Wellington, on 10 April 1832, judging the incipient act as "opposed to the sentiments of all the gentlemen, of the yeomanry, and of the middling classes throughout the country."[6] In fact, the language used by the members of both Houses remained in flux throughout the debate and occasionally within individual speeches, thereby calling attention to the formal uncertainty that accompanied the legal recognition of society's newest enfranchised constituency.

Reform-era MPs' terminological confusion had been fifty years in the making: since the 1780s, the formal vocabulary used to describe the nation's unequal distribution of social, economic, and cultural capital also had changed, from a rhetoric of "ranks," "orders," "degrees," and "estates," each with its own "interest," to a language of "classes" defined by their relationships to systems of production.[7] For most of the eighteenth century, those occupying the social middle had been referred to as "middling people" or "middling sorts," with the "most successful of them," according to Asa Briggs, "easily absorbed into the 'gentry,' that most English of social groupings."[8] In the last quarter of the century, however, a preference for a "middling" or "middle" "class" or "classes" began to emerge, with the new label intended to convey "a space, a 'between' . . . a grouping that fails, or refuses, to fit the dominant social division between upper and lower, rich and poor, land and labour."[9] The fact that this new set of terms was also "politically and morally loaded" only added to the potential confusion.[10]

Since members of this misfit social middle were active participants in the myriad debates over their own proper place in the nation, this taxonomic predicament represented, for them at least, an urgent epistemological if not existential dilemma. Were they one class or many? How did they differ from other classes? What limits bound them, both above and below? Could these limits be breached? On what basis might those in the social middle claim legitimacy for their aspirations to public authority? Their responses to these and related questions – which only intensified as the eighteenth gave way to the nineteenth century and anxieties over social revolution were redirected into concerns about the spread of democracy, and which ranged from agonized to triumphant and often did not distinguish between class as defined by production and relative position as determined by status – appear throughout the diverse archive left to their descendants, us, by the Victorians.

That many professional writers, especially novelists, self-identified as middle class, means that the record of this ongoing attempt to define, legitimate, and otherwise differentiate society's newest stratum appears with particular acuity and provocative creativity throughout the period's voluminous literary output, most especially of fiction.[11] In many ways, this later corpus represents the mature expression of the earlier process of "novelization" and of forms of "novelistic usage" described by Michael McKeon in *The Origins of the English Novel*. According to McKeon, the novel as we understand it emerged in the seventeenth century in response to "the curse of modernity," identified as the "sociohistorical condition of status inconsistency."[12] By one account, some 60,000 novels were published during the reign of Victoria, and the vast majority of them continued to encode within themselves the only-expanding "nagging uncertainty" about traditional forms of "status hierarchy" that had given birth to the form in the first place.[13] Novelists built their own legitimacy upon their ability to secure readers, since without them writers could neither maintain middle-class standards of respectability nor mobilize changes to public policy. Unfortunately, this need for a degree of popularity threatened the very status they hoped to achieve: popular approval had long been associated with facile aesthetics and uncritical thought.[14] Moreover, professional writers of fiction faced the additional impediments that any influence they enjoyed originated in the reception of their work in a historically low-status genre, and that the principle of utility so favored by their middle-class counterparts working in other fields remained largely unavailable, since classic utilitarianism eschewed all but a didactic function for imaginative literature.

Victorian novelists, therefore, had an unusually long row to hoe in order to obtain the middle-class status to which they aspired, and their novels present a supple record and strategic re-presentation of the complexities of asserting middle-class identity during the Age of Reform. Concentrating on this rough half-century from the 1830s to the 1880s and employing a methodology with roots in historical, sociological, and literary theory, this book reconstructs the unusual, at times even paradoxical attempts of Victorian fiction writers to define the limits of middle-class status. Ultimately, their collective efforts lead me to propose a new and newly historicized theory of status grounded in absence and articulated through negative assertions of value, by which I mean self-conscious repudiations of both conventional sources of legitimacy such as consanguineous relations or significant wealth, as well as more recent standards like numerical preponderance or rational sufficiency. Epistemologically uncertain, this representational and ideological strategy was also professionally efficacious, since it was grounded in appeals to a disinterested, because noncompetitive and already dominated, broad public, whose assent, whether fictional or material, modeled and justified the approval implied by such writers' popular readership.

A Middling History of Class

With relatively few exceptions, historians have traced the comparatively recent and definitionally messy emergence of the language of class to eighteenth-century Britain.[15] Building upon the foundational work of Briggs, Penelope Corfield describes an "endless debate about the number and nature of social classes" in this period, prompted by the emergence of a recognizably modern "mobile society in which origins and eventualities did not inevitably match."[16] Similarly, Eric Hobsbawm asserts that the "language of class replaced the language of ranks precisely when the growing distance between social groups and their conflicting interests began to push their supposed common interests into the background."[17] "Upper," "middle," and "lower" or "working" became convenient adjectives with which to subdivide this increasingly conflicted social arena, but, as David Cannadine remarks, even in the eighteenth century, "few Britons believed that there was one single middle class or one single working class, and they were right to be thus incredulous."[18] Those in the rapidly growing, diversifying, and urbanizing social middle presented particular problems of classification, since they simultaneously lacked an aristocratic pedigree, were obliged to work for a living, and yet engaged in predominantly mental rather than manual labor. Hence, "middle class came increasingly into use from the mid-eighteenth century onwards to distinguish growing numbers of people from the aristocracy above and the workers below. But, this was an essentially negative usage from which it does not necessarily follow that those in the middle were in any way homogeneous."[19] Members of the new middle class(es), then, were distinguishable only in relation to other more established social strata, from which they might draw their members and to which they could perhaps rise or fall according to their fortunes in Britain's progressively more complex industrialized market economy.[20]

Such financial and social insecurity only intensified during the Napoleonic wars, with their deleterious effect on trade and disproportionately imposed income tax. After Waterloo, middle-class voices were among the most insistent in calling for legal and political reform, often on Utilitarian principles.[21] In fact, most historians, regardless of their ideological commitments or position on the field's so-called "linguistic turn," describe this campaign for reform, culminating in the debate over the First Reform Bill, as the crucible in which a distinctively Victorian middle-class identity took form.[22] Thus Norman Gash, in *Politics in the Age of Peel*, still the standard history of the passage of the First Reform Act 1832, attributes the perseverance of the Whigs throughout the two-year-long debate to "the need to bring the middle classes within the orbit of the constitution," not least because their exclusion "strengthened popular discontent and disorder" by forcing them "into an alliance with the lower classes."[23] Fifty years later, Simon Gunn and Rachel Bell similarly describe the principal effect of Reform as a deliberate split, between "merchants and professional men" on the one side and "working men and women" on the other, accomplished by "giving the vote to those with property while continuing to exclude the propertyless masses."[24] Establishing the £10 franchise meant creating in law an effective minimum threshold for membership in the middle class, whereas before there had been only an unstable social or rhetorical boundary.[25]

Perhaps the most influential, and controversial, account of how the debate over Reform accomplished this transformation of class rhetoric into legal reality appears in Dror Wahrman's *Imagining the Middle Class*. Written during the first heady swerve of the linguistic turn, Wahrman's book seeks to answer the question, "why and when did the British come to *believe* that they lived in a society centered around a 'middle class'?" by retracing the discursive construction of the social middle in parliamentary oratory, periodical prose, and other publications especially invested in political commentary that appeared in England between roughly the French Revolution and the First Reform Act.[26] The "middle-class idiom" that emerges from these sources, Wahrman argues, presents its subject as a sort of Barthesian myth, one amorphous and adaptable enough that "in the hands of political moderates the 'middle class' – whether absent or present – always came out looking good."[27] From the 1790s, when "the anti-war rhetoric of the respectable opposition repeatedly highlighted the existence of the 'middle class', its virtues, its wisdom and its moderation, as well as its umbilical link to liberty," to the 1820s, when the "'middle class' – by now confirmed as 'tame', anti-popular and committed to political stability – could readily be made to fulfil the part of that social sector for which . . . an adjustment of the electoral map was required," England's mythic middle was repeatedly deployed to justify both the need for and the inevitability of measured social and political transformation.[28] *Imagining the Middle Class* devotes considerable space to citations from the prolonged parliamentary debates over what would become the First Reform Act, following the passage of which, according to Wahrman, "a very large number of the British people came to see the 'middle class' as a statement of fact, contentious not in itself but only in its evaluative implications, a purportedly objective and readily observable presence in the world around them. The invention of the Barthesian myth . . . was completed."[29]

Although this conclusion, and the methods that enabled it, have been both praised and panned by subsequent historians – who, whatever their reaction, now find Wahrman unavoidable in the study of class in Britain – what seems to me both most useful and most frustrating about *Imagining the Middle Class* is its focus on the parliamentary debates of 1831–2.[30] On the one hand, Wahrman both includes copious excerpts from and admits the "versatility" and "indeterminacy" of the "middle-class idiom" during this period of parliamentary grandstanding.[31] On the other hand, he persistently flattens the actual vocabulary deployed by various speakers to describe those in the soon-to-be-enfranchised social middle, bracketing all of the competing terminology under the generic label "middle class." This means that he unfortunately obscures the very productive variability that he elsewhere asserts and that I have reproduced above.

For this new bloc of voters to achieve Wahrman's "objective and readily observable presence in the world," it would ultimately require more than just the possession of a minimal standard of wealth, whether in the form of an explicit property qualification or an assumed annual income.[32] In addition to remaining a key rhetorical figure in post-Reform political debates, from global abolitionism to the repeal of the Corn Laws to further expansions of the franchise, the middle class also asserted its material presence through distinctive patterns of consumption and recognizable institutions of public culture.[33] Church attendance, especially in an urban congregation, was central, as was the employment of at least one domestic servant and self-improvement via lectures, reading, and visits to cultural institutions, with additional prescriptions segregated by sex. Men held membership in voluntary societies, whether civic, professional, or cultural; subscribed to one or more clubs, both social and political; and received a superior education, preferably at one of the "public" boarding schools. Women were involved in charitable activities and organizations; committed to ideals of domesticity, most notably household management and childbearing; and expected to show social accomplishments, including "lesser" artistic abilities, conversational grace, and polite knowledge of French.[34] Once one had achieved a certain minimum standard of wealth with respect to systems of production, in other words, one's middle-class identity needed to be performed through affirmative demonstrations of status.[35]

Written overwhelming for, by members of, and largely about, this earnest, productive, respectable, aspiring, self-improving social middle, Victorian fiction meticulously records, subtly prescribes, and knowingly parodies its individual, institutional, and class-fractional efforts to construct status through its own forms of culture.[36] Read before the hearth at home, in the omnibus or train while commuting from new suburbs, and during the hours of leisure created for those performing mental, as opposed to manual, labor in the industrial economy, Victorian novels accrued popularity by representing the middle class to itself. In addition to documenting and frequently editorializing upon the clothes, food, diction, domestic entertainments, public activities, social forms, and other realistic details of middle-class life, fiction synthesized the ideological affirmations that made such a life distinctive and sought to legitimate the claims to public authority made by those who lived within its bounds. Among the most important of these were the complementary claims made by members of the middle class to gentlemanliness and character, rhetorical moves traced by Robin Gilmour and Lauren Goodlad, respectively. Gilmour, in *The Idea of the Gentleman in the Victorian Novel*, convincingly shows how the eighteenth-century notion of gentility, based in birth and wealth, was challenged in the nineteenth century by the idea of gentlemanliness, grounded in conduct, itself with a moral and an aesthetic component. Gentlemen were said to possess "character," and Goodlad's *Victorian Literature and the Victorian State* reveals a "profound shift" from prescriptive to descriptive theories of character – or from character as something to aspire towards to character as something already possessed – between 1820–30 and 1850–70. Whereas, at the beginning of the period, character focused on "a theoretically limitless potential for inner development, catalyzed by interpersonal relations," by the second half of Victoria's reign, character had grown "noticeably stationary" and more dedicated to securing social privilege against the increasing pressures of materialism.[37] Visualized as a Venn diagram, Gilmour's gentlemanliness overlaps with portions of both the prescriptive and descriptive phases of Goodlad's character, and this zone of intersection represents a powerful discursive strategy for affirming that the middle class possessed a superior degree of culture and therefore the legitimacy to translate their growing economic and productive power into political, moral, and cultural capital.

Sociological Theories of Status

Such affirmative assertions of status, whether historical or fictional, remain especially amenable to explanation by sociological theory in general, and by the work of Max Weber and Pierre Bourdieu in particular. In *Economy and Society* and *Distinction*, respectively, these two theorists elucidate a variety of individual and collective strategies designed to assert social dominance on the basis of "style of life" or "cultural capital," and thus both are remarkably well positioned to account for the myriad status-building activities undertaken by members of the intermediate strata of Victorian society in the Age of Reform.[38]

At pains to establish the limits of the discipline, Weber's magisterial *Economy and Society* seeks to differentiate sociology from other, more established fields of study that also purport to explain how and why individuals and societies behave the way they do. Thus, in contrast to history, "which is oriented to the causal analysis and explanation of individual actions, structures, and personalities possessing cultural significance," sociology, according to Weber, "seeks to formulate type concepts and generalized uniformities of empirical processes."[39] Focusing on types rather than persons, on uniformities rather than exceptionalities determined by cultural prominence, and on processes rather than particular actions requires the sociologist "to treat all irrational, affectually determined elements of behavior as factors of deviation from a conceptually pure type of rational action."[40] Although he stresses that he intends this assumption of rationality "only as a methodological device" rather than a categorical statement about the "actual prominence of rational elements in human life" or about the uniformity of rationality itself across times and cultures, Weber appears to have little doubt about his own or his discipline's ability to detect the specific form of rationalization that motivates a given social action and to declare as deviant any irrational departures from the types and uniformities that underlie that action.[41]

Weber thus treats society as a coherent system that functions according to collectively recognized, even if unarticulated, rules for domination, or the exercise of authority. Partly derived from "material or affectual or ideal motives," each system of domination also attempts "to establish and to cultivate the belief in its legitimacy," to secure consent from those whose freedom of action is somehow constrained that their obedience is warranted.[42] Weber then proposes three systems of domination, each claiming its own type of legitimacy. The most primitive is "charismatic" domination, which begins with the nonrational, apparently magical power of a single leader, who must continuously "prove" his legitimacy by obtaining "recognition on the part of those subject to authority."[43] For charismatic domination to continue after the death of its founder, charisma must be institutionalized and secured through the ongoing performance of ritual action by institutional office holders. This state of affairs can therefore develop into a second, preindustrial "traditional" domination built upon "status," an "effective claim to social esteem" that is typically founded on "style of life," formal education, or "hereditary or occupational prestige" and that is expressed through conventions that "create economically irrational consumption patterns and fetter the free market."[44] Conversely, modern "rational" domination relies upon a robustly developed and recognizably complex "free market" to generate "money power," or wealth as expressed through the control over the production and acquisition of material goods.[45]

It is important to note that, although I have presented these different systems of domination in an order that might suggest how each grows out of its predecessor, for Weber, they are not necessarily linked genealogically and the existence of one does not preclude the contemporary presence of one or both of the others. In such a case, different conceptions of "social honor" or "prestige" would potentially clash with each other, leading in extreme instances to regional or international conflict – "Experience teaches that claims to prestige have always played into the origin of wars" – and in more peaceful circumstances to social dislocation and anxiety about competing claims to social authority.[46] In a point that would be contested by his successors, including Bourdieu, Weber clearly separates and outlines the potential points of disagreement between modern rational systems built upon class difference and more traditional systems that rely upon status hierarchies. Fundamentally, class difference is grounded in productive power and expressed through the economic order (who possesses wealth and of what sort), whereas status hierarchies are expressed through patterns of consumption and manifested via the social order (who holds social honor and how they advertise its possession). Thus, even though there are historical examples in which "social honor, or prestige" derived from status "very frequently" has been "the basis of economic power," according to Weber, the "status order would be threatened at its very root if mere economic acquisition and naked economic power still bearing the stigma of its extra-status origin could bestow upon anyone who has won them the same or greater honor as the vested [status] interests claim for themselves."[47] Such potential conflicts between class and status become especially likely in periods of great "technological repercussion and economic transformation" that push "the class situation into the forefront."[48] Little wonder, then, that Victorian England struggled to come to terms with its ascendant social middle, which itself both deployed the language of class and enacted the consumption patterns of status.

As announced by its subtitle, *A Social Critique of the Judgement of Taste*, and explained in its Preface, Bourdieu's *Distinction* offers a materialist challenge to Kant's third *Critique* that is also "an endeavour to rethink Max Weber's opposition between class and *Stand* [status]."[49] Grounded in empirical evidence gathered from statistical surveys and ethnographic observations of 1217 "Parisians and provincials" between 1963 and 1968, the text argues that "taste," in all senses of the word – from aesthetic judgement to gustatory preference, and everything in between – is inextricably bound up with class.[50] For Bourdieu, class is a matter of capital, "understood as the set of actually usable resources and powers – economic capital, cultural capital and also social capital," all of which are mobilized into practices designed to express available degrees of distinction through consumption.[51] Arranged vertically by their relative distance from economic necessity, classes are sub-dividable horizontally into fractions according to their members' differentiated distributions of types of capital. These fractions struggle constantly with one another for dominance, with one of the primary points of conflict being the "exchange rate" for the potential conversion of one sort of capital into another; that is, whether at a given historical moment, economic, cultural, or social capital is the "dominant principle of domination."[52] Each fraction seeks legitimacy through and for its habitus, defined by Bourdieu as "necessity internalized and converted into a disposition that generates meaningful practices and meaning-giving perceptions; it is a general transposable disposition which carries out a systematic, universal application."[53] Because "the work of art is the objectification of a relationship of distinction," fractions of the dominant class tend to contest with one another most visibly over the meaning, value, and appropriation of aesthetic objects.[54] Such interested disagreements of taste include not merely debates over the worth of individual works of art, but also over the comparative value and cultural capital invested in whole categories or genres, such as that ongoing in the Victorian period over the artistic value of prose versus poetry.[55]

The robust philosophical discourse on aesthetics represented synecdochally by Kant's *Critique of Judgment* evinces the durability of this struggle for what Bourdieu labels "misrecognition." From a materialist perspective, the "dialectic of conditions and habitus is the basis of an alchemy which transforms the distribution of capital, the balance-sheet of a power relation, into a system of perceived differences, distinctive properties, that is, a distribution of symbolic capital, legitimate capital, whose objective truth is misrecognized."[56] Misrecognition remains possible because taste, the primary term of the underlying contest for social power, remains largely "below the level of consciousness and language, beyond the reach of introspective scrutiny or control by the will."[57] Taste is conveyed from one generation of members in a class fraction to the next indirectly, through countless experiences accumulated in everyday life and both formal and informal systems of education.[58] Acknowledging his debt to Weber, Bourdieu does briefly allow for the agency of charismatic individuals, those with the power "to impose their own self-image as the objective and collective image of their body and being; to persuade others, as in love or faith, to abdicate their generic power of objectification and delegate it to the person who should be its object, who thereby becomes an absolute subject, without an exterior (being his own Other), fully justified in existing, legitimated."[59] However, it is far more typical in *Distinction* for agency to be attributed to the class, class fraction, or habitus itself.[60] Individual artists or intellectuals may approach a particular work of art with great self-consciousness and theoretical acuity, but for Bourdieu they almost always remain unaware of the "past and present material conditions of existence which are the precondition of both" their "constitution and ... application" of the "aesthetic disposition."[61] In other words, class always underwrites *Stand*, even in apparently "pure" aesthetic struggles between charismatic individuals over objects, genres, or institutions of culture that are markers of status.

Despite being written a half-century apart and in Bourdieu's case with the explicit goal of revising Weber's earlier work, both *Economy and Society* and *Distinction* share the fundamental assumption that status is both grounded in and detectable by affirmative demonstrations of its possession. Even Weber's "negatively privileged status groups," whose "social honor" is not acknowledged by the society of which they are a part, maintain their "belief in a providential mission and . . . a specific honor before God" by means of an observable style of life.[62] All such life-styles, whether positively or negatively privileged, "are stratified according to the principles of their *consumption* of goods," including "wearing special costumes . . . eating special dishes . . . carrying arms," etc.[63] Similarly, although Bourdieu allows that in "matters of taste, more than anywhere else, all determination is negation; and tastes are perhaps first and foremost distastes, disgust provoked by horror or visceral intolerance ('sick-making') of the tastes of others," he still imagines such distastes operating according to a substitutive logic of binary opposition.[64] Thus, the members of one class fraction will profess disgust at the choice of food, clothing, music, etc. of a rival group while always asserting their own "superior" preference for an alternative. Whether as an element of a style of life or as an object of distinction, such evidence is consistently represented by Weber and Bourdieu as a positive sign of legitimacy: I do/have/prefer X, therefore I am an individual of status.

Negative Assertions of Value

Although the theories of Weber and Bourdieu have tremendous heuristic potential to elucidate the more public and collectively constructed elements of the Victorian status economy, transferring their twentieth-century conceptual categories onto nineteenth-century society is not without its challenges. The linguistic and historical evidence, cited earlier, of the Victorians' singularly unclear sense of their own intermediate social strata, greatly problematizes some of the broad generalizations and should trouble the epistemological confidence evident in both of their work. For instance, Weber's three systems of domination, each grounded in its own strategies of legitimacy and forms of rationalization, appear coterminous and indistinguishable during the semantically and epistemologically confused nascence of the muddled Victorian middle. Members of this newly enfranchised constituency simultaneously participated in the creation and expansion of the free market, while also somewhat incongruously seeking to legitimate their claims to authority by claiming a type of status that can only be secured through public recognition like that normally reserved for holders of charisma.[65] Moreover, the apparently inevitable triumph of the modern system remains, during this period at least, effectively deferred by institutions of middle-class professional prestige about which I have written at length elsewhere.[66]

Hedging somewhat his methodological bets, Bourdieu does acknowledge both that "the system of distinctive features which express or reveal economic and social differences ... varies considerably from one period, and one society, to another," and that "a true comparative study would have to take account of the specific forms that the struggle and the themes in which it is expressed take on when the objective relations between the class fractions change."[67] Perhaps most pressing among the "distinctive features" and "specific forms" of the amorphous Victorian middle is its similarity, in self-consciousness and aspirational trajectory, to those whom Bourdieu labels petit bourgeois. Describing these upwardly mobile members of relatively new or renovated occupations in 1960s France as equidistant "from the two extreme poles of the field of the social classes, at a neutral point where the forces of attraction and repulsion are evenly balanced," Bourdieu explains that "the petite bourgeois are constantly faced with ethical, aesthetic or political dilemmas forcing them to bring the most ordinary operations of existence to the level of consciousness and strategic choice."[68] This indeterminacy places acute pressure on his account of systems of classification that operate below consciousness and absent introspection, but the petit bourgeois ultimately do not imperil his theory because they remain dominated and because Bourdieu posits that their strategic choices are all directed towards assuming the habitus of their social superiors. At precisely these points, however, the similarity between twentieth-century France and nineteenth-century England breaks down, since those occupying the middle strata of Victorian society experienced increasing success in making universal and normative their particular standards of taste.

The disciplinary distinctions made by Weber – sociology's necessary focus on "generalized uniformities" and classification of behavior according to a binary notion of rationality – preemptively prevents the analysis of individual cases in which status appears grounded in something other than its affirmative, objective demonstration.

Literary texts are particularly difficult for a "pure" sociological critique. Stylistically idiosyncratic, structurally arbitrary if not blatantly irrational, characterologically reliant upon affect, literature is by nature deviant even when otherwise aspiring to respectability. And many works of Victorian fiction approach their society's intermediate – one might well say central – imbrication of class and status in a strikingly peculiar way, through what we might productively recognize as an historically-specific form: the negative assertion of value. For all of their ability to multiply examples of gentlemanliness, to delineate the complexities of character, to represent or ironically re-present performative patterns of consumption, Victorian novels often also warrant their claims of and about middle-class status not in presence but in absence, not in displays of legitimating possession, but in repudiations of alternative rationales for social authority.

A brief nonfictional example may help to illustrate this process of assertion-through-negation of status.[69] In 1842, opportunistic American editor and critic Rufus Griswold published the first edition of *Poets and Poetry of America*, among the first and unequivocally the largest anthology of American poetry assembled to date. Clearly intended as a demonstration of status – on behalf of Griswold himself, the individual poets included (especially the eighty-six for whom Griswold provided authorial headnotes), American poetry more generally, and the United States of America as a politically and culturally independent nation – the book was produced to an unusually high standard, indicating its aspirations to an international audience. *Poets and Poetry of America* did, in fact, receive extensive attention in the January 1844 issue of London's *Foreign Quarterly Review* but not of the sort for which Griswold must have hoped. Former *FQR* editor John Forster savagely judged the volume "the most conspicuous act of martyrdom yet committed in the service of the transatlantic muses" and the nation it synecdochally represented as "accustomed to contemplate without emotion the vicissitudes of a semi-barbarous mode of society."[70]

Both Griswold's editorial paratexts and Forster's review essay are full of negations. Most of these operate according to the logic of binary substitution featured in Weber's *Economy and Society* and Bourdieu's *Distinction*. Thus, Griswold denigrates colonial American poetry in order to glorify American poetry written after independence, and he rejects "that vassalage of opinion and style" that binds "the subjects of kings" so that he can embrace America's democratic republicanism.[71] Similarly, Forster dismisses the "euphonious brood of American jinglers" featured in *Poets and Poetry of America* as vastly inferior to even such minor verse as might be culled from English magazines and annuals of the previous seventy or eighty years, and he negates Griswold's claims on behalf of American literature by invoking the pejorative judgments of his more critical countryman, William Ellery Channing, in "Remarks on American Literature."[72] At least one of Forster's negations operates somewhat differently, however. Americans, Forster argues, have no business aspiring after literary status, because they have chosen to subscribe to an entirely different standard of value. As "there must be an aristocracy everywhere of some sort, of blood, or talent, or titles," Forster writes, "so America has made her election, and set up her aristocracy of dollars—the basest of all."[73] Although he does offer potential alternatives, in the form of "blood, or talent, or titles," Forster neither expresses any preference among them nor explicitly rules out further possibilities, apparently trusting his readers to make up their own minds on the strength of their shared repudiation of American materialism. His readers' collective status at this moment thus depends primarily upon a shared negative.

Forster's review thus furnishes a singular instance of a rhetorical move, a form, that I shall demonstrate was widespread throughout Victorian literature, particularly novels, and that I shall argue was ideologically key to authors' constructions of Victorian middle-class status. Exemplary of a negative assertion of value, Forster's explicit rejection of one contemporary basis for legitimacy – in this case, the indiscriminate accumulation of wealth, "utter indifference to the honesty of means of acquisition giving additional impetus to the naked passion for gain" – also includes an appeal for recognition from a broader public.[74] That this public is intimately bound up with literary popularity is evident from Forster's identification of those members of the aspiring middle class whom America's "aristocracy of dollars" hurts the most:

> A bag of dollars is a surer introduction to the "best society" in America than the highest literary reputation. A famous author will be stared at, and jostled about, and asked questions, and have his privacy scared and broken in upon by impertinent curiosity; but a rich man moves in an atmosphere of awe and servility, and commands every thing that is to be had in the way of precedence, and pomp, and circle-worship.[75]

Almost certainly derived from Dickens's 1842 reading tour, about which Forster received ample news through personal correspondence, this passage expects the comfortably well-off readers of the

FOR to accept that Dickens's multitudinous admirers – some of them equally assured members of the middle class, but many falling below £10 pound householder status – legitimate his claims to domination, in this case in the form of an inalienable right to privacy.[76]

Such acknowledgments of popular readership were both necessary and risky for Victorian authors. Novelists' pretentions to improve the society in which they lived and about which they wrote were predicated upon the size of their readership. These same authors' ability to maintain their own households in a degree of middle-class comfort was dependent upon the income they derived from their books, and hence from sales to circulating libraries and private individuals. And yet, as Richard Salmon observes, "Dickens and other writers of the 1840s and 1850s sought to define Literature as a profession precisely in terms of its relative distance and insulation from the market."[77] In other words, publishers and printers might chase sales numbers and advertise their wares to potential readers, but authors dedicated themselves to the disinterested mental labor of writing just as physicians dedicated themselves to medicine or barristers to the law.

That authors felt the need to eschew their own paying customers emerges not just from the emulation of professionals' disdain for "trade," but also from the persistence with which literary popularity had come to be associated with flaccid writing and thinking. Thus, in the 1800 Preface to *Lyrical Ballads*, William Wordsworth regrets that "the literature and theatrical exhibitions of the country have conformed themselves" to "a multitude of causes, unknown to former times ... now acting with a combined force to blunt the discriminating powers of the mind, and ... to reduce it to a state of almost savage torpor."[78] Even blunter in the "Essay, Supplementary to the Preface" of 1815, he declares,

> Away, then, with the senseless iteration of the word, *popular*, applied to new works in poetry, as if there were no test of excellence in this first of the fine arts but that all men should run after its productions, as if urged by an appetite, or constrained by a spell![79]

Writing in 1830 and attempting to advance the reputation of his then-relatively unknown friend Alfred Tennyson, Arthur Henry Hallam argues that "it is the fate of genius to be unpopular," because "those writers will be always most popular who require the least degree of exertion."[80] An author more famous for his "obscurity," and hence the exertion required to read him, than for his popular reception in 1852, Robert Browning, in his "Essay on Shelley," similarly observes that "the misapprehensiveness of his age is exactly what a poet is sent to remedy," and thus no one should be surprised at "the interval between his operation and the generally perceptible effect of it."[81] Widely read and considered for the laureateship after Wordsworth's death, even Elizabeth Barrett Browning has her semi-autobiographical surrogate, Aurora Leigh, wonder, in 1856, "If virtue done for popularity / Defiles like vice, can art, for praise or hire, / Still keep its splendor and remain pure art?"[82] Such statements, which only proliferated once aestheticism had taken root in Britain, made legitimating one's claims to social authority on the basis of one's appeal to a broad public a tricky business. It was, nevertheless, a consistent strategy by which Victorian prose writers sought to insert themselves and their aspirations for middle-class status into the absences they had created through negative assertions of value.

Novel Approaches to Status

The five chapters that follow each center on one of the categorical negations that Victorian novelists used to justify and define a peculiarly literary construction of middle-class status.[83] All follow a similar format, first reconstructing the generic and historical pressures particularly salient to the basis of legitimacy being novelistically repudiated, second suggesting the pervasiveness and representational versatility of the negative assertion of value under discussion through a series of pithy interpretations of period fiction, and third offering an extended close reading of a single Victorian novel in which the unconventional validation of one or more iterations of middle-class status assumes particular prominence in the narrative. Necessarily anecdotal, the argument is also intended to be synecdochal, using individual texts to suggest a more widespread, if never entirely systematic response to the problem of status grounded in absence and legitimated only retrospectively by public assent.

Chapters 1 and 2 concentrate on Victorian novelists' challenge to the two categories of social identity traditionally invoked to warrant privileged forms of status. Chapter 1 deploys Charles Dickens's *Oliver Twist* (1838), Charlotte Brontë's *Jane Eyre* (1847), Anthony Trollope's *Doctor Thorne* (1858), and Wilkie Collins's *The Woman in White* (1860) and *No Name* (1862) as the primary texts through which to track middle-class Victorian efforts to claim legitimacy by denying the overdetermining force of ancestry. The figures of the orphan, a child without parents, and the bastard, a child without parentage, loom large in these texts, representing the dilemma of a middle class largely without historical warrant. *No Name*, at least, also stages, quite literally, the problem of popularity in low-status genres through its protagonist, Magdalen Vanstone, a talented actress who attempts, futilely, to use her facility for disguise to swindle her way back to membership in the middle class.

Industrialism provided an alternative means for attaining social prominence through the accumulation of capital, regardless of consanguineous relations, and yet the growth of Britain's market economy created as many problems of status as it solved. Chapter 2 matches William Makepeace Thackeray's *The History of Samuel Titmarsh and the Great Hoggarty Diamond* (1841), Dickens's *Dombey and Son* (1848), Charles Reade's *Hard Cash* (1863), and Trollope's *The Way We Live Now* (1875) with William North's *The City of the Jugglers* (1850) to show the wariness with which middle-class writers approached Weber's "'naked' money power" as a source of public authority. Ultimately, North proposes poetic genius, of the sort described in Shelley's posthumous "Defence of Poetry" (1840), as a cure for money-grubbing and a warrant for social status, even as he worries, with good reason, that his novel will fail to attract enough readers to legitimize either his social analysis or his personal genius.

Chapters 3 and 4 focus on sources of legitimacy of a more recent vintage, one of potential benefit to England's historically underprivileged and the other a more "scientific" approach whose rationalism threatened to exclude imaginative writers altogether. Chapter 3 reexamines middle-class Victorians' anxieties over the foreseeable consequence of continued franchise reform: the numerical preponderance of working-class voters and the possibility, in Alexis de Tocqueville's durable phrasing from *Democracy in America* (1835–40), of a "tyranny of the majority." Displaying an interested fascination with working-class crowds as dangerous mobs, Dickens's *Barnaby Rudge* (1841), Brontë's *Shirley* (1849), Charles Kingsley's *Alton Locke* (1850), Elizabeth Gaskell's *North and South* (1855) and George Eliot's *Felix Holt: The Radical* (1866) frequently conflate numerical superiority and the potential for violence in order to maintain middle-class status through categorical negation. Eliot's subsequent "Address to Working Men, by Felix Holt" (1868), which seeks to use a fictional character to influence actual electors recently enfranchised by the Second Reform Act 1867, demonstrates exactly what is at stake for Victorian novelists in their epistemologically fraught legitimation of their own and their middle-class characters' power of domination.

Numbers of a different sort take center stage in Chapter 4, which reconstructs Victorian novelists' skeptical response to the growing prominence of quantifiable knowledge as the principal basis for public policy and middle-class legitimacy. Framed against the rise of what Mary Poovey denominates the "modern fact" – represented by the penetration of statistics and the continued influence of Utilitarianism in social and political life – this chapter reads Brontë's *Villette* (1853), Elizabeth Barrett Browning's *Aurora Leigh* (1856), Trollope's *The Three Clerks* (1857), and Dickens's *Hard Times* (1854) for their shared rejection of what they represent as a narrowly conceived and misguided reliance upon empiricism to overdetermine patterns of domination. Long read as an unsatisfying condition-of-England novel, *Hard Times* is repositioned as a sophisticated sociological novel with a clear function for its apparently anomalous outsider characters: rather than serve as a simple-minded panacea for the manifold ills of England's factory system, Sleary and his fellow circus performers emerge as key figures for the disinterested legitimation of Gradgrind, and by extension Dickens, as representatives of middle-class authority.

Chapter 5 revisits many of the novels featured in earlier chapters in order to uncover the largely unarticulated gendered assumptions that inform their constructions of status. Negative assertions of value focused on birth, wealth, force, and fact had tangible benefits for middle-class men's status, which was, itself, predicated upon a fifth repudiation, of the symbolic phallus, to be made by contemporary middle-class women. I argue that women's legitimacy in the period marked by the mid-century "surplus women" crisis, widespread opposition to the Contagious Diseases Acts 1864, 1866, 1869, the passage of the Married Women's Property Act 1870, and the consolidated Central Committee of the National Society for Women's Suffrage (1872) rested upon a rejection of claims to equal public authority. Focusing at length upon Charlotte Yonge's *The Clever Woman of the Family* (1865), this chapter reveals how, in order to legitimate the middle-class perspective of her titular "clever woman," Rachel Curtis, Yonge studiously strips her of any claims to masculine authority; this anti-feminist pattern, I assert, is perceptible even in novels with very different ideological investments.

Finally, in a brief afterward I consider some of the changes to the novel and to society in the 1880s that rendered status grounded in absence and granted through disinterested recognition a less urgent matter for middle-class late-Victorians. I also suggest a direction for future research that challenges the boundaries of what we mean by novelization and the novelistic in the Age of Reform.

Notes

1. In *Forms*, Caroline Levine "makes a case for expanding our usual definition of form in literary studies to include patterns of sociopolitical experience," each possessing its own unique "affordances," defined via design theory as "the potential uses or actions latent in materials and designs" (2, 6). According to Levine, such latent potentialities appear at moments of "'collision' – the strange encounter between two or more forms that sometimes reroutes intention and ideology," and that is particularly well captured in narrative, where the relationship between politics and aesthetics becomes both visible and fungible (18).
2. According to David Cannadine in *Class in Britain*, "When Britons have tried to make sense of the unequal social worlds they have inhabited, settled and conquered, across the centuries and around the globe, they have most usually come up with versions or variants of these same three basic and enduring models: the hierarchical view of society as a seamless web; the triadic version with upper, middle and lower collective groups, and the dichotomous, adversarial picture, where society is sundered between 'us' and 'them'" (19–20).
3. *Hansard's Parliamentary Debates*, 3rd Series, II.1191, II.1196, II.1199.
4. Ibid. III.63.
5. Ibid. III.136.
6. Ibid. II.1338, VI.556, XII.162.
7. Asa Briggs was the first to outline this shifting "Language of 'Class' in Early Nineteenth-Century England," which Steven Wallech connects explicitly to eighteenth-century economic theories of production in his "Class Versus Rank." See also Seed and Corfield.
8. Asa Briggs, "The Language of 'Class' in Early Nineteenth-Century England," 45.
9. John Seed, "From 'Middling Sort' to Middle Class in Late Eighteenth- and Early Nineteenth-Century England," 115.
10. Simon Gunn, *The Public Culture of the Victorian Middle Class*, 16.
11. According to Richard Salmon, in *The Formation of the Victorian Literary Professional*, a fundamental ambiguity attended "the social position and class status of professional authors: should authorship be viewed as an ordinary form of wage-labour (either 'noble' or 'degrading' depending on one's perspective) or as a professional service guaranteeing membership of the respectable middle classes?" (213).
12. Michael McKeon, *The Origins of the English Novel 1600–1740*, 210.
13. This estimate appears in John Sutherland's *Stanford Companion to Victorian Fiction* (v); digitization efforts undertaken since the book's 1989 publication date suggest that this number should be even higher.
14. For a recent study of the "vexed" problem of popularity as applied to poetry, See Clara Dawson's *Victorian Poetry and the Culture of Evaluation* (6).

15. In *The Making of the English Middle Class*, Peter Earle asserts a much earlier, seventeenth-century pedigree for the English middle classes, and does so with a confidence in his own definitions and occupationally-determined methodology than is unmatched by subsequent historians. More circumspect in his exceptionality is Peter Calvert. In *The Concept of Class*, he identifies the "first public use of the word 'class' in the English language to refer to divisions in *modern* society" as being "made simultaneously in Scotland and England in 1767, by Adam Ferguson and Jonas Hanway, respectively," but he is more interested in class as a concept with complex and contradictory roots in ancient Athenian and Roman jurisprudence, Aristotelean philosophy, Medieval Christianity, and, above all, the French Enlightenment (14). Ultimately, Calvert is highly skeptical of class as a useful descriptive or analytical category, preferring instead to rely upon status.
16. Penelope J. Corfield, "Class by Name and Number in Eighteenth-Century Britain," 103, 112.
17. Eric Hobsbawm, "The Example of the English Middle Class," 127.
18. David Cannadine, *Class in Britain*, 60. Twentieth and twenty-first century social historians' awareness of the methodological difficulties of social description has only increased their skepticism of simple class divisions: "The formation of social strata always poses fundamental difficulties of analysis in social history, because it is not enough simply to show that people shared a common characteristic such as a certain level of income or a certain occupation. If stratification is to be shown then there is an axiomatic requirement to prove it through identifying actual social relationships and commitments" (Crossick, "The Emergence of the Lower Middle Class in Britain," 12).
19. Alana Kidd and David Nicholls, eds., *The Making of the British Middle Class?*, xxiii. As Roy Lewis and Angus Maude noted succinctly in *The English Middle Classes* in 1950, "nobody has ever found a definition of the English middle classes which is short, satisfactory, and watertight" (3).
20. Summarizing existing historical scholarship for the BBC2 series *Middle Classes*, which aired February to March 2001, Simon Gunn and Rachel Bell acknowledge that almost "everyone who has studied the middle classes has acknowledged the difficulty of defining them" (13).
21. Among the "several factors" enumerated by Briggs as "encouraging the development of a sense of middle-class unity where hitherto there had been a recognition of (imperfect) mutual interest" are "the imposition of Pitt's income tax," the financial burdens of war with Napoleonic France, and Utilitarian ideals of reform (53–5).
22. Although he identifies "the second quarter" of the nineteenth century as the period in which that portion of the social middle composed of "the northern employer class" was "made," Patrick Joyce primarily links this coalescence of identity to "the completion of the mechanisation of

factory production . . . confirming the historical inevitability of industrial capitalism in the mind of the employer as much as in the mind of the operative" (*Work, Society and Politics*, 3).
23. Norman Gash, *Politics in the Age of Peel*, 14–15. Gash's claims have been reiterated more recently by Chris Vanden Bossche, who writes that the "intention of the Act, as understood by contemporary politicians, was to enfranchise the newly risen middle class" (*Reform Acts*, 1). See also Crossick, "From Gentleman to the Residuum," 155–6.
24. Gunn and Bell, 18.
25. In *The Bourgeois*, Franco Moretti offers empirical evidence from the Google Books corpus that ties the rise of the term "middle class" to debates surrounding Reform: "in the years immediately preceding the 1832 Reform Bill—when the relationship between social structure and political representation moves to the centre of public life—'middle class' and 'middle classes' become suddenly two or three times more frequent that 'bourgeois'" (11). Although Moretti does not employ Levine's vocabulary of "affordances," he similarly asserts that "once the baptism had occurred and the new term had solidified, all sorts of consequences (and reversals)" followed (12).
26. Dror Wahrman, *Imagining the Middle Class*, 1.
27. Ibid. 27.
28. Ibid. 54, 226.
29. Ibid. 375–6.
30. Devoting roughly five of its twenty-two pages to an explication of Wahrman's *Imagining the Middle Class*, James Thompson 's "After the Fall: Class and Political Language in Britain, 1780–1900" lauds Wahrman's "wealth of material" and asserts that "Wahrman powerfully demonstrates that after the 1790s the 'middle-class idiom" was primarily concerned to emphasize the pacific and conservative nature of these groups in society" (797–8). Ultimately, Thompson judges that "Wahrman is making a strong argument for the absolute centrality of 1832 to subsequent notions of the rise of the middle class" (800). By contrast, Gunn finds Wahrman's book much less worthy of space or praise, asserting that "studies [like Wahrman's] that concentrate on class as a discursive or rhetorical construct tend to neglect the issues of power and inequality that are central to any effective understanding of the concept" (4).
31. Wahrman, 317.
32. According to Seed, by the 1830s "there was a broad consensus that £300 per annum was the minimum for sustaining a middle-class standard of living" (121).
33. Gunn asserts that, beyond "the fact of property ownership what served to unify the middle class, above all, was culture, conceived from the early nineteenth century as a sphere of consensus and reconciliation" (24).

34. This is a highly selective list of some of the primary features of middle-class culture, aspects of which are treated in greater detail and at much greater length by numerous social historians, including Gunn, Gunn and Bell, R. J. Morris, Seed, and many others.
35. "Thus the middle classes were structured by the variety of different relationships to capital available to them, the fixed and circulating capital of the manufacturers and craftsmen, the finance and variable capital of the merchant, the stock of the retailer, the human capital of the professional man and the rentier assets of the 'independent' income group. Within all of these groups thus defined by the nature of their relationship to capital, there existed a range of status rankings. Status itself was an important influence upon options and preferences for social action" (Morris, *Class, Sect and Party*, 319).
36. "The novel was an art form which grew in popularity alongside the expansion of the middle classes; commuting created a whole new time in the day for men to read, while many middle-class women now had quiet leisure time at home which could be filled by novels. While much popular literature was, of course, escapist, novels concerned with family and domesticity often addressed the minutiae of life in such a way as to allow their readers to learn" (Gunn and Bell 37).
37. Lauren M. E. Goodlad, *Victorian Literature and the Victorian State*, 130. More recently, Aeron Hunt has more specifically positioned character as central to "the problems of representation not only in the Victorian economy but in the writing, literary and nonliterary, that engaged and helped to produce it"; this writing, Hunt argues, "centers on character: the social, performative, and textual form through which the personal emerges in practice and discourse as a crucial vector of power within economic life" (*Personal Business*, 4).
38. This relevance of sociological theory has been noted by numerous previous critics, including Goodlad and Hunt, whose accounts of character build perceptibly upon Weber's work, and Gunn, who subtly deploys Bourdieu in his historical reconstruction of middle-class public culture.
39. Max Weber, *Economy and Society*, I.19.
40. Ibid. I.6.
41. Ibid. I.7. On Weber's diachronic and explicitly historicized concept of rationality, as well as his confidence in his own abilities to discern rationality in whatever form it appears, see also his *Protestant Ethic and the Spirit of Capitalism*, 39. On rationality as the "ideal type," rather than the objective condition, of human action, see also Weber's *Basic Concepts in Sociology*, 32–3.
42. Weber, *Economy and Society*, I.213.
43. Ibid. I.242.
44. Ibid. I.305–7.
45. Ibid. II.927.

46. Ibid. II.910–11. Weber does appear to imagine that conflicts between modern rational systems of domination, grounded in what he calls "discipline," and charismatic or status-based system will almost always result in the triumph of the modern system: "The force of discipline not only eradicates personal charisma but also stratification by status groups; at least one of its results is the rational transformation of status stratification" (*On Charisma and Institution Building*, 28).
47. Weber, *Economy and Society*, II.926, II.936. On the opposition between class and status, see also *On Charisma and Institution Building*, 177.
48. Weber, *Economy and Society*, II.938.
49. Pierre Bourdieu, *Distinction*, xii.
50. Ibid. 505.
51. Ibid. 114.
52. Ibid. 125.
53. Ibid. 170.
54. Ibid. 227.
55. As Bourdieu observes, "of all the objects offered for consumers' choice, there are none more classifying than legitimate works of art, which, while distinctive in general, enable the production of distinctions ad infinitum by playing on divisions and sub-divisions into genres, periods, styles, authors, etc" (16).
56. Ibid. 172.
57. Ibid. 466.
58. "Two basic facts were thus established: on the one hand, the very close relationship linking cultural practices (or the corresponding opinions) to educational capital (measured by qualifications) and, secondarily, to social origin (measured by father's occupation); and, on the other hand, the fact that, at equivalent levels of educational capital, the weight of social origin in the practice- and preference-explaining system increases as one moves away from the most legitimate area of culture" (Bourdieu, 13).
59. Ibid. 208.
60. Bourdieu's preference for language expressing collective as opposed to individual agency appears most strained in his discussion of the petite bourgeoisie, a point to which I shall return later.
61. Ibid. 53.
62. Weber, *Economy and Society*, II.934.
63. Ibid., II.937, emphasis in original; II.935.
64. Bourdieu, *Distinction*, 56; see also 468.
65. This reliance upon charisma in Victorian business, where transactions at a distance were predicated upon trust in individuals, is precisely what Hunt means to highlight by the term "personal business," the acknowledgment of which means that our "understanding of Victorian business—even Victorian 'big business'—must be flexible enough to comprehend the uneven, constantly transforming patterns

of impersonality and abstraction, personalization and embeddedness, that coexisted in tension in representations and in economic practice" (*Personal Business*, 14).
66. See Pionke, *The Ritual Culture of Victorian Professionals*.
67. Bourdieu, *Distinction*, xii, 73.
68. Ibid. 345.
69. For a much lengthier account of the publication and English reception of *Poets and Poetry and America*, see Pionke, "'Horn-Handed and Pig-Headed.'"
70. [John Forster], "American Poetry," 297, 301. Advertising his own much finer judgment of poetic quality, Forster exempts from his otherwise sweeping dismissal of American poetry the work of Ralph Waldo Emerson, Fitz-Greene Halleck, William Cullen Bryant, and, supremely, William Wadsworth Longfellow.
71. Rufus S. Griswold, ed., *The Poets and Poetry of America*, v.
72. [John Forster], "American Poetry," 298.
73. Ibid. 296.
74. Ibid. 297.
75. Ibid. 296.
76. See, for instance, Dickens's letter to Forster of 24 February 1842 in *The Letters of Charles Dickens*, 81–90. Not only did Forster receive regular updates from Dicken by letter, but the English public was in the midst of reading a fictional re-presentation of Dickens's experience in January, 1844, when not only Forster's review of Griswold's anthology but also Dickens's thirteenth monthly number of *Martin Chuzzlewit* appeared in print.
77. Richard Salmon, *The Formation of the Victorian Literary Professional*, 12.
78. William Wordsworth, Preface to *Lyrical Ballads*, 128.
79. William Wordsworth, "Essay, Supplementary to the Preface," 83.
80. Arthur Henry Hallam, "On Some of the Characteristics of Modern Poetry, and on the Lyric Poems of Alfred Tennyson," 616, 619.
81. Robert Browning, "Essay on Shelley," 143.
82. Elizabeth Barrett Browning, *Aurora Leigh*, 5.258–60.
83. It is important to acknowledge that the five middle-class-specific negative assertions of value that occupy this book were, themselves, predicated upon a broader repudiation grounded in a broadly racialized national chauvinism. That is, one's legitimacy as a middle-class Victorian presupposed that one was English – as opposed to American, Austrian, French, Italian, Prussian, Russian, or of any other national origin – and white. Indeed, the assurance with which middle-class Victorians pursued reputation and fortune within Britain's global colonial empire suggests a relative absence of anxiety over their supposed natural superiority to the peoples of color with whom they came into contact.

Chapter 1

The Orphan Narratives of a Class Lacking Antecedents

Victorian fiction is disproportionately populated by orphans and bastards. According to demographic historians, there were an average of approximately 38,000 of the former in state care at any one time between 1844 and 1877, a period in which the total population grew from between sixteen to twenty-five million; whereas at no point in nineteenth-century history did the illegitimacy ratio, the percentage of registered baptisms recorded as unsolemnized by parental marriage, rise above seven percent.[1] Although there is room for considerable debate about these numbers, no amount of methodological revisionism will account empirically for the proliferation or prominence of characters without parents or without legitimate parentage in the mid-nineteenth-century novel. Among the embarrassment of illegitimate riches is Emily Brontë's *Wuthering Heights* (1847), which recounts the disruptive introduction of a presumably orphaned, illegitimate, and racially suspect foundling brought home from Liverpool, Heathcliff, on successive generations of families at adjacent country estates.[2] In *Bleak House* (1853), Charles Dickens offers a veritable catalog of orphans, from Jo, the poor crossing sweeper; to Ada and Richard, the wards of John Jarndyce who are also competing plaintiffs in the novel's Chancery case; to Esther, who, it turns out, is also illegitimate. Elizabeth Gaskell's contemporary novel, *Ruth* (1853), features an eponymous orphan who gives birth to an illegitimate son and ultimately dies from a fever caught from the rakish father of her child. At the end of the decade, George Eliot similarly constructs the plot of *Adam Bede* (1859) around the seduction of a working-class orphan by a member of the squirarchy, although in this case the birth and death of their bastard child creates a different set of legal problems for the rural community of Hayslope.

In so centrally featuring fictional individuals with a tenuous relationship to their consanguineous pasts, Victorian novelists were both doubling down on and subtly remaking a characterological trend with a significant pedigree in English literary history. As critics often note, Shakespeare's *King Lear* provides an early-modern prototype for the literary bastard as "sexy scoundrel" in Edmund, who consistently outshines his legitimate half-brother Edgar even as he schemes to inherit lands and titles to which he has no legal claim.[3] Edmund's fictional heirs came into their own in the eighteenth-century novel, which features a lively cast of (sometimes only apparently) illegitimate, eponymous, and frequently picaresque protagonists, from Daniel Defoe's *Moll Flanders* (1722) to Henry Fielding's *Tom Jones* (1749) to Fanny Burney's *Evelina* (1778) to Robert Bage's *Hermsprong* (1796). Critics such as Jenny Bourne Taylor, Wolfram Schmidgen, and Lisa Zunshine have sought to historicize this fictional fascination with bastardy, which they have convincingly yoked to various cultural instabilities brought about by dramatic growth in the numbers and inheritable wealth of the middle ranks of eighteenth-century society. Taylor focuses on the challenges this demographic and economic transformation posed to traditional notions of patriarchy, opening up "a particular kind of symbolised and social space for the mother – albeit one which is never straightforwardly oppositional," whereas Schmidgen positions the literary bastard as a liminal figure whose "curiously disembodied" social mobility exposes without radically upsetting the century's "vertical solidarities of property and patronage," including, presumably, those grounded in gender difference.[4] Further elaborating upon "the multiplicity of cultural meanings of bastardy," Zunshine ambitiously reconstructs four concomitant views of illegitimacy in eighteenth-century culture. The two most productive for period fiction both articulate apprehensions centered on society's middle strata: the first in the form of a "threatening pretender" with the capacity "to disrupt the smooth transfer of property and to poison the emotional well-being of the family"; the second under the more pathetic guise of an illegitimate child abandoned by its serving-class mother, historically a ward of London's newly-created Foundling Hospital and fictionally "a correlative to the middle-class family anxiety about the encroaching illegitimate children of its philandering patriarch."[5]

As these and other literary and cultural historians have observed, a subtle shift in the rhetoric surrounding illegitimacy, including its representation in the novel, occurred during the last decades of the eighteenth and the first decades of the nineteenth century. Foundling narratives began to outpace those centered on the picaresque and/or sexy scoundrel, and the highly unlikely figure of the "fictional 'crypto-bastard,'" the foundling who is ultimately discovered to have been born to legitimately wedded parents, appeared with greater frequency.[6] Simultaneously, and in keeping with both the ethos of Romanticism and the growing imbrication of sexual reputation and social status among England's middle ranks, there was also an increasing number of stories about orphans in search of their true selves, which may or may not relate to their true parentage, whose personal stories are bound up with broader striving for societal amelioration. The first of these trends leans heavily upon melodramatic convention, while the second borrows from and contributes to the growth of the bildungsroman.[7]

Leavening their melodrama with social realism and their narratives of development with more prescriptively ambitious calls for social reform, Victorian novelists elevated the orphan to new prominence, continued their predecessors' fascination with the foundling, and inverted the previous century's appraisal of the bastard by introducing the more sympathetic figure of the "natural" child.[8] These and other trends in the numerous Victorian fictions of (il)legitimacy have remained objects of critical interest since Nina Auerbach's rather sweeping survey of "Incarnations of the Orphan" in a 1975 *ELH* article. Although she lumps together the orphan, the foundling, the bastard, and the natural child – figures whom subsequent scholars have taken pains to distinguish from each other – Auerbach establishes some of the key points of entry for later inquiries, including a provocative metaphorical connection between the orphan and the novel, a generic link between the orphan and the picaro, and a social-historical foundation for the dramatic upsurge in characters "without precedent or visible sanction" in a Victorian period "orphaned ... of its sense of its own past."[9] Taylor, Lydia Murdoch, and Laura Peters have extended and refined Auerbach's argument on both theoretical and historical grounds. Marrying her feminist approach to illegitimacy, outlined above, with a nuanced appreciation for the dynamics of secrecy and cognition surrounding its fictionalization, Taylor suggests that "by the middle of the nineteenth century, 'illegitimacy' has become a particularly powerful means of figuring the transmission of hidden memories within a family and from one generation to the next."[10] Attentive to the fiction and propaganda depicting, as well as the institutional practices governing, the urban poor, Murdoch "examines the surprising disjunction between the popular representations of Victorian poor children and the ways in which families actually used state and philanthropic welfare services" and connects this incongruity to a growing ideological gap between middle-class ideals of domestic and imperial citizenship and working-class appeals to "the traditional rights and liberties of freeborn Englishmen, among which parental rights were central."[11] In *Orphan Texts: Victorian Orphans, Culture and Empire*, Peters offers perhaps the most robust study of fictional orphanhood currently available. Highlighting the central representational role of the family in Victorian culture, she positions the orphan as a convenient scapegoat capable of diffusing widespread anxiety over what was, in many ways, an unrealizable but nevertheless normalizing ideal of consanguineous middle-class domesticity, and observes that "the linking of orphanhood and illegitimacy persists and challenges the middle classes themselves."[12] Peters also helpfully reconstructs the Victorians' capacious notion of orphanhood, a vulnerable state brought on not just by the death of both parents, or even only one parent, but also by the loss of "protection, advantages, benefits, or happiness, previously enjoyed."[13]

Taylor, Murdoch, and Peters all agree that the watershed event coloring the Victorians' understanding of orphans, bastards, and illegitimacy more generally was the passage of the 1834 Poor Law Amendment Act, most commonly remembered as the New Poor Law. An instrumental attempt to reduce the number of poor dependents on the parish, and hence to protect financially vulnerable middle-class residents from rising taxes, the New Poor Law institutionalized the workhouse and sought to legislate a Malthusian solution to lower-class illegitimacy. The Act's infamous bastardy clauses removed the ability of mothers to publicly name and seek financial support from the fathers of their illegitimate children.[14] This dramatic legal revision of England's historical reliance on canon law was quickly cast as the "philanderer's charter" by critics, who mobilized both melodramatic conventions surrounding the upper-class libertine and middle-class anxieties about master-servant relations. As Lisa Forman Cody asserts, these same critics also "pointed out the defenseless third party—the innocent child born out of wedlock—involved in such squabbles," thereby raising the profile of abandoned and orphaned children more broadly.[15] That the newly enfranchised middle-class Members of Parliament continued to debate the bastardy clauses until 1844, when a new Act re-empowered mothers of illegitimate children to sue for compensation from fathers in the Petty Sessions, suggests that at stake in this durable public conversation over workhouse orphans, parish rates, and illegitimacy was more than just the welfare of the poor.

Victorian fiction writers were well aware of the middle-class subtext to this ostensibly working-class-focused debate, and frequently used the figures of the orphan, the bastard, the foundling, and the natural child, to explore the fragility and novelty of middle-class status. This chapter reconstructs their efforts in two ways. First, a series of brief readings of novels published in the three decades after the passage of the New Poor Law hints at the ubiquity, representational potential, and middle-class valence of various incarnations of the orphan in period fiction.[16] Second, a detailed interpretation of Wilkie Collins's *No Name* (1862), a novel particularly interested in the interanimating problems of status, orphanhood, and illegitimacy, offers a case study for the primary negative assertion of value by which Victorian writers sought to disconnect middle-class status from the overdetermining power of birth.

Novel Forms of Victorian (Il)Legitimacy

If the myriad orphans of Victorian fiction can be said to have a single father, that novel paterfamilias is surely Charles Dickens. By turns melodramatic and realistic, often juxtaposing narratives of individual development with broader plots imprecating institutions or social conditions in desperate need of reform, Dickens's novels manifest a consistent fascination with children who have lost, become separated or estranged from, or been abandoned by their parents, whether living or dead.[17] Wildly popular in their own day and impressively durable in ours, many of Dickens's unfamilied protagonists have grown into iconic progenitors of Victorian fiction and Victorianist criticism. And none enjoys a larger place than Oliver Twist, the eponymous hero of Dickens's 1838 novelistic assault on the New Poor Law.[18] Orphaned on the day of his birth in the workhouse, his unidentified mother dead after imprinting a single kiss on his forehead, Oliver is "left to the tender mercies of churchwardens and overseers," who, it turns out, have very little to spare (Dickens, *Oliver Twist* 19). After famously incited by his fellow child sufferers to request more food, Oliver is apprenticed to an undertaker, from whom he runs away to London, where he is recruited into the Jewish fence Fagin's criminal gang to be trained as a thief.

Saved, then lost, then saved again with the aid of a repentant prostitute, Nancy, and her saintly, middle-class, and orphaned counterpart,

Rose, Oliver melodramatically suffers from persecution by another character, Monks, who conspires with the workhouse beadle, Mr Bumble, to conceal Oliver's patrimony. The truth nevertheless emerges – despite all that Monks, Bumble, and the bastardy clauses of the New Poor Law can do to prevent it – that Oliver is Monk's illegitimate half-brother and Rose's nephew.[19] With his philandering father and virtuous maternal aunt identified, his legitimate half-brother discredited, and his own minority unstained "with any public act of dishonor, meanness, cowardice, or wrong," Oliver enters the middle class not through birth, but via adoption by Mr Brownlow, the original target of his first, failed attempt at pickpocketing.[20] Dickens's remarkable reworking of previous fictional conventions for representing orphanhood, bastardy, (il)legitimacy, melodrama, mystery, and criminality established a new, eminently imitable Victorian pattern for orphan stories. At the same time, as Susan Zlotnick asserts, this tale of "The Parish Boy's Progress" also provided "an origin myth for the birth of the middle class."[21] Uncoupled from patrilineal consanguinity and hence from aristocratic notions of birth, Oliver's middle-class status principally emerges out of other characters' recognition that he deserves it.[22]

Oliver's counterpart, and perhaps the most famous female orphan in Victorian fiction, is Charlotte Brontë's Jane Eyre, whose own 1847 story is replete with children (and adults) who have been severed from their consanguineous pasts.[23] Unlike Oliver, whose mother's death consigns him immediately to the workhouse, Jane begins her narrative already adopted by wealthy middle-class relatives, the Reeds, after her own parents' untimely demise. Her adoption does not save her from orphandom, however, in either of the senses defined by Peters. A childhood confrontation with her cousin John precipitates her expulsion from the Reeds' family home of Gateshead and her relocation for the rest of her childhood to Lowood, among the least charitable of charity schools. Here, a dearth of wash basins, an excess of burnt porridge, and a system of instruction in which public humiliation plays a large part constitute a significant loss of "protection, advantages, benefits," and this before an outbreak of typhus reduces the "Orphan Asylum" from a "seminary into an hospital."[24] At eighteen, having survived Lowood's initial deprivations and subsequent reforms and risen to the rank of teacher, Jane leaves the school to become a governess at Thornfield Hall, where her pupil is Adèle, the illegitimate French daughter of the ex-mistress of the property's owner, Edward Rochester (who is not, however, Adèle's biological father). Estranged from his own father and elder brother, now deceased, Rochester presides over this unusual nuclear family of orphans, grooming Jane into nearly accepting his illegitimate, because secretly bigamous, offer of marriage. Fleeing Thornfield in the middle of the night after she discovers the truth, Jane finds herself orphaned once again; after she leaves her belongings in a coach, she is even suspected by the villagers in Morton of being a fallen woman and nearly dies of exposure before finding refuge with the Rivers siblings at Moor House. Mary, Diana, and St. John have, themselves, recently lost their parents, who died without leaving a significant patrimony, and so all are preparing for a life of labor, the sisters as governesses and the brother as an overseas missionary.

The significance of this novel family of the unfamilied is to show the ability of its constituent members to counteract the overdetermining power of their own orphanhood and nevertheless attain middle-class status. The Rivers siblings manage their reascent up the class ladder by their capacity for self-denying charity even when in comparative want themselves, taking in the friendless Jane under an assumed name despite the suspicions of their lone remaining servant. Jane eventually discovers that she is, in fact, related to her companions, with whom she divides an unexpected legacy from the same childless uncle who had denied her cousins an inheritance, thereby preserving the sisters, at least, from the need to work. Undeterred from his purpose, St. John almost succeeds in compelling Jane to accompany him as his wife, before she is saved from what she foresees as her own certain death in India by a supernatural summons back to Rochester. She discovers Thornfield destroyed by Rochester's legitimate and insane wife, Bertha, herself now dead; Rochester physically disfigured and presumably financially reduced by his loss; and their own mutual love augmented by their greater physical and financial equality and shared orphan state.[25] Told retrospectively by Jane ten years after their marriage, *Jane Eyre* appears motivated by a desire to establish the legitimacy of their union, Jane's independent rise to the upper-middle class, and the status of their child, who will eventually inherit their combined material and emotional wealth.

The marriage and inheritance of another female orphan occupies the majority of attention in Anthony Trollope's *Doctor Thorne* (1858), the principal plot of which seems designed to prove that wealth, coupled with character, outranks even unambiguous bastardy. The illegitimate daughter of the titular doctor's rakish younger brother, Henry Thorne, and a working-class woman, Mary Scatcherd, whom Henry had seduced precisely because she was engaged to be married – according to Trollope's narrator, "the devil had tempted him to tempt her" – Mary Thorne was orphaned before birth. Her maternal uncle, Roger Scatcherd, beat Henry Thorne to death in a drunken rage induced by the discovery of his sister's pregnancy.[26] While this uncle was incarcerated for manslaughter, her mother received and was brought to accept a renewed offer of marriage and emigration from her former fiancé, who stipulated that the infant be left in England. As the narrator recounts, Mary Thorne might at this point have been "left to live or die as a workhouse bastard," not unlike Oliver Twist, but she was instead adopted by her paternal uncle, Dr Thomas Thorne.[27] Raised at a local farm house until age six and then sent to boarding school in Bath until age twelve, Mary is brought home to live full time with the doting doctor in Greshamsbury, where she completes her education – in music, French, German, and the subtler arts of performing the role of a young lady – alongside the privileged daughters of the town's most prominent family, the Greshams.

These local worthies are both related by marriage to the Earl de Courcy and deeply in debt, which facts cast a disapprobrious shadow over the young heir, Frank Gresham, and his affection for the reciprocally affected Mary. Frank is even brought by his materialist relatives to propose, however halfheartedly, to another orphan, the wealthy Miss Dunstable, heir to a fortune accrued by her father selling a patent medicine, the "Ointment of Lebanon"; too ethical to accept his offer, she instead invites him to confess to her of his love for Mary. Meanwhile, the now-released and still-alcoholic Roger Scatcherd somewhat improbably rises from convicted murderer to wealthy railway developer and becomes the Gresham's largest creditor. His even more implausible will states that his great wealth, including his mortgages on the Gresham estate, will be inherited by his legitimate but unappealing son, Louis Philippe, on the latter's twenty-fifth birthday. When Louis, who might well remind Victorian readers of a dissolute Monks, drinks himself to death before coming of age, Scatcherd's riches duly pass to his absent sister's eldest child, who, it is legally proven, is Mary Thorne. Frank and Mary's marriage is approved by the elder Mr Gresham before news of the inheritance emerges, allowing Mary to enter the family of "the first commoner in Barsetshire" on her own merits.[28] Once her newfound wealth is more widely publicized, even the de Courcys allow that Frank has made a good match, despite the fact that "birth and blood are very valuable gifts."[29]

Published at the start of the "sensation sixties," a decade of which it was a herald and for which it would serve as a pattern, Wilkie Collins's *The Woman in White* (1860) ends on the same note as

Jane Eyre and *Doctor Thorne*, with the birth of the next generation of England's landed gentry.[30] Unlike its predecessors, however, Collins's novel presents this happy event as equal parts question and exclamation, such that proving Walter and Laura's child the legitimate "Heir of Limmeridge" becomes, arguably, the *raison d'être* of the text.[31] That little Walter's legitimacy remains at risk after an appropriate nine months of serial gestation in the pages of *All the Year Round* and *Harper's Magazine* testifies to the thoroughness with which *The Woman in White* deploys its interanimating and epistemologically destabilizing themes of orphanhood and bastardy.[32] The story features a robust cast of incarnations of the orphan, all of whose "true" fictional identities have been further obscured by the use of "feigned names": Walter Hartright, the romantically ambitious drawing-master protagonist, has already lost his father and, once sent on his masculine quest to Honduras, swiftly leaves his modest "protections, advantages, benefits" behind in the Central American jungle; half-sisters Laura Fairlie and Marian Halcombe have no living parents and both experience a precipitous, if temporary, decline in circumstances from Limmeridge House to "furnished lodgings of the humblest kind" in London's East End; Laura is additionally confined for a time in a private lunatic asylum when her identity is purposefully confused with that her other, illegitimate half-sister, Anne Catherick, the titular "woman in white"; Anne and Laura's captivity serves the interests of Sir Percival Glyde, baronet, the "natural" child of unmarried parents who seeks to preserve his fraudulent claim to his family's property and status by falsifying a parish register and ruthlessly protecting the "Secret" of his status as a bastard.[33]

The final third of the novel chronicles Walter's efforts to expose the conspiracy by which Laura has been defrauded and to force the inhabitants of Limmeridge House and its estate to recognize her original identity, regardless of "the machinery of the Law."[34] Both representing and unravelling this tangled skein of illegitimacies moved Collins to invent a new method of novelistic narration whereby a fictional master narrator, Walter, purportedly compiles a series of first-person witness statements from multiple subsidiary narrators, himself included, supposedly in order to "present the truth always in its most direct and most intelligible aspect ... word for word."[35] Incredibly successful as a novelistic conceit – Collins increased the circulation of *All the Year Round* above the level it had attained while serializing Dickens's *A Tale of Two Cities*, and *Woman-in-White*-themed merchandise was sold across London – this complex narrative method foregrounds (il)legitimacy at the level of form. The novel, in effect, becomes its own offspring, an orphan whose worth is determined not by its writerly birth but by its readerly consumption.

The Middle Class as *Filius Nullius* in *No Name*

The quasi-legalistic narrative structure invented by Collins for *The Woman in White* has among its advantages that it effectively allows for two authorial prefaces. That provided by Collins's master narrator, Walter Hartright, famously opposes the "Law," too often suspect for serving as "the prearranged servant of the long purse," and literature, as represented by a story the fathoming of whose truth shall be left not to a "Judge" but to the "Reader."[36] Hartright's preamble lays the groundwork for a novel centered on identity theft, sensational death, and status reversal in which a would-be baronet is revealed as a bastard and a lowly drawing master's son is elevated to the gentry. Collins's authorial preface to the second edition then acknowledges his own "very large circle of readers" for their "public approval," explains the "pains" he took to avoid "misleading" them – in the process claiming them by means of a strategically deployed personal possessive – and cites the "reception accorded to *The Woman in White*" as confirmation of his theory of fiction (32). Readers thus substitute for presiding lawyers within the text and legitimate the author of that text within the broader circuit of Victorian letters.

The voluminous audience for *The Woman in White* – it outsold rival/mentor Charles Dickens's contemporary novel *Great Expectations* (1861) – also stood Collins in good stead when he negotiated the sale of his next book, *No Name* (1862).[37] Purchased by Sampson & Low for £3,000, a sum ironically equal to the annual revenue of the Limmeridge estate in Collins's prior fiction, *No Name* is indebted to its predecessor for more than just the value of its volume publication rights. Law is once more placed in opposition to justice on the subject of inheritance, and both personal identity and social status remain central topoi.[38] Collins also employs a similar conceptual framing mechanism; although, in the case of *No Name*, which relies upon a more traditional strategically omniscient singular narrator, as opposed to the multiple first-person witness-narrators of *The Woman in White*, Collins functionally combines the previously doubled complementary paratexts into a single authorial preface. In it, he juxtaposes "the truth as it is in Nature" with the implied standards of an artificial society, which, among other flaws, often fails to sympathize with "a pathetic character" if that character manifests "perversity" or "errors" and persists in dogmatizing "that there is no such moral phenomenon as unmixed tragedy to be found in the world" (5). Collins then invokes "the experience of my readers" to reinforce his binary opposition and thereby confirm his "laws of Art" (5). This prefatory strategy denaturalizes polite society while naturalizing Art, effectively legitimating the now financially secure novelist "on the authority of [his] many readers" (5).[39]

Near the end of the preface, Collins explains that in *No Name* he has followed "a new course . . . to enlarge the range of my studies in the art of writing fiction" (6). Although the primary example of novelistic innovation cited concerns the de-emphasis of secrecy in favor of rousing "the reader's interest in following the train of circumstances by which . . . foreseen events are brought about" (6), an equally significant change from *The Woman in White* is a slight slide down the social scale into a region more recognizable as middle class.[40] No hereditary title will be imperiled by documentary fraud and no tenanted estate will be the object of a criminal conspiracy; instead, two middle-class women living comfortably near the top of that stratum will have their status stripped away by an act of English inheritance law. *No Name* might therefore be read as an experiment in the representation of class deprived of the legitimating affirmation of birth.

"A compound of negatives"[41]

This severance of social standing from consanguineous relation is first raised while the plot remains in its initial expository stage through the character of Mr Clare. The "satirically indifferent" neighbor of the upper-middle-class Vanstones, Clare belongs "to the younger branch of a family of great antiquity," from whom he has inherited "a magnificent library" and little else (35–6). This self-described "pauper with a pedigree" claims to have "outlived all human prejudices," including that prescribing special favoritism towards his three sons, whom he regards as little more than "a necessary domestic evil" perpetually threatening "the sanctity of his study and the safety of his books" (36). Dismissing "the unimportant accident of their birth from all consideration," Clare judges his progeny "below average in every respect" and "addle-headed from infancy" (37). An unenthusiastic father and thoroughly cynical pragmatist, he imagines making "Frank a butcher, Cecil a baker, and Arthur a grocer—those being the only human vocations I know of which are certain to be always in request" (37). That such occupations would entail a precipitous descent down the social ladder and a virtual abdication of their inherited status does not appear to concern him at all. In fact, his aggressive neglect plays upon the "ordinary prejudices" of Mr Vanstone, who practically adopts all three boys, playing the father's part to the eldest so far as to apprentice him to a civil engineer of his acquaintance (37). Clare thus makes a "compound of negatives" out of the status-legitimating force of birth on three levels: first, he assumes the role of "impartial spectator" with respect to his sons; second, he envisions transforming his young gentlemen by birth into tradesmen by profession; and third, he resigns the role of parent and patron to a neighbor with whom he shares no blood relation (38).

Fortunately for Clare's sons, their virtual adoption does not require much sacrifice on their part, as the Vanstones thoroughly affirm their affluent middle-class status through patterns of conspicuous consumption and cultural participation. The novel opens in the early morning on the ground floor of the family's "country residence in West Somersetshire, called Combe-Raven" (7). Located fashionably one county south of Bristol and Bath, the house is divided into public rooms on the ground floor – among them the entry hall, library, breakfast-room, and morning-room – with family bedrooms immediately upstairs and servants' quarters "in the higher regions of the house" (7).[42] The hall is marked by a clock and the family also owns a piano; moreover, the grounds include "a garden and paddock ... a stream, some farm-buildings," and a conservatory (12).[43] The family's indoor servants are, in order of appearance, a cook, a housemaid, a lady's-maid, a kitchen-maid, and a footman, as well as a governess, "not one of the forlorn, persecuted, pitiably dependent order of governesses," but rather a trusted friend of the family who now oversees the "entire management of the household ... and to those duties she was free to add what companionable assistance she could render ... and what friendly superintendence she could still exercise" with respect to the Vanstones' two grown daughters (10, 24). The hall-clock reveals that the household is off to a late start as a result of the principals' attendance at the previous evening's Beethoven symphony, performed in Bristol, where the family also evidently attends the theatre.[44] Combe-Raven is, in short, a country estate worthy of the wealthy son of a now-deceased "manufacturer in the North of England" (124).

Although one might argue that the affirmation of upper-middle-class status through the acquisition and domestic display of expensive furnishings already includes a significant performative element,

No Name much more explicitly imbricates theatricality and legitimacy in its opening pages. The Vanstones' younger daughter, Magdalen, who possesses a "plastic, ever-changing face" and a natural talent for accurate and amusing mimicry, first reveals her full performative potential in a private theatrical put on by the neighboring Marrable family (14). Initially cast as Lucy, the scheming maid, in Sheridan's *The Rivals*, Magdalen's efforts at her first rehearsal prompt the hired director to proclaim her "a born actress, if ever there was one" (57). The resignation of another of the players ultimately promotes Magdalen to a leading position as she absorbs the additional role, triumphantly displaying her "rare faculty of dramatic impersonation" by acting as both Lucy and Julia, the play's pure and long-suffering female romantic, to the acclaim of "two hundred exiles from the blessings of ventilation, all simmering together in their own animal heat" (63). Unfortunately for Magdalen, affirmatively demonstrating that she is a "born actress" implies a social, if not ancestral, relation to entirely the wrong class of people. As her former governess, Miss Garth, informs her in a letter written after Magdalen has begun acting professionally, "Your way of life, however pure your conduct may be . . . is a suspicious way of life to all respectable people" (313).[45] In her own dramatic way, then, Magdalen invokes the same disjunction between inherited and performed social standing as did Mr Clare's hypothetical vocations for his sons.

The original dramatic staging of the play-within-the-novel occurs in "The First Scene," set at "Combe-Raven, Somersetshire" (7). In fact, *No Name* is conceived in eight scenes, each limited to a specific location in Collins's paratextual headings, as well as a corresponding number of connecting epistolary sections labeled "Between the Scenes."[46] Heavily indebted to theatrical convention at the level of structure, the novel is also focalized around characters with clear antecedents in popular melodrama. Perhaps not surprisingly, *No Name* was immediately adapted for the stage. Collins initially paid American expatriate playwright and critic William Bayle Bernard to produce a five-act play based on the novel, which was duly published in 1863 to protect Collins's dramatic copyright.[47] In 1870, Collins unsuccessfully attempted to write his own theatrical version, ultimately surrendering the work to actor Wybert Reeve, whose four-act adaptation premiered without apparent effect at Newcastle upon Tyne in 1877. The example set by Sheridan with *The Rivals* was not to be repeated. And although the state of copyright law in the 1860s made it a sensible financial decision to publish a dramatic adaptation as quickly as possible, Collins's enduring dalliance with the theatre in *No Name* potentially imperiled his own claims to middle-class professional status, first by yoking his novel to an even more suspect genre in melodrama and, second, by failing to obtain an audience that might justify his descent from page to stage.

No Name may not have legitimated Collins's avocation as a dramatist, but it certainly demonstrated his training as a lawyer. The novel's turn from exposition to necessary action pivots on English inheritance law, explained at length in the twelfth and thirteenth chapters of "The First Scene" by the Vanstones' family lawyer, Mr Pendril, to Miss Garth. Meeting only one day after the funeral of Mr and Mrs Andrew Vanstone, they "confront each other in the silence of the summer's morning—both dressed in black," and they engage in a "formal interchange of question and answer . . . customary inquiries, and the customary expressions of sympathy," all conducted with a sense of "ceremony, in . . . conventional tone" (117–18).[48] Their affirmative demonstrations of middle-class propriety are raised to such prominence – and even, perhaps, subtly mocked by means of the homophonic morning/mourning – that they at first impede these otherwise worthy characters' sympathy for each other. Appropriate to the earlier theatricality of the novel, their conversation remains at first constrained by a set of socially prescribed behaviors that, because of their explicitness in the narrative, render somewhat indistinct the boundaries between convention and performance.

The requisite social forms observed, Mr Pendril gets down to the business of rescinding the association between the status and birth of the Vanstones' adult daughters, twenty-six-year-old Norah and eighteen-year-old Magdalen. Both are not merely illegitimate, their parents not having been married to each other when the children were born, but the offspring of adultery, as for most of their lives their father remained bound within an imprudent marriage contracted while a young army officer stationed in Canada.[49] As Mr Pendril didactically observes, the former condition would be sufficient under England's "abominable" laws of legitimacy to make Norah and Magdalen "Nobody's Children"; the latter fact, however, places them "out of the pale of the Civil Law of Europe" (138–9).[50] Their consanguineous connection to Andrew Vanstone, then, is insufficient to guarantee that his upper-middle-class status, in the form of the Vanstone family name, extends to them. For the first sixteen days of the narrative, they preserve their ability to inherit the hall clock, piano, and other real and personal property that would enable them to affirm their status through public acts of consumption, thanks to their father's will, which had been duly executed five years prior to the opening scene. After 20 March, 1846, however, Norah and Magdalen are unknowingly placed at risk by their parents' secret marriage in London, since, according to English law, "a man's marriage . . . destroys the validity of any will which he may have made as a single man; and . . . renders absolutely necessary the entire reassertion of his testamentary intentions in the character of a husband" (136). When their father dies intestate, two thirds of his £80,000 fortune bypasses them for Andrew Vanstone's legally recognized next of kin, briefly their newly-legitimated newborn sibling, who is succeeded at death by the child's paternal uncle, Andrew's estranged elder brother Michael. The remaining one third passes to their mother, who dies in childbirth, also without a will, leaving Norah and Magdalen with nothing.

The remainder of the novel occupies itself with the question of whether, deprived of the guarantee of birth, the sisters can retain or regain their middle-class status. Their first response to their disinheritance consists of a joint appeal, made on their behalf by Mr Pendril, to their uncle. His rude epistolary rejection of their affecting story reinforces the novel's delegitimation of consanguinity as a basis for inheritance, whether of status or money: not only does Michael Vanstone claim their inheritance as his "by right," but he also asserts this right as "a proper compensation" for his original estrangement from his own father, an estrangement which he continues to attribute to "the vile intrigue" of his deceased younger brother (155). He goes on to recommend that Norah and Magdalen should, "as becomes their birth, gain their bread in situations," offering to "assist them to start virtuously in life, by a present of one hundred pounds each" (155). The lawyer's announcement of his lack of success occurs in a scene, at the beginning of which Magdalen's face, "always remarkable for its want of colour, was now startling to contemplate, in its blank bloodless pallor"; after she reads the letter itself, her face undergoes a further undefined change to a degree that, momentarily at least, "made the familiar features suddenly look strange, even to her sister" (152, 156).[51] Cast aside by their uncle, they are nevertheless succored by their former governess, who offers to house them in London at a prosperous school that she owns with her sister, "until time has helped us to bear our affliction better than we can bear it now," after which she will aid them to "earn their own independence . . . as a gentleman's daughters should," by becoming private governesses in some of the "best families in this land" (162–3). That in so doing she should, in fact, reinforce Michael Vanstone's advice, is an irony that goes unremarked.

"Triumph in the art of self-disguise"[52]

After this point, the sisters' respective responses to their new statusless status diverge. Norah accepts Miss Garth's help and finds work as a governess, effectively renouncing her claims on the inheritance and ceasing to perform or otherwise affirmatively assert her former social privilege. At her first position – supervising two "sullen and intractable" girls in an unpleasant London family governed by a "domineering" grandmother – her mourning attire suits "her altered station; her black gown was made of stuff; her black shawl and bonnet were of the plainest and cheapest kind" (312, 272). A confrontation with the family about Magdalen (about whom more in a moment) precipitates Norah's resignation and her return to Miss Garth's establishment. Within a month, she enters into a second and more successful situation with the Tyrrels, who treat her "with as much kindness and consideration as if she was a member of the family," taking her with them to the south of France, later giving her leave to attempt to trace her sister in Aldborough, and ultimately showing themselves "heartily interested in Norah's welfare" (519, 684). Recounted mainly by others in the epistolary "Between the Scenes" sections of the novel, Norah's story offers a synecdochal example of McKeon's "sociohistorical condition of status inconsistency" met by what I have termed negative assertions of value: repudiations of birth or wealth as foundational to the middle class. Bearing "her hard lot with patience, and sweetness, and courage," Norah retains "the modest grace and neatness which no misfortune could take from her," thus performing Gilmour's gentlewomanliness and Goodlad's character to a degree that demands recognition of her now-naturalized status from the characters and readers of No Name (648, 272).

Magdalen's approach is more active, more elaborate, more susceptible to censure, and narrated at much greater length throughout the remainder of the novel. After bribing one of the servants at the school to assist her, she sells her dresses and jewelry and sets out to try her fortune on the stage.[53] This desire to move from private theatricals to public performances brings her to York, where she joins forces with Captain Horatio Wragge, who, though he claims a family connection to the now-deceased Mrs Vanstone, is, in fact, "the son of her mother's first husband, by that husband's first wife," and, therefore, "not even the widest stretch of courtesy could have included him at any time in the list of Mrs Vanstone's most distant relations" (30). Their non-consanguineous partnership begins with matrimonial parody, as Wragge declares, "'Place your departure from York, your dramatic career, and your private inquiries under my care. Here I am, unreservedly at your disposal. Say the word—do you take me?'" to which Magdalen replies succinctly, "'I do'" (226).[54] He then requests an audition, cuing Magdalen to reenact Lucy (crucially, not Julia) from *The Rivals*; with "desperate self-command" and "angry resolution," Magdalen, willfully determines to "harden" herself, then "dashe[s] at it, with a mad defiance of herself . . . The native dramatic capacity that was in her, came, hard and bold, to the surface" (228). Unlike her sister, Magdalen self-consciously strips her character "of every softening allurement which had once adorned it," electrifying Wragge into a recognition of her talent but also precipitating a "vague sense of some serious change having taken place in herself and her position" (228, 232–3). She goes on to perform a series of "At Homes" – essentially a succession of character sketches – in Derby, Nottingham, Sheffield, Manchester, Liverpool, Preston, Lancaster, Birmingham, and elsewhere, and is particularly acclaimed for her "old north-country lady," the particulars of which she borrows from Miss Garth. In her own way, then, Magdalen, too, ironically follows Michael Vanstone's advice, transforming herself into a simulacrum of her former governess to gain her bread. After slightly more than five months, she earns roughly one thousand pounds.

However, Magdalen's pecuniary sights are set considerably higher. The third element of Wragge's initial proposal concerns certain "private inquiries" he will undertake on his new partner's behalf. These consist of discovering the location, habits, and associates of Michael Vanstone. Unlike Norah, who renounces her claim on their father's £80,000, Magdalen remains committed to "her desperate purpose of recovering the lost inheritance, at any risk, from the man who had beggared and insulted his brother's children" (222). Once armed with Wragge's intelligence, she plans to insinuate herself into her uncle's household at Brighton, to usurp the place of domestic confidante currently occupied by his housekeeper Mrs Lecount, to induce her now-adopted father to accept Wragge as his new man of business, and then to take advantage of his propensity for financial speculation by swindling from him "'the fortunes of which he had robbed my sister and myself. To the last farthing'" (336). Although she accepts the legitimacy, if not the justice, of the legal authority which deprives her of her name – and thus the insufficiency of birth to determine social standing – Magdalen discerns that wealth offers its own gilded path back to privileged middle-class status. She actively directs all of her considerable energies, then, to regaining the material foundations of her former position.

Unfortunately for Magdalen, neither the immediate results nor the broader consequences of this initial strategy are quite what she had hoped. Practically, her scheme is rendered moot by Michael Vanstone's premature death, tidings of which appears in the newspaper on the eve of Magdalen's departure for Brighton. Mortality places him beyond the reach of even the most skillfully practiced misrepresentation. Socially, Magdalen's foray into public performance has tarnished not only her own, but also her sister's image. Miss Garth's epistolary judgment about the respectability of acting is written in response to the circumstances surrounding Norah's first job as a governess. Norah's employer, along with his wife and mother, upon learning of Magdalen's appearance on stage, mandate that the younger Vanstone never be allowed in their house or near their children, prompting Norah to resign. "For all you know," Miss Garth writes to Magdalen, "the harm may go on. What has happened in this situation, may happen in another" (313).[55] Moreover, in pursuance of her plan, Magdalen has found it necessary to connect herself with Wragge, whom she immediately recognizes as a "Rogue," one who unashamedly admits that his practice of "moral agriculture" most commonly brings him into contact not with "Sir John, with property in half a dozen counties," but rather with servants, small clerks, and "that woman who is crying stale shrimps in Skeldergate at this moment" (200, 212, 215). Thus, although she may convincingly impersonate a legion of respectable young and old ladies on stage, her own daily associations come with those occupying a considerably more marginal social position.

Undeterred from her "Purpose," Magdalen adjusts her means from swindling her uncle to seducing her cousin, the congenitally weak-hearted and compulsively miserly Noel Vanstone. She effectively transfers her skill at mimicry from the stage to the home, first capitalizing upon her most popular public role by visiting Noel Vanstone in London under the guise of Miss Garth to gather information about her new mark. Although eventually betrayed by her temper during the interview and goaded by the formidable Mrs Lecount into speaking with her own voice, her appearance is "a triumph in the art of self-disguise . . . nobody who now looked at Magdalen could have suspected for an instant that she was other than an ailing, ill-made, unattractive woman of fifty years old at least" (269). Magdalen then conspires with Wragge to encounter Noel again in Aldborough, where she foresees that the "short way and the vile way lies before me. I take it . . . and marry him," counting on his poor health to leave her a wealthy widow (338). In this more elaborate and sentimental plot, Magdalen allows her own youthful beauty to appear – minus the two identifying moles on her neck – while shrouding her identity in that of Miss Susan Bygrave, one the many "*Skins to Jump Into*" borrowed from "individuals retired from this mortal scene" by the fraudulent Wragge (322).

The unconventional courtship that ensues consists largely of a fencing match between Wragge and Lecount, who since the London interview has been on the lookout for a conspiracy. Thus, he distracts her with factoids and simple experiments taken from *Joyce's Scientific Dialogues* and designed to appeal to her vanity, thereby allowing Magdalen to flatter Noel into paying her compliments. She then attempts to ferret out the details of their household, only to have her own brother's illness in Switzerland disclosed by her already-smitten employer. Later, on a day trip to Dunwich, Wragge contrives to get himself and Mrs Lecount lost while walking, leaving Magdalen time to "'tie the miserable wretch to your apron string'" (382); whereupon Lecount, in the carriage on the return journey to Aldborough, surprises Magdalen with a question about Miss Garth, provoking just enough hesitation in response "to confirm Mrs Lecount's private convictions" (386). Mrs Lecount then writes directly to Miss Garth, enlisting her unwitting aid in the form of a minute personal description of Magdalen, whose exposure is saved only by Wragge's expert application of makeup to Magdalen's neck.[56] After this, Wragge plays his greatest and cruelest trick, forging a letter from Switzerland that recalls Mrs Lecount to her supposedly dying brother's bedside just long enough for Magdalen "to wring an offer of marriage out of that creature," Noel Vanstone (413). She succeeds, they wed in Mrs Lecount's absence, and then all decamp from Aldborough leaving no forwarding addresses for the housekeeper to follow.

The evident practical success of her new role as Miss Bygrave does not come without characterological cost for Magdalen, who suffers increasingly severe psychological stress the nearer she approaches the altar. Choosing her dress for her first public encounter with Noel, she already finds herself "'worthless in my own estimation,'" and this sense of self-censure manifests itself physically on the way home from Dunwich, when she "shuddered from head to foot" while informing Wragge, "'He has kissed my hand,' she said. 'Does that tell you enough? Don't let him sit next to me on the way home! I have borne all I can bear—spare me for the rest of the day'" (355, 384).

Once a kiss of the hand has grown into an offer to take her hand, Magdalen admits to having "'bad nights . . . I rise haggard and worn,'" and bad nights are succeeded by bad days, as her growing horror of the impending marriage drives her to demand that Wragge "'take me somewhere where I can forget it, or I shall go mad! Give me two days' rest . . . I'll go through with it to the end! Only give me two days' escape from that man and everything belonging to him! Do you hear, you villain?' she cried, seizing his arm and shaking it in a frenzy of passion—'I have been tortured enough—I can bear it no longer!'" (418, 437–8). The final weekend prior to the wedding, after Lecount has been dispatched on her fallacious errand and the legal notice of marriage publicly made, Magdalen appears ready to join her alter ego not just by but in the grave. Told that the ceremony will occur in four days, "fear—all-mastering fear—[takes] possession of her, body and soul," leaving "her face stiffened awfully, like the face of a corpse" (473). By that evening, she comes to realize that events have gotten away from her, that the "backward path had closed behind her," and that her purpose – revenge and the restoration of hers and her sister's status through her recovery of her father's wealth – has become "a part of herself: once she had governed it; now it governed her. The more she shrank, the harder she struggled, the more mercilessly it drove her on. No other feeling in her was strong enough to master it—not even the horror that was maddening her; the horror of her marriage" (484–5).[57] Magdalen even contemplates suicide, going so far as to buy a bottle of laudanum for the purpose, writing a suicide note to her sister in which she declares, "'Don't grieve for me, Norah—I am not worth it,'" and ultimately allowing whether she will live or die to be determined randomly by the number of ships that pass within sight of her window (497). When she is saved, she cannot decide whether it is "'Providence . . . Or chance'" that has preserved her (500).[58] As readers, we know that the agent responsible is none other than Wilkie Collins, whose own status as comfortably middle-class author requires a suitably dramatic conclusion for this serial installment, and a need to keep up readerly investment in his "pathetic" heroine, regardless or perhaps because she enmeshes herself in "perversity" and "error."

Even once the marriage is accomplished by an almost scandalously brief "It was done," and Magdalen's former panic is replaced by "icy resignation," her purpose remains fraught with difficulties (511, 512). As Wragge informs her, the fact that she married under a false name means that Noel "can appeal to the Ecclesiastical Court to have his marriage declared null and void" (508). So long as one spouse dies before any application to the court can be made, however, the marriage would remain legally valid even if the deception were subsequently discovered. On top of this, as Magdalen has learned from her own original experience of disinheritance, if Noel dies intestate, his property would be divided by the court, which would award his widow only one-third of his fortune and leave the remaining two thirds to his legal next-of-kin. In order to secure what her father originally intended for her inheritance, therefore, Magdalen must compel Noel to craft a new will before he dies and before her falsified identity comes to light, as it is likely to do once Mrs Lecount returns from Switzerland. Her success at the first of these objects is communicated to the reader in a letter from Alfred de Bleriot, an agent employed by Mrs Lecount to trace the newlyweds, in the "Between the Scenes" interlude prior to the "Fifth Scene," which transports the action to Dumfried, Scotland. The identity between Noel's last will and testament and Magdalen's own will emerges from the details of the final bequest: she, "in the very hour of her triumph . . . had rigorously exacted her father's fortune from him to the last farthing and had then turned her back on the hand that was tempting her with tens of thousands more!" (554). Insisting upon the eighty thousand pounds and no more, she effectively reconstructs her former social status as Miss Vanstone, a name denied to her by the legalities surrounding birth in the novel, on the basis of wealth alone.

Once again, however, and despite all of her self-assertion, her plan unravels. Mrs Lecount succeeds in discovering Noel alone at their new Scottish residence – Magdalen has left to attempt a reconciliation with her sister – convinces him irrevocably of his wife's deception, and dictates to him a new will that leaves the false Mrs Vanstone disinherited. The shock of learning about the true motives behind his own marriage prompts Noel to suffer an apparent heart-attack, and in the course of reviving him Magdalen's laudanum, labeled "Poison" by the chemist who prepared it, is discovered. This leads Mrs Lecount to presume that Magdalen's original plot included Noel's murder, and it is with this false knowledge that she browbeats him into the final arrangement of his affairs. Ostensibly leaving everything to his father's friend, Admiral Bartram, Noel creates a "Secret Trust" that wills his property to his cousin, the admiral's nephew, George Bartram, provided that he marries within six months of Noel's death. Mrs Lecount thus seeks to counter any future seductions by Magdalen by leaving her in the dark about the money's true destination and with too little time to complete another mercenary and presumably fraudulent marriage. Noel dies of another heart attack at the end of the "Fifth Scene," preventing his marriage from being annulled, but also setting the new will into motion, and leaving Magdalen "in unavailing remorse, in hopeless isolation, and in irremediable defeat" (600). Her change in status from "Nobody's Child" to "Somebody's Wife" has not, in fact, helped her to achieve her purpose (590); what it has done is to publicize her previous fraud and to class her among the century's numerous would-be poisoners.[59] From an upper-middle-class young lady she had sunk to an actress, and now from an actress she has become a widowed criminal.

Despite these considerable setbacks, Magdalen does not renounce her goal, but rather changes tactics once again. As she writes to her lawyer, Mr Loscombe – whose name one is tempted to read as "Lost Combe," as in Andrew Vanstone's house, Combe-Raven – "I am strong enough to win my way through worse trials than these. My spirits will rise again, and my time will come. If that Secret Trust is in Admiral Bartram's possession—when you next see me, you shall see me with it in my own hands" (598). In order to accomplish this new object, she determines to enter the admiral's household at St. Crux-in-the-Marsh disguised as a parlor-maid. After two months of training by her own lady's-maid, Louisa, whose name she borrows and to whom she gives her remaining earnings from her days as an actress to pay for Louisa's emigration to Australia with her illegitimate child and fiancé, Magdalen succeeds in assuming her new position and beginning her clandestine search. Her determination to regain her former upper-middle-class status by the reacquisition of her father's fortune has thus transformed her into an affirmative indicator of that status in someone else. Moreover, her readiness to part with the last of her savings means that Magdalen's transition from one served by domestic servants into a domestic servant herself will likely be permanent, absent the complete success of her third secret scheme.

It is with a special sense of urgency, then, that Magdalen conducts her search for the Secret Trust. She is, in this portion of the novel, almost entirely alone, possessed of neither family connections nor allies, not even dubious ones like the Wragges. The other servants at St. Crux, out of a "vague conviction which possessed them all alike, that the new comer was not one of themselves," watch her "with the untiring vigilance of malice and distrust" (636). Her only social interaction comes with Mazey, "known, far and wide, as 'the admiral's coxswain,'" a hard-drinking naval veteran secretly charged with frustrating Bartram's somnambulism (622). Scouting the ample property for over four weeks, Magdalen makes no progress, at which point the "bountiful gifts of health and strength, so prodigally heaped upon her by Nature, so long abused with impunity," begin to fail her (655).[60] Desperate and possessed by "an animating shame that nerved her to go on," she enters the uninhabited half of the house that night, encounters a sleep-walking Admiral Bartram, purloins his keys, and obtains the Secret Trust, which in her excitement she begins to read haphazardly and without full understanding (664).

At this precise moment, with Noel's instructions in her grasp, "a Hand passed suddenly from behind her, between the letter and her eye, and gripped her fast by the wrist in an instant" (672). Although too drunk to have slept in his accustomed place outside the admiral's door, Mazey has nevertheless caught her in the act of burglary. Labeling her a "young Jezebel," he threatens her with a court of inquiry in the morning, but finally relents enough to allow her to flee without any of her possessions before the household awakens (672). Ultimately, the results of this last assertion of her purpose are directly at odds with Magdalen's goal: she knows the Secret Trust exists but not precisely what it says; meanwhile, Admiral Bartram sickens and dies from a "severe inflammatory cold" contracted as a result of his nighttime wandering, without revealing the final location of the document that Magdalen held in her hand (686); and his death renders the trust lost, with the result that "the whole of his estate, both real and personal (that is to say, all the lands he possesses, and all the money he possesses, at the time of his death)," including Andrew Vanstone's £80,000, passes to George Bartram and thus outside the bounds of Magdalen's twin desires for vengeance and restitution (694). A letter from Mrs Ruddock, a London lodging housekeeper, to Mr Loscombe that is included in the final Between the Scenes section reveals that this last failure of all her plans has left Magdalen's "circumstances . . . fallen very low," her "looks and conduct . . . altered most shockingly," her health "on the eve of a serious illness," and herself "utterly deserted and friendless" (695).

"The last sacrifice of the old perversity and the old pride"[61]

The unnumbered "Last Scene" of the novel, set in Aaron's Buildings, a poor lodging house in London's East End, discloses the fate of both sisters and in so doing reflects upon the durability of middle-class status deprived of the guarantee of birth. As Mrs Ruddock had feared, the overthrow of all of Magdalen's schemes for recovering her father's money and, with it, hers and her sister's former status has led to a serious "illness which had struck her prostrate, mind and body alike," with "all the ordinary functions of her brain . . . in a state of collapse" (701, 704). From the most active character in the novel, Magdalen has been reduced to the most passive, forced to rely upon others for basic necessities. Much to the consternation of some of *No Name*'s early critics, Margaret Oliphant among them, however, Collins does not punish her social and sexual transgressions with death.[62] She is, instead, providentially nursed back to health by Captain Robert Kirke, the sea-faring son of the army officer who had helped to hush up the scandal of her father's improvident Canadian marriage. Magdalen and Kirke had briefly encountered one another back in Aldborough, where he had unaccountably fallen in love "with an electric suddenness" at first sight and had retained his feelings throughout his intervening months at sea (330). From earning her own money as an actress to securing her own legacy as a seductress to attempting to burglarize the means of contesting her second disinheritance as a disguised domestic, Magdalen is forced during the weeks of her illness to rely upon Kirke to pay for her food, her lodgings, and her medical care. He also succeeds in reuniting her with the Wragges and, through them, with her sister.

Norah has fared much better than Magdalen. As she recounts in a letter sent to prepare the way for her arrival at Aaron's Buildings, she has fallen in love with and married George Bartram, whom she had first met while fruitlessly attempting to trace Magdalen's movements in Aldborough. Collins has Magdalen reflect upon this news in a way that explicitly juxtaposes the sisters' responses to their original loss of status and the respective results of their conduct:

> Norah, whose courage under undeserved calamity, had been the courage of resignation—Norah, who had patiently accepted her hard lot; who, from first to last, had meditated no vengeance, and stooped to no deceit—Norah had reached the end which all her sister's ingenuity, all her sister's resolution, and all her sister's daring, had failed to achieve. Openly and honourably, with love on one side and love on the other, Norah had married the man who possessed the Combe-Raven money—and Magdalen's own scheme to recover it, had opened the way to the event which had brought husband and wife together! (725)

There is little ambiguity about the point being made here with respect to middle-class status, which apparently yields to a combination of renunciation and character but is not accessible through active assertions and dishonest schemes.[63] Further reinforcing the point, Norah has also discovered the Secret Trust, quite by accident, while on a tour of St. Crux, where it was unconsciously buried amidst the ashes in a charcoal brazier. In accordance with "the general perversity of all lost things," it has revealed itself not as a result of active seeking but rather after a period of passive waiting (734). Ironically, the passage of time and Admiral Bartram's and another relative's death have made Magdalen the legal heir to the Vanstone fortune after all. Unwilling to accept the money on these terms, however, Magdalen makes "the last sacrifice of the old perversity and the old pride" by tearing up the Trust and renouncing her claim, whereupon Norah presents her with her share of their father's fortune as a sororal gift. Norah's repeated enactment of what I have termed negative assertions of value allows not only her but also her sister to regain the middle-class status they had lost. Norah's rights to claim this status are recognized relatively early on by the Tyrrels and George Bartram, whereas Magdalen's final deserts come through the eyes of Kirke, who one month after her recovery meets her again at Aaron's Buildings and realizes that she "had never looked lovelier in her best days, than she looked now," and who, we presume, is on the cusp of proposing to her as the novel ends (737).

Somewhat more ambiguously and in addition to the happy endings achieved by both Norah and Magdalen, the final fates of Mrs Lecount and Captain Wragge subtly endorse Magdalen's original sense that wealth can substitute for birth as a means of legitimating middle-class status. Successfully obtaining through Noel's final will the £5,000 legacy promised to her by Michael Vanstone, Mrs Lecount retires to Zurich and establishes two charitable bequests that will absorb her investment principal after her death: a named scholarship at the University of Geneva and a scheme for the maintenance and vocational training of orphan girls in Zurich. For this she receives public recognition, in the form of a write-up in the Swiss newspapers, which extol her as "a Paragon of public virtue" with whom "William Tell, in the character of benefactor of Switzerland, was compared disadvantageously" (637). Wragge has done even better for himself, reinvesting his share of the money earned by Magdalen while on stage together with a small legacy from a recently deceased relative of Mrs Wragge in a patent medicine empire. From "Moral Agriculture" he has shifted to "Medical Agriculture," and in so doing has become a "Grand Financial Fact," employing "four-and-twenty young men, in white aprons, making the Pill" and "three elderly accountants, posting the vast financial transactions accruing from the Pill, in three enormous ledgers" (709–11).[64] Neither Mrs Lecount nor Captain Wragge alter their characters one jot – she remains the viperish ex-housekeeper of Michael Vanstone and he continues a Rogue, albeit in a new field – and yet both attain middle-class status, she as a public philanthropist and he as a successful entrepreneur.[65] All that has changed is their relative wealth, and neither begins their new social life with more than a small fraction of Magdalen's £80,000 objective. Middle-class status, *No Name* seems to imply, requires no grand antecedents nor spotless virtues, provided that one has sufficient coin.

Notes

1. On the number of mid-nineteenth-century orphans, see Laura Peters, *Orphan Texts*, 7; on the percentage of illegitimate children in the period, see Alysa Levene, Thomas Nutt, and Samantha Williams, eds., *Illegitimacy in Britain, 1700–1920*, 6.
2. The historical setting and specific mention of the port of Liverpool make Heathcliff a powerful if unstable signifier for Britain's central role in the global enslavement of Africans in the century prior to the abolition of the slave trade within British territories via the Slave Trade Act 1807, the abolition of slavery itself throughout most of the Empire after the passage of the Slavery Abolition Act 1833, and Britain's aggressive pursuit and enforcement of international anti-slavery treaties in the mid-1830s and after. Critical treatments of the ways in which Heathcliff invokes the topic of slavery specifically and the topic of race more generally include Matthew Beaumont, "Heathcliff's Great Hunger"; Sarah Fermi, "A Question of Colour"; Susan Gillman, "Remembering Slavery, Again"; Christopher Heywood, "Yorkshire Slavery in Wuthering Heights"; and Elsie Michie, "From Simianized Irish to Oriental Despots."
3. Martha C. Nussbaum, "The Stain of Illegitimacy," 151.
4. Jenny Bourne Taylor, "Representing Illegitimacy in Victorian Culture," 124; Wolfram Schmidgen, "Illegitimacy and Social Observation," 142, 159.
5. Lisa Zunshine, *Bastards and Foundlings*, 2–5.
6. Jenny Teichman, *Illegitimacy*, 132. Zunshine's exhaustive survey of novelistic examples allows her to generalize, "When eighteenth-century fictional narrative featured an abandoned child, his or her gender served as a largely reliable predictor of whether at the end of the story, he/she would turn out to be a legitimately born foundling or a bastard. Lost male children, such as Tom Jones or Humphrey Clinker, were allowed to stay illegitimate. The majority of their female counterparts, on the other hand, suffered the threat of illegitimacy throughout the story, only to discover at the end that their parents had been married at the time of their conception" (8).

7. On the concern with sexual reputation among the middle ranks, see Levene, Nutt, and Williams, 13; and Lisa Forman Cody, "The Politics of Illegitimacy in an Age of Reform," 133. On late-eighteenth and early-nineteenth-century orphans in search of self-fulfillment, see David Floyd, *Street Urchins, Sociopaths, and Degenerates*, 3. On orphan literature and melodrama, see Jenny Bourne Taylor, "Nobody's Secret," 573–4; and Lydia Murdoch, *Imagined Orphans*, 15. On the growth of the European bildungsroman, see Franco Moretti, *The Way of the World*.
8. The growing intensity and diversity of orphan literature from the late eighteenth century through the early twentieth century has led Floyd to propose the "long nineteenth-century" as "the century of the orphan," a "potent literary type . . . remarkable for its consistent recurrence and its metamorphosis as a register of cultural conditions" (1).
9. Nina Auerbach, "Incarnations of the Orphan," 409–10 (on the orphan and/as the novel, see 395). See also Margot Finn, Michael Lobban, and Jenny Bourne Taylor, eds., *Legitimacy and Illegitimacy in Nineteenth-Century Law, Literature and History*, 9.
10. Taylor, "Nobody's Secret," 566.
11. Murdoch, 2, 8.
12. Laura Peters, *Orphan Texts*, 23.
13. Ibid. 1.
14. Numerous critics provide helpful summaries of the debates surrounding the New Poor Law and the issue of bastardy. See, for example, Taylor, "Representing," 129–32 and "Nobody's Secret," 573; Cody, 133–57; and Susan Zlotnick, "'The Law's a Bachelor,'" 134–8.
15. Cody, 146.
16. Orphans of all sorts remained prominent in novels of the second half of the Victorian period and the Edwardian period as well, during which they were increasingly imbricated within the imperial ideals suggested by Murdoch. See Floyd's *Street Urchins, Sociopaths, and Degenerates* and Peters's "Popular Orphan Narratives" on later incarnations of the orphan in genre and juvenile fiction, respectively.
17. The strength of Dickens's fascination leads Auerbach to generalize that, "All Dickens' novels constitute variations on the theme of orphanhood" (411). Baruch Hochman and Ilja Wachs similarly ground *Dickens: The Orphan Condition* in their assertion that, "However complex the plot of a Dickens novels, however florid its rhetoric, however urgent its moral statement, the orphan condition, with its pain and its pathos, is always close to the center of its concerns" (11).
18. Oliver's iconic status is such that Murdoch deploys him in the opening sentence of *Imagined Orphans* as the representative "portrait of the workhouse child that remained the standard image for the Victorian age" (1). While acknowledging the "moral passion" of Dickens's critique of the workhouse, Zlotnick also argues that the ways in which

"Rose (along with her avatars Nancy and Agnes) are ultimately judged according to the 'classificatory categories' allied with realism and the New Poor Law," suggests *Oliver Twist*'s "status as an anti-poor law novel may have to be reconsidered" (132–3).
19. As Taylor notes, "The sinister, epileptic Monks, Oliver's legitimate sibling, self-consciously enacts the role of envious, displaced bastard brother and inverts this structure," which Dickens had inherited from earlier English literature, including *Lear* and numerous eighteenth-century novels (Taylor, "Representing," 135).
20. Charles Dickens, *Oliver Twist*, 344.
21. Zlotnick, 143.
22. Rose's deserts are also rewarded in the same scene, as she, whom everyone had thought an illegitimate orphan, is revealed to be a legitimate foundling.
23. Just as Oliver does for Murdoch, so Jane serves both as Auerbach's point of entry into nineteenth-century incarnations of the orphan and as Mary Jean Corbett's argumentative focus for "Orphan Stories and Maternal Legacies in Charlotte Brontë." Corbett ranges widely among Brontë's juvenilia and mature novels in order to provide a contextualized reading of *Jane Eyre*, which turns out to be one of a vast array or orphan stories, many with racialized subtexts, produced by Brontë over the course of her life.
24. Charlotte Brontë, *Jane Eyre*, 79.
25. Jane's triumphant transcendence of her own orphanhood relies upon a simultaneous repudiation of direct involvement in Britain's colonial empire, in the form of St. John's mission, and of too-close contact with colonized peoples, represented by Bertha, while still allowing for sharing the proceeds of colonial labor, in the form of her uncle's legacy from his years in the Portuguese colony of Maderia. On the significance of colonialism in *Jane Eyre*, see, among many choices, Carolyn Vellenga Berman, "Undomesticating the Domestic Novel"; Elaine Freedgood, "Souvenirs of Sadism"; Susan Meyer, "Colonialism and the Figurative Strategy of *Jane Eyre*"; Philip Rogers, "'My Word Is *Error*'"; and Alexandra Valint, "Madeira and *Jane Eyre*'s Colonial Inheritance."
26. Anthony Trollope, *Doctor Thorne*, 23.
27. Ibid. 27.
28. Ibid. 479. According to Nussbaum, Trollope's meticulous ordering of the novel's dénouement proves that in Barchester, which is "the image of a sane England, an England where lives are not ruined by youthful error," Mary Thorne can be classed "with Miss Dunstable, an heiress whose father rose from the lower middle class by making a fortune on a patent medicine called the 'oil of Lebanon,' and with another wealthy tradesman, Mr Moffat, a fine catch in the local marriage market" ("The Stain of Illegitimacy," 168).

29. Trollope, *Doctor Thorne*, 538. Among the guests at Frank and Mary's wedding are the doctor's formerly estranged relatives, the venerable Thornes of Ullathorne, including the family's maiden-aunt matriarch, Miss Monica Thorne, who, could she "have spoken her inward thoughts out loud . . . would have declared, that Frank would have done better to have borne his poverty than marry wealth without blood" (556). Not everyone in Barsetshire, then, is convinced that status can dispense with birth.
30. After Rochester's sight partially returns, he is able to see that his first-born, a boy, "had inherited his own eyes, as they once were—large, brilliant, and black" (Brontë, *Jane Eyre*, 476); similarly, after Frank and Mary return from their honeymoon, "Another event is expected . . . of such importance to the county" (Trollope, *Doctor Thorne*, 557).
31. Marian's last words are literally punctuated with two exclamation points and two question marks before she settles on a period for her final declarative sentence: "'Child!' she exclaimed, with all her easy gaiety of old times. 'Do you talk in that familiar manner of one of the landed gentry of England? Are you aware, when I present this illustrious baby to your notice, in whose presence you stand? Evidently not! Let me make two eminent personages known to one another: Mr Walter Hartright – the Heir of Limmeridge'" (Wilkie Collins, *The Woman in White*, 646). Marian's triumph here is predicated upon the very real impediments of Laura's own unstable identity throughout the narrative, the circumstances surrounding her second marriage, and the large status gap between herself and her former-drawing-master husband.
32. In their introduction to *Legitimacy and Illegitimacy in Nineteenth-Century Law, Literature and History*, Finn, Lobban and Taylor write that "*The Woman in White* is a striking example of the uses of illegitimacy as a narrative device, and the power of the novel hinges on its success in bringing together apparently disparate understandings of the term" (2).
33. Collins, *The Woman in White*, 563, 433, 303. On the motif of the masculine quest, see Herbert Sussman, *Victorian Masculinities*.
34. Collins, *The Woman in White*, 33.
35. Ibid. 33.
36. Wilkie Collins, *No Name*, 33. Hereafter cited parenthetically in the text.
37. For an account of the writing of *No Name*, which was complicated by illness and serial publication deadlines and spurred on by Sampson & Low's offer for the book publication rights, as well as of the novel's fictional re-presentation of Wilkie's mother, Harriet Collins and her autobiographical fragment and life experiences, see Catherine Peters, *The King of Inventors*, 249–52.
38. According to Jonathan Loesberg, in "The Ideology of Narrative Form in Sensation Fiction," the anxious interleaving of personal identity and

social status is a defining feature of sensation novels, which "evoke their most typical moments of sensation response from images of a loss of class identity. And this common image links up with a fear of a general loss of social identity as a result of the merging of the classes—a fear that was commonly expressed in the debate over social and parliamentary reform in the late 1850s and 1860s" (117).

39. In a perceptive close reading of the opening pages of *No Name*, Daniel Hack argues that Collins's prefatory appeal to Nature, his emphasis on his own narrative labor, and his assertion that the novel's popularity justifies his intentions aligns the novel with a much less reputable although no less widespread fictional genre in Victorian England, the begging letter, and lays the groundwork for a later identification between the novelist and the "moral agriculturalist," and thus between Collins and his roguish character, Captain Horatio Wragge (*The Material Interests of the Victorian Novel*, 136–7). That Collins legitimates his own performance by referring to his many readers is hardly exceptional. As Sue Lonoff observes in *Wilkie Collins and His Victorian Readers*, "All the great mid-Victorian novelists were immensely concerned with their public" (1). Quoting Collins's own essay from *Household Words* on "The Unknown Public" (1858), Lyn Pykett further expounds this point: "Collins was not the only novelist of the 1860s who self-consciously sought to reach that 'unknown public', the 'the monster audience', the 'unfathomable, the universal public', who avidly consumed the racy, soap-opera-like narratives in the penny weeklies which they purchased from 'small stationer's or tobacconist's shops' in 'second and third rate neighborhoods'" ("Collins and the Sensation Novel," 51).

40. As Christine Bolus-Reichert explains in "The Foreshadowed Life in Wilkie Collins's *No Name*," the ease with which a comfortably middle-class woman could be forced from her home by a change in financial circumstances over which she had no control means that "Collins does not expect his readers to foresee the specific circumstances that drive Magdalen into the world, but rather to anticipate what the loss of home will mean to a woman like the character he invents" (24). Commenting upon the de-emphasis of secrecy in favor of the narration of generally foreseeable circumstances, Deirdre David argues that Collins's "narrator collaboratively offers a chance to see how plot comes into being, an opportunity to experience plot-in-progress, so to speak, rather than plot-as-product" ("Rewriting the Male Plot in Wilkie Collins's *No Name*," 188).

41. Collins, *No Name*, 38.

42. By providing these geographical and architectural details, Sundeep Bisla argues, "Collins has done a very good job – showing himself a kindred spirit to his chameleon-like heroine – of impersonating, or mimicking, a writer of domestic fictions," and may, in fact, be "setting his sights on a particularly famous representative of his chosen

drama, Jane Austen's *Sense and Sensibility*, a more 'serious' treatment of the theme of disinherited girls of contrasting natures" ("Over-Doing Things with Words in 1862," 2). In *Dead Secrets*, focusing less on the opening setting and more on the "recurrent image of buried writing" and the anxious play of "female power and subversion" throughout the narrative, Tamar Heller identifies an alternative, but contemporary, literary antecedent for Collins's novel in Radcliffean Gothic (1, 8). Both the early domestic novel as defined by Bisla and the Gothic novel as treated by Heller are manifestations of the late eighteenth-century novel of sensibility. It is from such prior fictions, according to Tamara Wagner, that Collins constructs his "enervated (male) victims of sensation," his "weak antihero," and his exemplar of a notably sensitive "heroic manliness," Captain Kirke, in *No Name* ("'Overpowering Vitality,'" 472, 481).

43. In its attention to expensive and status-advertising features like the clock and the piano, this initial description of Combe-Raven is of a piece with what Kimberly Harrison describes as sensation fiction's awareness of the new, industrial consumer culture and patterns of consumption: "consumption itself was not a new social phenomenon, but what was new within industrial society was the quantity of commodities produced, the plethora of discourse about commodities, and the commodities' cultural force. Not just a form of exchange, commodities became spectacle, with representation qualities, decontextualized from their place and process of production" ("'Come Buy, Come Buy,'" 528).

44. At breakfast, Mr Vanstone declares, "'If I am to be allowed my choice of amusements next time, I think a play will suit me better than a concert,'" after which his younger daughter, Magdalene, whispers in his ear "'*The Bristol Theatre's open, papa*'" (16, 18).

45. As Nina Auerbach notes in *Private Theatricals*, "reverent Victorians shunned theatricality as the ultimate, deceitful mobility," and looked upon the actor as "one image of the Victorian anti-self, capering and mocking sincere emotion. The actor is associated too with bestial, with monstrous, vampiristic, and spectral mutations" (4, 114). More soberly, Lonoff observes that for much of the century, "the English stage lacked the novel's vitality, and in any case many middle-class people avoided the theater on moral and religious grounds" (23).

46. Numerous critics have commented upon the novel's dramatic structure and its relationship to character and theme: "It comes as little surprise then that *No Name* should be written on the plan of a stage-drama. This theatrical frame establishes . . . the appropriate backdrop for Magdalen's many acts of taking on disguises throughout the story" (Bisla 4); "structure makes all of the characters into actors, even those who do not adopt false identities" (Simpson, "Selective Affinities," 119); "With its heavy reliance on melodramatic conventions and scenes

that take place in the theatre, *No Name* makes sisterhood into spectacle" (Michie, "'There Is No Friend Like a Sister,'" 408). As Lonoff asserts, however, numerous novels of the period took advantage of their readers' familiarity with dramatic convention without exposing them to the moral suspicion attached to the theatre: "The frequently dramatic confrontations and disclosures" in Victorian fiction "offered the pleasures of the theater at home to people who rarely went out. . . . But the theater was stagnant, playwrights were ill-paid, and respectable people still distrusted the stage, while the capacious novel transposed the excitement of the drama to the hearth" (9).

47. According to Jim Davis, "Learning from the experiences of such authors as Dickens, multiple adaptations of whose novels at home and abroad secured him little monetary advantage, Collins sought to protect his copyright and income by adapting his own novels" ("Collins and the Theatre," 173).

48. It is, perhaps, noteworthy that neither of Andrew Vanstone's wives is provided with a first name. Whether this omission represents a subtle facet of Collins's critique of marriage, with its legal subsumption of the wife's identity into that of her husband, or silently attests to Collins's own patriarchal impulses, remains open for debate. Bisla finds in *No Name* a "relentless attack on the institution of marriage" (3); Amy Leal, in "Affirmative Naming in *No Name*," asserts that Collins "uses names and their absence to comment on the powerless position of women in general" (6); and Debra Morris, in "Maternal Roles and the Production of Name in *No Name*," similarly reads the novel as illustrative of "how maternal power is threatening not only to men but to the women who find themselves trapped in maternal discourse simply by virtue of being daughters themselves" (271). Somewhat less sanguinely, Pykett acknowledges that "if Collins's representation of Magdalen challenges some gender stereotypes, it reproduces others. This heroine is full of purpose and passion, but she is also manipulative, scheming, duplicitous and histrionic – in short, she displays many of the negative traits associated with femininity in the mid-nineteenth century" (57). Finally, Heller explains that Collins's often divided representations of female characters are connected to his own "position as a male writer in the Victorian literary marketplace" and his "investment in the ideology of professionalism, which, as historians have argued, strongly reinforces the division between male labor and female domesticity" (4, 8).

49. For Simpson, this dramatic set of revelations about the Vanstones "reveals the ideal family to be no more than a sham spectacle—a promise of happiness and stability that distracts characters, particularly Magdalen Vanstone, and readers alike" (115).

50. In "Wilkie Collins and British Law," Douglas MacEachen explains that in England "the bastard was legally an outcast. Only a special act of

Parliament could make him legitimate, and such an act was very rarely passed. In respect to bastardy the English law had remained unchanged since the Middle Ages," before going on to find *No Name* an "unmistakable and convincing . . . illustration of the injustice of the English law of illegitimacy" (123–4).
51. Norah declines to read the letter itself, but when its terms are briefly summarized for her by Mr Pendril, her face "crimsoned with indignation" (159): both sisters, then, register in their faces Michael Vanstone's nullification of blood as a basis for their social position.
52. Collins, *No Name*, 269.
53. As a literal actress, Magdalen becomes, according to Melinda Huskey, a figurative "paradigm for the sensation novel's heroine—the resourceful, energetic, powerful, and deceptive woman who abandons one life, one role, one identity after another in pursuit of a goal" ("*No Name*: Embodying the Sensation Heroine," 6). For Anna Jones, Magdalen's acting is only one facet of her broader practice of masochism, a "perverse" form of agency that requires Magdalen to be "an active agent in her own suffering" ("A Victim in Search of a Torturer," 203, 201).
54. This exchange is one example of what Bisla identifies as Collins's tendency "to revel in the failures of speech acts rather than to prop them up through the deliberate and desperate imposition onto the system of language of unworkable proprieties (or falsifying normalizing conventions)" (8).
55. It is as if Magdalen's embodiment of "three major Victorian anxieties about acting and actresses – the blurring of distinctions between fiction and reality, the promiscuous multiplication of (especially female) identity, and the corporeal and erotic dimension of life on stage" – is a contagion that might be transmitted to Norah and, though her, to her young charges (H. Michie, 412).
56. Laurence Talairach-Vielmas reconnects this scene to the novel's original periodical context, revealing how Wragge's timely application of make-up connotes far more than it appears to (or covers over): "Interestingly enough, an article entitled 'Paint, and No Paint,' which was published alongside the instalments of Wilkie Collins's *No Name* in *All the Year Round* on August 9, 1862, merges further make-up and waste: it denounces blush, made with alloxan, a chemical substance derived from the foetal membranes of animals, together with other examples of recycled refuse that fashionable women use" (62).
57. According to Amanda Anderson's account of the Victorians' "rhetoric of fallenness" in *Tainted Souls and Painted Faces*, this sense of being overmastered by circumstances makes Magdalen a fallen woman even before she sexually compromises herself by consummating her false marriage to Noel Vanstone.
58. As Christopher Kent observes in "Probability, Reality and Sensation in the Novels of Wilkie Collins," Magdalen's near-suicide and

post-survival uncertainty reflect how, in the nineteenth century, "thinking about probability underwent a significant reorientation . . . . For the first time huge quantities of statistical information became available on matters of life and death through the information-gathering agencies of government. They also provided some striking illustrations of the so-called law of large numbers, as regularities began to appear in events," including rates of mislabeled postage and suicide, "which had long been regarded as quintessentially accidental and random . . . . Did such regularities in actions assumed to be freely willed indicate that society was somehow determined by mysterious laws of social mechanics?" (260). I will return to such subjects at greater length in Chapter 4.

59. "Two varieties of clever crime particularly obsessed mid-Victorians," John Sutherland asserts in "Wilkie Collins and the Origin of the Sensation Novel," "secret poisoning and forgery" (244). Among the more famous examples of the former are the 1856 trial of William Palmer and the 1857 trial of Madeleine Smith. On the effects of these and other sensational trials on Collins's fiction, see Sutherland, "Wilkie Collins," 148–58; Kent, 262; and Pykett, 52.

60. As Kylee-Anne Hingston remarks, "In the novel, nearly all bodies—even the apparently healthy ones—reveal themselves to be uncontrollable and atypical, and managing one's identity and body preoccupies every character" ("'Skins to Jump Into,'" 118).

61. Collins, *No Name*, 737.

62. In addition to Oliphant's much-quoted remarks from her 1862 *Blackwood's* article on "Sensational Novels," the critic for *The Athenaeum* found Magdalen a "perverse heroine . . . let off with a punishment gentle in proportion to the unscrupulous selfishness of her character" ("No Name," 10), whereas the otherwise sympathetic notice in *The London Review* pronounced all the novel's characters "moral monstrosities; not shocking only because they are too monstrous to suggest the idea of their possibility, while the resemblance to real life is the very faintest possible, and only just sufficient to enable author and reader to forget the fictitiousness of the whole" ("No Name," 46). Reviews in the *Saturday Review* and the *Examiner* both focused on Collins's plot, judged with increasing severity as "ingenious" and "wholly artificial" ("*No Name* and *Thalatta*," 84; "No Name," 54).

63. On the novel's final juxtaposition of the Vanstone sisters, see, in order of publication, H. Michie, 409; Huskey, 9; A. Jones, 200; Wagner, "'Overpowering Vitality,'" 484; Leal, 13; and Pykett, 59.

64. Reinforcing his earlier identification between Collins and Wragge, Hack argues that in the latter's successful pill-making operation, "we see Collins promoting an awareness of the self-promotional nature of his own strategy. It is not just plate glass but transparency itself that Collins's reader is invited to see through" (144).

65. Adopting a less socio-historical perspective on the fates of Wragge and Lecount, William Marshall writes in *Wilkie Collins*, "Since she no more than Wragge is concerned with moral considerations in attaining her ends, there are no restrictions upon the devices each uses to abort the schemes of the other . . . . Neither is punished, for more than any of their villainous predecessors, Captain Wragge and Mrs Lecount illustrate Collins's view of the relativity of evil, the mixed nature of virtue and vice" (68–9).

Chapter 2

Repudiations of Wealth in Victorian Financial Fiction

If, instead of suddenly and unexpectedly dying, Michael Vanstone had survived long enough to have been swindled by the defrauding duo of Magdalen Vanstone and Horatio Wragge, then *No Name* might well have evolved into another recognizable subtype of the nineteenth-century novel: the novel of financial speculation. In this counterfactual fiction, the seduction of Noel Vanstone and the dissimulation before Admiral Bartram might have been replaced by a sequence of confidential after-hours consultations in the neighborhood of Threadneedle Street, where Wragge, posing as the agent of a broker-member of the Stock Exchange, would have puffed fallacious shares representing government consols, Exchequer Bills, an array of joint-stock companies, and foreign securities (including the highly suspect sovereign debt of Brazil, Chile, Colombia, Mexico, Peru, and Spain). Alternatively, Vanstone could have been seduced by the potential profits to be had on Lombard Street by setting up his own discount house for buying and selling bills of exchange, whose amounts might then have been altered or whose endorsers' names discreetly forged as necessary to recoup the familial debt owed to Magdalen and Nora. Add to this hypothetical the untimely failure of one or more undercapitalized banks, an ephemeral overseas infrastructure scheme (mines and railways were particularly popular), and perhaps an opportunistically sunk and unfortunately underinsured merchant ship, and one would have a familiar set of narrative conventions representing the frightening array of lived possibilities for middle-class readers.[1] Generally bereft, although perhaps not to the extent of the Vanstone sisters, of the benefits of gentle birth, these readers quite often did not possess what lawyers refer to as "real" property – land – but instead relied upon their own intellectual capital and individual credit. When these somewhat intangible sources of income succeeded in generating wealth, one had to do something with it – invest, speculate, or even gamble – in order to maintain one's social position, and the need to do so exposed one to myriad risks in a largely unregulated financial system. A keen awareness of the fragility, even disingenuousness of middle-class status legitimated principally by wealth pervades Victorian fiction, which often cautions against over-reliance on the cash nexus by revisiting the crashes of the distant and recent past.[2]

Writers and readers with especially long memories might have recalled the financial scandals of the previous century. Conceived at the same time that Defoe was making his transition from pamphleteer to novelist, the Mississippi Bubble grew out of Scotsman John Law's experiments linking his Compagnie des Indes, which enjoyed monopolistic control over colonial trade in French Louisiana; with his Banque Générale, which had the authority to print paper money; with France's national debt, which Law planned to pay off through the sale of Compagnie shares whose purchase would be financed by the new national currency he was producing with the approval of the French government. The resulting financial feedback loop prompted widespread speculation, since it appeared that Compagnie stock was guaranteed by the French government, and rampant inflation, as Law printed ever greater amounts of currency, the value of which was no longer supported by France's gold reserves, leading to the eventual rupture of the French stock market bubble in 1720.[3] The more general economic crash that followed also hit closer to home, encompassing England's South Sea Company, which had been founded in 1711 and which, under the leadership of John Blunt, adapted the model of and sought to directly compete with Law's Compagnie des Indes. Like its French counterpart, the South Sea Company assumed responsibility for its home nation's debt, which it sought to convert into company stock, to be traded at a profit through four rounds of increasingly public offerings. Overseen by the same government ministers and members of parliament to whom it "sold" stock without requiring a deposit – essentially a bribe – the South Sea Company enjoyed a rapid rise and spawned a host of smaller "bubble" companies with business plans ranging from the merely unlikely to the blatantly fanciful. Nearly all failed after the value of South Sea Company shares collapsed in September 1720, once rumors of disagreements among the directors and a shortage of available capital put an end to the rampant momentum of speculation. Subsequent investigations revealed the extent of Blunt's fraud and the complicity of the company's four MP-directors and the Chancellor of the Exchequer, Sir John Aislabie.[4] Although over £2 million was eventually recovered from the board of directors, this did not begin to cover the losses sustained by the company's numerous shareholders, who, according to Edward Chancellor, "came of every social class," and included King George I, the Prince of Wales, "an assortment of jobbing dukes, marquises, earls, and barons," and myriad "country gentlemen and rich farmers," as well as prominent intellectuals and writers such as John Gay, Sir Isaac Newton, and Alexander Pope.[5] The South Sea Bubble, as it came to be known, both acted as a traumatic check on joint-stock company founding, short selling, and speculating in futures and options through the 1810s, and served as a yardstick by which to measure later, nineteenth-century examples of financial malfeasance.

Almost one hundred years later, the successful conclusion of the Napoleonic wars brought about a widespread fall in prices, a corresponding rise in liquidity, and a renewed sense of collective financial confidence. All those who had, themselves, accrued losses in the South Sea Bubble were dead, and the nation's appetite for speculation had returned. From the 1820s through the 1870s, England experienced a series of boom-and-bust cycles that recurred roughly every ten years, with speculative fervor and easy credit combining to produce what were often retrospectively characterized as manias or bubbles, themselves succeeded by rapid losses and widespread bankruptcies. Often, acts of parliament accompanied these gyrations in the markets as either contributing causes or belated reactions.[6] The first of these financial paroxysms occurred in 1824–6 and, according to Norman Russell, "was to be remembered throughout the century with the same intensity that its famous ancestor, the South Sea Bubble, had created in the minds of those who had either lived through it, or heard of it as part of national folklore."[7] Simón Bolívar's successful campaign against the fading Spanish empire had created a cluster of newly independent, resource-rich, but capital-poor states in Central and South America. Foreign bond offers for Columbian, Chilean, and Peruvian national debt appeared on the London Exchange and were followed swiftly by opportunities to invest in joint-stock mining companies created to extract the entire region's legendary gold and silver reserves. The Bubble Act of 1720, which had been passed while England was in the throes of the South Sea debacle, required parliamentary review of every joint-stock incorporation. With over 250 companies applying for a charter by April 1825, Parliament was overwhelmed, and so in June the Company Act was passed and the Bubble Act repealed. In all, over 600 new companies were founded in 1824–5, and there was insufficient hard currency to purchase the resulting shares, which were, instead, bought largely on credit provided by London and provincial banks.[8] By November, bullion reserves held by the Bank of England had declined over seventy percent from the previous year, and so the Bank sharply curtailed its lending and raised its rates. Numerous bank failures followed, share prices collapsed in the absence of fresh investment, hundreds of companies declared bankruptcy, the South American loans slid into default, and many thousands of Britons lost their savings.[9] For the first generation of Victorians, who came of age in the 1820s, the 1824–6 cycle of speculative excess and subsequent insolvency served as a powerful reminder of the fragility of financially-warranted status.

Even more so than the default in Spanish bonds, failed joint-stock banks, and spectacular Independent West Middlesex Life and Fire Assurance Company fraud of the 1830s, the so-called Railway Mania of the 1840s offered a similar lesson in the dangers of speculation for the second generation of Victorians.[10] Railways had actually gotten their start in Britain in 1825, at the height of the South American bubble, with the founding of the Stockton and Darlington line and had already experienced a minor mania in 1836–7, but it was in 1845–7 that railways matured into the primary object of speculative enthusiasm, financial fraud, and, eventually, catastrophic collapse. Explicitly excluded from the various Company Acts passed since 1825, railways still required individual parliamentary review and an act of Parliament prior to their incorporation as joint-stock companies. Even before and certainly during this official process, however, railway companies could advertise to attract speculative investors, and many did so using a range of fraudulent tactics, including larding their prospectuses with prominent "guinea pig" directors, sometimes without their consent or knowledge; "puffing" the embryonic line's likely profitability in periodicals ranging from *Railway World* to *The Times*; and "rigging" the price of shares through secret buyback schemes by the railway's promoters.[11] In 1844, recognizing the potential for fraud but unable to persuade MPs committed to free trade of the need for industry-wide regulation, then-President of the Board of Trade, William Ewart Gladstone, pushed through passage of the Railway Act, which called for the formation of a Railway Advisory Board to examine all applications for new lines. Led by Lord Dalhousie, this body reviewed 240 such applications representing £100 million of proposed investment in the month of May 1845 alone, but as the board's recommendations were not binding on Parliament, its function was largely moot, and it was disbanded in July that same year. In 1846, Parliament approved a further 270 applications for railway incorporation representing over £131 million of future construction. Available capital began to run short when the repeal of the Corn Laws prompted speculation in the future price of grain and the Bank of England raised its lending rates. Railways then issued calls on their shares, requiring speculators who had purchased on deposit to deliver the outstanding balance. In 1847, a good harvest caused the price of corn to fall, and those who had speculated on grain found themselves financially squeezed from two directions at once. By October, the Bank of England had nearly exhausted its reserves, and only the suspension of the Bank Act allowed the nation to avoid insolvency. Subsequent parliamentary commissions and shareholder investigations revealed the extent of fraud committed by shady railway promoters, directors, and MPs, including George Hudson, the "Railway King" member for Sunderland.[12] Meanwhile, because the Railway Mania "drew in the whole nation of investors," the financial consequences of the 1840s boom and bust cycle were felt wherever the speculative race in track had been run, which is to say, everywhere.[13]

In the 1850s and 1860s, Parliament sought to modernize Britain's financial sector and reduce the risk to individual participants by legislating into being a new standard of limited liability. At the same time, several high-profile examples of misconduct by the nation's bankers and two economic crises precipitated by failures in the banking and insurance industries reminded Victorian depositors and policyholders of the continued vulnerability of their hard-earned wealth, even when soberly invested rather than more recklessly speculated.[14] Prior to the passage of the Limited Liability Act of 1855 and the Joint Stock Companies Act of 1856, individual stock holders could be held responsible for the total debts of any company of which they held even a single share; the aftermath of the 1840s Railway Mania thus exposed many first-time investors to tremendous fiscal risk. After the acts were passed, those same investors could lose their principal to a company's creditors, but the remainder of their assets would remain untouched. The Joint Stock Companies Amendment Act of 1858 and the Companies Act of 1862 explicitly extended limited liability protection to stockholders of banking and insurance companies, respectively.[15] Unfortunately, no amount of legislation could prevent individual bankers from behaving recklessly, even fraudulently, with their clients' money. As Parliament was working on limited liability in 1855, the longstanding and highly respected private bank of Strahan, Paul and Bates failed spectacularly, the partners having lost £750,000, including through bad loans to collieries, and, to cover their losses, having sold £100,000 of their clients' securities without their consent. They were tried in the Old Bailey, convicted of false conversion, and sentenced to fourteen years transportation.[16] The next year, John Sadleir, then MP for Sligo and junior Lord of the Treasury, was found to have forged deeds to cover the fact that he had embezzled over £200,000 from Ireland's Tipperary Bank, which was run by his brother James. Sadleir infamously died by suicide on Hampstead Heath rather than face prosecution, and the bank failed for £400,000.[17] Also in 1856, the Royal British Bank failed for over £650,000 after its manager and two directors used its assets to make unsecured loans to themselves and their friends. Since these were "loans" – even though they went unpaid and were covered up by means of falsified accounts and bribery – the men received much lighter sentences (of one year or less) than the partners of Strahan, Paul and Bates actually did or than Sadleir would have had he lived.[18] The broader banking crisis came in 1857 and was set into motion by an American institution, the Ohio Life Insurance and Trust Company, the insolvency of which triggered the collapse of over 5000 banks in the United States and Canada, "the almost total collapse of American commerce" for the next two years, and numerous British bank failures.[19] Ensuing parliamentary investigations revealed widespread mismanagement and fraud, to the extent that, suddenly, Sadleir began to appear representative. Once again, the government and the Bank of England intervened and the business cycle reset from bust to boom, until it was undone again in 1866 by a second banking crisis, this one predicated upon the financial collapse, in another period of low liquidity and high interest rates, of Overend, Gurney and Company, the largest issuer of accommodation bills in London and second only to the Bank of England in offering credit to other banks. Although the directors were eventually tried for fraud, they were acquitted thanks to what George Robb describes as "the inadequate provisions of company law," with the result that "Overend's shareholders consequently lost millions of pounds, and the company's debts were not fully discharged until 1893."[20]

In light of this and other longitudinal evidence of moral turpitude and financial skullduggery, Victorian novelists should probably be excused for the consistency with which they represented Mammon as abroad in the land. Whether they had personally experienced the slings and arrows of outrageous financial fortune – and some writers, including three of those discussed in the following section, Charles Dickens, Anthony Trollope, and William Makepeace Thackeray, had – many were observant enough to see that wealth was an unstable basis on which build one's place in Victorian society. Certainly, the tragic example of Sir Walter Scott – who assumed responsibility for and essentially wrote himself to death discharging his manager, James Ballantyne's, debts, themselves caused by the collapse of his London bank in the aftermath of the South American bubble – provided a prescient reminder of the precarious nature of writing as a profession.[21] Money was not necessarily the problem, as the numerous novelistic happy endings achieved through a fortuitous inheritance or provident marriage demonstrate; instead, it was the pursuit of wealth as an end in itself that could transform an abstraction of value into filthy lucre and its possessor into an unsympathetic miser, a profligate gambler, a villainous fraud, or a pathetic bankrupt.[22]

Novel Speculations

In a method reminiscent of the earlier discussion of novelistic orphanhood and the rejection of birth as a source of legitimacy, this chapter discusses Victorian novelists' disarticulation of wealth from middle-class status in two phases. First, tightly focused interpretations of select novels published between the 1837–9 and 1878 crashes reconstruct the prevalence of financial subplots in period fiction and reveal novelists' consistent repudiation of wealth as a necessary and sufficient element of middle-class social position. Second, an extended reading of an all-but-forgotten Victorian text, William North's *The City of the Jugglers; or, Free-Trade in Souls: A Romance of the "Golden" Age* (1850), recounts the surprising representational dividends paid by an exclusive investment in financial fraud. Ultimately, North stages a novelistic revolution against any form of status guaranteed by wealth; that his paean to poetic genius as a viable alternative falls afoul of his text's own generic confusion only highlights the dangers of aesthetic speculation in an age of scrip.

Set during the speculative mania of the 1820s and leavened by an impossible-to-miss allusion to the more recent financial crisis of the 1830s, Thackeray's *The History of Samuel Titmarsh and the Great Hoggarty Diamond* (1841) satirically dismantles the apparent link between wealth and status on multiple levels at once. By September 1841, the month in which the novel began its serialized run in *Fraser's Magazine for Town and Country*, Thackeray had already experienced his own severance from inherited prosperity, losing his fortune through a combination of gambling debts incurred while an undergraduate at Cambridge in 1829–30, the collapse of the Indian bank at which his and his step-father's assets were deposited in 1834, and the failure of his newspaper, the *National Standard*, in 1837; as a result, he lived "for more than a decade . . . in a chronic state of insolvency."[23] Told twenty years after the fact by the titular Titmarsh but informed by Thackeray's own first-hand knowledge of financial hard knocks, the serial fiction recounts its narrator's youthful misadventures while working at the West Diddlesex Fire and Life Assurance Company.[24] The young Sam begins as the thirteenth of twenty-four clerks at this seemingly successful but, as Thackeray's readers would have easily recognized, almost certainly fraudulent seller of annuities, his position secured by his mother's investment of her life's savings of £400 in exchange for a suspiciously high nine percent rate of return (Sam's initial clerk's salary of £80 per year raises the annual rate of return on his mother's investment to an almost incredible twenty-nine percent!).

Sam receives the "Great Hoggarty Diamond" – really an ostentatious gold and enamel brooch containing a miniature of his uncle, thirteen locks of hair, and a diamond, which he has reset into a pin – from his rich aunt Mrs Hoggarty, and then experiences a meteoric rise both at work and in fashionable society once he begins wearing his new diamond pin to the office. His boss, the parvenu director-promoter Mr Brough, who also speculates in foreign sovereign debt and directs a bubble's worth of companies, mistakes him for a wealthy heir, and even the cousin of the Countess of Drum. Sam is invited to Brough's country estate in Fulham, introduced to a variety of those whom Thackeray would later christen snobs, and receives a significant promotion up the ladder of clerks. On the strength of his new salary, Sam marries his sweetheart Mary Smith, who moves to London to be with him. Eventually, Brough's speculative empire begins to collapse when a number of his companies fail even as two suspicious fires and one unforeseen death cause claims to come due at the West Diddlesex. Brough absconds to the continent, leaving Sam to be arrested for debt, confined to Fleet Prison, and forced to testify before the Bankruptcy Court Commissioner, who absolves him of criminal responsibility but also cautions, "if you had not been so eager after gain, I think you would not have allowed yourself to be deceived . . . Directly people expect to make a large interest, their judgment seems to desert them."[25] The commissioner's moral is appropriate, as the misalignments between status and wealth in the novel are legion, and range from various characters' misapprehensions of Sam fomented by his diamond pin to society's embrace of Brough on the strength of his speculative wealth to Sam's mother's initial investment in the West Diddlesex and her willingness to surrender her son to the caprices of his wealthy aunt.[26] After a month, Sam and Mary's baby dies while Sam is imprisoned, but they are rescued from penury by Mary's own maternal assets, as she becomes a wet nurse to the wealthy Tiptoffs, true relatives of the Countess of Drum, who eventually pay Sam's debts and employ him as the family steward. He is reconciled with his aunt on her deathbed, and she leaves him a valuable inheritance, the money now purged of the taint of the active pursuit of wealth for its own sake and Sam's status already secured by his legitimate reputation for honesty.[27]

Published the same year as Thackeray's *History of Samuel Titmarsh and the Great Hoggarty Diamond*, Scottish journalist Charles MacKay's *Memoirs of Extraordinary Popular Delusions and the Madness of Crowds* (1841) provides in its first volume popular histories of the Mississippi Scheme and the South Sea Bubble, reintroducing Victorian readers to the antecedents for their more recent company mania and speculations in foreign debt. As his title implies, MacKay adopts a predominantly psychological approach to these foundational examples of financial crisis, which serve as the leading examples of "popular delusions" of all kinds, from alchemy to witch burning to the crusades. The book was sufficiently popular in MacKay's lifetime (1814–89) to justify subsequent editions in 1852, 1856, 1869, and 1880, and it continues to be cited by economic historians of the twentieth and twenty-first centuries.[28] MacKay and Dickens were friends, correspondents, and professional associates, and it seems certain that the novelist benefitted from the journalist's knowledge and approach when crafting his own numerous speculative subplots and financial fictions. These most famously include the swindle surrounding the Anglo-Bengalee Disinterested Loan and Life Assurance Company in *Martin Chuzzlewit* (1844), Dickens's adaptation of the Independent and West Middlesex; the dramatic descent into bankruptcy of the eponymous West Indian trading firm in *Dombey and Son* (1848), itself self-consciously written in the aftermath of the Railway Mania; and, in *Little Dorrit* (1857), the rise and fall of the colossal speculator Mr Merdle, in whom Dickens combines the qualities of George Hudson and John Sadleir.

These and numerous other examples scattered throughout Dickens's fiction warn readers against overinvesting in characters who appear to be able to convert wealth into social position. Such socio-financial alchemy, he warns, may be popular but is also delusional: real, durable status can only be earned in a Dickensian novel through renunciation of, not speculation in, the things of this world. This turns out to be an exceedingly difficult lesson for

Mr Paul Dombey, whose "one idea of . . . life" is that the "earth was made for Dombey and Son to trade in."[29] Indeed, Dombey must undergo what Barbara Weiss memorably phrases "salvation by bankruptcy," before he can be brought even to appreciate his firstborn daughter, Florence, as more than, in the words of Dickens's narrator, "a piece of base coin that couldn't be invested—a bad Boy."[30] Recast in generic terms, Dombey commences the story believing himself to be the hero of an economic epic but concludes by being impressed into his role as the grandfather of a domestic fiction.[31] In between these two narrative endpoints, the novel repeatedly depicts the problems that arise from overvaluing wealth. In the first of two crucial scenes featuring Dombey and his children, the sickly "Son" of the family firm, also named Paul, disconcerts his father with the seemingly simple question, "'Papa! what's money?'"[32] After two false starts, Dombey settles on an enumeration of money's social functions: "money cause[s] us to be honoured, feared, respected, courted, and admired, and ma[kes] us powerful and glorious in the eyes of all men."[33] After Paul's death, Dombey recalls this exchange, reflecting on "the feebleness of wealth . . . what *could* it do indeed: what had it done?"[34] What it has done already is to estrange him from his daughter, who, in the second key filial scene only two chapters earlier, had sought to commiserate with him over their common loss and been repulsed. "Let him remember it in that room, years to come," the narrator intones.[35] Dombey will do so, but not before driving Florence from him altogether by striking her "crosswise, with that heaviness, that she tottered on the marble floor," displacing his rage at his recently fled second wife, Edith, upon his daughter.[36] Eventually, after his bankruptcy has severed him from his wealth, Dombey is diverted from thoughts of suicide by Florence's dramatic reappearance and is moved by her entirely unwarranted pleas for forgiveness to admit, "'Oh my God, forgive me, for I need it very much!'"[37] He is, thus, saved, and if no longer "powerful and glorious in the eyes of all men," becomes, at least, the object of affection for his granddaughter's "earnest eyes."[38]

Over the next fifteen years, Dickens infused cautionary financial subplots into his own novels and edited additional fictional examples and newsy articles provided by other writers for his weekly journals *Household Words* and *All the Year Round*. Serialized in the latter from March through December 1863, Charles Reade's *Very Hard Cash*, simplified to *Hard Cash* when it appeared in volume form at the end of that year, was originally conceived as an exposé of the abuses inherent in private asylums. Following the main plot,

Alfred Hardie, a promising Oxford undergraduate, has his engagement broken by his banker-father, who then has him committed under false pretenses; Alfred subsequently undergoes horrific treatment that Reade claimed to have lifted directly from documented cases of contemporary medical practice. Also confined in the asylum is David Dodd, who is suffering from cataleptic shock and as a result has forgotten his own identity. The two become friends and eventually escape from their incarceration during a fire, after which Alfred Hardie proves his sanity in court, Richard Hardie loses his grip on reality to a monomaniacal miserliness, Dodd regains his memory, and their two families unite through the long-delayed marriage of Alfred to Dodd's daughter Julia. All of this sensationally tinged action revolves around the novel's central metonym, the titular hard cash, paper money that seems always on the verge of being lost.[39]

The money's fragile status expresses the larger fragility of status when built upon wealth in a society riddled with financial fraud. The cash gets its start in India, where Captain Dodd had, "under advice of an Indian friend . . . during the last few years, placed considerable sums, at intervals, in a great Calcutta house, which gave eight per cent for deposits."[40] With an interest rate on a level with those offered by Brough at the West Diddlesex, the bank runs into difficulties, and Dodd succeeds in withdrawing his "hoard" on the very day that legitimate currency begins to run short.[41] He must then transport the cash back to England, along the way repulsing repeated attempts to steal it, including during a maritime attack by literal pirates.[42] Unfortunately, an unduly relieved Dodd next deposits the money with Richard Hardie, who turns out to be a buccaneer of the financial sort; realizing his mistake too late is what triggers Dodd's first attack of catalepsy. Hardie's own now-false status as a reputable banker dates to the 1820s, when he succeeded in piloting what was then his father's bank through that earlier financial storm. "'You have read of bubbles; the Mississippi Bubble and the South Sea Bubble,'" Mrs Dodd tells her daughter, perhaps thinking of MacKay's *Memoirs*, "'Well, in the year 1825, it was not one bubble but a thousand'"; she continues, enumerating those who placed their status at risk in the pursuit of wealth for its own sake as "'Princes, Dukes, Duchesses, Bishops, Poets, Lawyers, Physicians'" along with "'their own footmen.'"[43] A conservative investor for two decades, Hardie is tempted into speculation by the sight of "a prime minister with a spade delving [a railway] in the valley of the Trent" and "a parliament, which, under a new temptation showed itself as corrupt and greedy as any nation or age can parallel."[44] Even while advising his depositors against placing their savings at risk, Hardie joins the "motley crew of peers and printers, vicars and admirals, professors, cooks, costermongers, cotton-spinners, waiters, coachmen, priests, potboys, bankers, braziers, dairy-men, mail-guards, barristers, spinsters, butchers, beggars, duchesses, rag-merchants; in one word, of Nobs and Snobs" who "fought and scrambled pell mell for the popular paper; and all to get rich in a day."[45] Once his speculations go bad, Hardie tries everything to extricate himself and the bank from the threat of bankruptcy, even going so far as to embezzle money from Alfred's trust, the concealment of which drives him to forbid the original marriage to Julia and have Alfred declared insane. Cash turns out to be very hard – in the sense of "difficult to bear; causing suffering" as opposed to "high and stable; firm" (OED) – in Reade's novel, which reveals how even "a colossus of wealth and stability to the eye" can be "ready to crumble at a touch" in the wrong financial circumstances.[46] Ultimately, a fortuitous rise in Turkish consols allows *Hard Cash* to purchase a happy ending for the characters who deserve it, but this *deus ex machina* does not obscure the madness of those who bank their status alongside their wealth.[47]

At their respective financial nadirs, both Paul Dombey and Richard Hardie contemplate suicide; although neither imagine jumping in front of a train, both are, to varying degrees, brought to the edge of self-destruction by one. As a novel written while the wave of railway mania was still cresting, and then published in volume form during the period of parliamentary and shareholder investigations, *Dombey and Son* deploys trains historically and metaphorically. Thus, in chapter six, Dickens describes the "first shock of a great earthquake" of railway construction in Camden Town, representing the chaotic scene as ironic evidence for the encroachment of the "mighty course of civilisation" upon "the miserable waste ground" adjacent to the row of squalid houses known as Stagg's Gardens.[48] Later, in chapter twenty, Dombey travels by rail and, in his grief for his son, can see the train only as a "triumphant . . . remorseless . . . indomitable monster, Death."[49] Finally, in chapter 55, the fleeing Carker is literally "beaten down, caught up, and whirled away" by a train "that spun him round and round, and struck him limb from limb, and licked his stream of life up with its fiery heat, and cast his mutilated fragments in the air."[50] Carker's death catalyzes the slow collapse of Dombey's firm, leading to his bankruptcy and thoughts of "severing that other link" into "a lazy little pool" of his own blood.[51] The relationship between *Hard Cash* and the 1840s mania is more straightforwardly financial, with imprudent railway speculations leading the elder Hardie to arm himself with pistol and poison while waiting for the final price of the Old Turks. This link between railway mania, insolvency, and autophonomania extends beyond Dickens's and Reade's novels to Anthony Trollope's *The Way We Live Now* (1875), in which the collapse of a fraudulent speculation, the South Central Pacific and Mexican Railway, leads inexorably to the bankruptcy and death of Augustus Melmotte by his own hand.[52]

Often described by critics in superlative terms – as "the best known and the most bitter" novel about England's Railway Mania, as one of "the most memorable Victorian financial novels," and as "unequaled in its portrait of commercial venality"[53] – Trollope's novel indicts all of English society for its embrace of financial hypocrisy and individual dishonesty as necessary components of "the way we live now." As it chronicles the rise and fall of its representative new man, the "purse-proud ... bully" Melmotte, the narrative illustrates how limited liability has grown from a principle of business into the principal mode of living for almost all of its high-status characters.[54] Among the well-to-do, only Roger Carbury, Trollope's elegiac country gentleman, entirely refuses to join the general scramble for speculative lucre that surrounds Melmotte and his American mountebank partner Fisker.[55] Almost all of the other characters stand among the "many people [who] speak very badly of Mr Melmotte's honesty," who see him as " tower ... thought by many to have been built upon the sands," who, in fact, understand that a "fortune was to be made, not by the construction of the railway, but by the floating of the railway shares."[56] In other words, they are in on the swindle from the beginning, but are willing to sacrifice present honor for the sake of future wealth. Before the final unraveling of his speculative schemes, Melmotte succeeds in being elected to parliament and in purchasing a country estate; he is also reduced to forging signatures, attempting to steal from his own daughter (albeit money he has settled upon her in order to limit his own liability in bankruptcy), and destroying documentary evidence.[57] In chapter 83, when "a general feeling prevailed that the world was more than ordinarily alive because of Melmotte and his failures," he appears drunk in the House of Commons, where he is studiously ignored by all of its members, and then returns home to "deliver himself from the indignities and penalties to which the law might have subjected him by a dose of prussic acid."[58] The remaining seventeen chapters of the novel concern themselves with tying up loose ends, including the emigration of Melmotte's widow and daughter to America with Fisker, who resolves to buy up all remaining shares in the illusory railway, return to San Francisco, and begin "the work of robbing mankind by magnificently false representations" all over again.[59]

William North's *The City of the Jugglers* and the "Conventional Necessity" of Mid-Nineteenth-Century Fiction

Perhaps even more deserving of superlatives than Trollope's novel, William North's *The City of the Jugglers; or, Free-Trade in Souls: A Romance of the "Golden" Age* (1850) is one of the least read, strangest, and most extended treatments of financial fraud in Victorian fiction. Republished in 2008 after over 150 years of bibliographic oblivion by the University of South Carolina Press and reconnected in 2009 to the currents of academic debate through a dedicated issue of *Victorian Newsletter*, North's *City* significantly troubles the generic limits of the nineteenth-century novel. That is, in Butlerian terms, it parodically re-presents many normative elements of the dominant literary form of its day and in so doing reveals that form's fundamentally constructed, arbitrary, even grotesque character. On a first reading, *City* may appear to belong alongside those novels cited above and other works concerned with capitalist speculation and England's expanding credit economy. Even within the rapidly diversifying portfolio of works held to be proper objects of the "new economic criticism" managed by Tamara Wagner, Gail Turley Houston, Martha Woodmansee and Mark Osteen, and others, however, North's text stands apart.

Unlike its best-known contemporaries, *City* follows fraud for its own sake and not as a figure for other characterological or social concerns. In thus reversing "the typical emphasis, moving formally marginal material—the financial . . . plots—to the center of the narrative," North's fiction may well be "unique among novels of economic critique."[60] According to its modern editor, Patrick Scott, *City* is more even than that, however: "It is a book that, taken seriously, could reconfigure views about the literature of the 1840s."[61] The text's capacity to challenge our understanding of period fiction, in fact, grows out of its central fixation on London's financial juggle. By making financial speculation its sign rather than its signifier, *City* internalizes at the level of form the notion of unfettered free trade that it repudiates. That is, its critique of the market comes to look like the market, monstrously inclusive, with none of the aesthetic protections normally afforded to either the text or the reader by generic convention.

North's own relationship to period conventions, whether societal or literary, was a vexed one at best. As reconstructed by Allan Life and Page Life, North's life, in the years leading up to the publication of *City*, seems grounded in his long-running rebellion against patriarchal authority, punctuated by unwise professional choices, imprisonment for debt, a possible illegitimate child, and increasingly paranoid exchanges with his contemporaries. North's literary production over this same period manifests a similar disdain for polite standards. In 1844, at the age of 19, he published *Anti-Coningsby*, a heavy-handed parody of Benjamin Disraeli's first Young England novel most notable for its opportunistic anti-Semitism. The next year, North released *The Imposter*, a conventional three-decker in form whose characters, including the self-proclaimed bastard son of Lord Byron, rather surprisingly speak and act according to the phrenological organs that each represents. Praised, despite its flaws, for its "entire originality . . . a new theme—a new style" by *The Critic*, the novel is, according to Life and Life, "among the most fascinating might-have-beens of Victorian literature."[62] Arguably less fascinating and even more on the fringe of the literary market, the rest of North's authorial work from the 1840s includes his publication of a romance, *The Anti-Punch* (1847); his translations of *Travels and Adventures in Egypt* (1847) by Prince Pückler-Muskau and *Poetic Meditations* (1848) by Alphonse de Lamartine; and his contributions to the short-lived newspaper *The Puppet Show* (1848–9).

It is, then, from something of a position of disaffected experience that North wrote his overt fictional repudiation of mid-century financial and literary conventions, *The City of the Jugglers*. In this, his final book-length publication in England, North interrogates at length Victorian conceptions of power, status, and authority, in particular the heavily leveraged position reserved for those whom later social theorists would label the intelligentsia. Since even dedicated readers of period fiction likely remain unfamiliar with the book, I begin by offering a brief plot summary highlighting the commercial juggle that serves as its primary narrative arc and functions as the incidental scaffold of the narrative. The text's account of how markets work reveals significant imaginative affiliations with both Hegel and Marx and lends itself to sociological analysis by means of Max Weber's *Economy and Society*. *City* puts into fictional form Weber's conflict between market and status economies and ultimately seeks to resolve this problem of modernity by invoking the transcendental figure of the poet from Percy Shelley's "Defence of Poetry" (1840). Having thus situated *City* within its original intellectual and subsequent theoretical contexts, I offer an extended reading of the remarkable remainder of this unusual book, concentrating on the many ways in which North transgresses the generic boundaries of the mid-century novel. The unconventional features of *City* offer a highly self-conscious argument by example for the superiority of the status economy of genius over the free market. By its end, this argument begins to break down as, within the narrative itself, North worries, not without cause, about how to classify his book so that others might read it.

"It is in the souls of the living . . . I propose to speculate."[63]

Set in the aftermath of Chartism, the European revolutions of 1848, and the bursting of the railway bubble, the main financial plot of *City* traces the rise and fall of an audacious commercial speculation in human souls. The Soul Agency, directed by Ignatius Loyola Grey, commodifies the "feelings" and "principles" of everyone from cabinet ministers to struggling artists, and then sells them on the free market (7). Lauded by the press and the government, Grey attracts sufficient investment to warrant the construction of an entire Soul Exchange. With a market now required to quantify accurately the value of individuals, intellectualism and genius begin to appreciate. Taking advantage of their newfound leverage, a cabal of revolutionary thinkers and writers, led by poet Bernard Viridor and Arthur Bolingbroke Darian, the Duke of St. George, maneuver towards the collapse of the market in souls and, with it, England's reactionary social order. First, they arrange a "Grand Exposition of the Souls of All Nations," which exhibits a variety of deranged, and therefore honest, persons who represent every "phase of moral or intellectual aberration" attributable to materialism, selfishness, and instrumentality (213). Second, Darian publicly renounces his title even as, third, Viridor publishes a best-selling book, described by the narrator as "to this present volume what the sun is to a common gas lamp . . . its sale was measured by tens of thousands" (230). Fourth, they host a party at which individuals of intellect mingle without regard to hierarchical social distinctions. Fifth, they engineer a strike of all the journalists in London to end anonymous publication; when the writers return to work victorious, they are all so impressed with the "solemn responsibility" of "appending their signatures" that they uniformly write liberal articles about "their duties to their fellow men" (241).

The hated faux-liberal Whig ministry resigns and Viridor is elected to parliament, where he successfully pressures a government threatened with civil war to grant universal male suffrage to placate the revolutionary masses. In the aftermath, the Soul Exchange is shuttered, and Grey immigrates to the United States to become a slave trader.[64]

Even this brief summary begins to suggest that North's historical imagination takes its shape from the dialectical process of determinate negation at work in Hegel's *Phenomenology of Spirit*. This Hegelian genealogy is perceptible in Viridor's explicit statement, "'I am no despiser of Hegel'" (39); the unanticipated "one good effect" of the new market's attention to "the nature of the Soul," that "stupid people began to find their level, and comparatively honest men to rise in estimation" (101); and the consequent rise in intellectualism of all sorts, manifested in the transformation of the "cheap literature of the hour" from G. M. W. Reynolds's *Mysteries of London* to editions of Berkeley, Kant, Hegel, Spinoza, and Swedenborg (226). Ironically, this idealist shift in England's zeitgeist is an inevitable effect of the materialist desire to make as much money as possible on the soul market. At the same time, the speculative nature of this market makes it vulnerable to manipulation, and not just by Grey. Early in the narrative, Darian enters a bid at the Soul Agency for Viridor, whom he values "as high as ten thousand pounds, with a place worth from five to twelve hundred a year, a seat in Parliament, and an introduction to the first society in England" (17). This "*ruse*, the object of which was solely to increase his (Viridor's) importance and influence amongst the soul dealers," prompts Grey to call in person at the writer's apartment and makes Viridor an object of rampant speculation among all those with investments in the market (157, emphasis in original). Both of these factors, the general shift in England's way of thinking and Darian's inflation of the value of Viridor's soul, permit Viridor and Darian's revolutionary vanguard of "Supreme Illuminati" to assume power enough to liquidate the soul market.

North's debt to Hegel extends further, moreover, to include a textbook example of the master-slave dialectic in the relationship between the government and the press. Immediately after his visit to Viridor's chambers, Grey proceeds to the offices of the *Timeserver*, a transparent pseudonym for the *Times*, where he appears as the principal among the paper's three directors. The paper is currently the slave of the Austrian government, which has purchased its loyal publicity on the Soul Exchange. With all of Europe "smoking cigars on barrels of gunpowder," however, the nation has much more to lose than the newspaper, which initially withdraws its support when the week's payment falls short (173). Only the last-second arrival of a breathless courier with a packet full of "notes," presumably issued by the Bank of England, prevents the defection and prompts Grey to instruct his anonymous editorial writers, "*Butter for Austria, orders revoked*" (175). As represented in *City*, the same precarious affiliation extends throughout mid-century Europe. Speaking to his fellow Illuminati, Viridor thunders,

> "But what could ordinary statesmen, with their barren inventions, ignorant confidence in their limited experience, and cautious timidities, have done during the late revolutions in Paris, in Rome, in Hungary? . . . Without the venal slaves and reckless renegades of the press, they would vainly seek for Mamelukes to carry out their designs." (191)

When, after the Great Exposition, "journalists of all grades, editors, subeditors, compilers, financiers, reporters, and even penny-a-liners" all go on strike, even the English government cannot retain its mastery without the support of its former periodical "slaves" (238).

This affinity for Hegelian dialectic generally, and for the master-slave dialectic particularly, points to the intellectual, ideological, at times even rhetorical alignment between North and Karl Marx, whose *Communist Manifesto* (1848) had appeared only two years prior to the publication of *City*. For instance, in his account of that class of society to which Grey undoubtedly belongs, North merges Marx's figure of the capitalist with Carlyle's mechanical pejorative to describe the "Gold-worshipper, or Plutocrat" as "a slave and a slave-driver at the same moment. His task is to squeeze the largest profit out of the labour of poorer men than himself. But with all his squeezing he is a mere money-collecting machine" (114). Those being squeezed are also represented. During Grey's walk from Viridor's apartment to the offices of the *Timeserver*, he encounters a "thin mechanic" whose experience of alienated labor has given him a keen sense of class consciousness: "He caught the Soul Agent's glance, and an expression of defiant hatred darkened all his countenance. Chartist and Socialist as he was, the well-dressed lounger, the idle gentleman, was an abomination in his eyes. Hunger breeds hatred, and the poor man soon imbibes the belief that his poverty is the rich man's crime" (162). Presumably this mechanic is among those who join the mob pressing for universal suffrage at the end of the plot; in this final expression of popular discontent, *City* offers the vision of the *Communist Manifesto* fulfilled in "a unanimous rising of the working classes—a demonstration of their strength, and an assertion of their rights" (244). Even when the novel distances itself from socialism and communism, it does so in terms reminiscent of Marx. Thus, charged by Viridor with a household arrangement that "borders on Communism," Darian responds by rejecting "the schemes of Cabet, Louis Blanc, Considérant, and all other followers of Fourier, St. Simon, or Owen" (49), in his denial thereby echoing chapter three, section three, on "Critical-Utopian Socialism and Communism," from the *Manifesto*.[65]

Although it would be possible to multiply these examples of Marxist sentiment and language throughout *City*, it is ultimately more productive to read the book's central financial plot through the critical lens provided by a slightly later intellectual heir of both Hegel and Marx, early twentieth-century sociological theorist Max Weber. North certainly finds repugnant the excesses of capitalist speculation, and he sympathizes with the plight of the poor, but his social vision is grounded not in the opposition between capital and labor or the bourgeoisie and the proletariat, but instead in the contest between market and status economies. As already discussed in this volume's introduction, according to Weber's magisterial *Economy and Society*, the former are fully rationalized in their unlimited extension of the free market and their reduction of social hierarchies to the possession of "'naked' money power." Status economies, by contrast, make an "effective claim to social esteem" that is typically founded on "style of life," formal education, or "hereditary or occupational prestige" and expressed through conventions of consumption.[66]

Put in Weber's terms, the Soul Exchange represents England's free market taken to its rational end point, at which the components of individual status can be quantified as so much naked money power and then sold to appropriately wealthy speculators, who gain social honor through undisguised economic acquisition. Fueling North's moral outrage throughout *City* – an outrage at least equal to that of the *Latter-Day Pamphlets* of Thomas Carlyle, to whom North alludes repeatedly – is the fact that Grey's is not an original idea, but rather a refinement upon what already exists in mid-century England. Thus, in making his initial pitch for startup capital to his future partner, Robert Russel Brown, Grey observes,

> "Look about you—look at Downing-street, look at the Houses of Parliament, look at the Church, the Bar, the Press—aye, look at the leviathan *Timeserver* and its crew; and say whether there are not souls bought and sold, aye, and double-sold in London, wholesale and retail, to an extent beyond all ordinary powers of calculation? Now observe

how clumsily, how indelicately, how imperfectly the thing is managed—and mark how splendidly my scheme will come in to supply all the wants of the age." (9)

Grey's choice of examples is telling, since he implicates as soul-dealers nearly all those with traditional professional and gentlemanly pretentions, who might be expected to invest most heavily in status economies because they may otherwise lack the guarantee provided by aristocratic birth. Before the end of his first chapter, then, North renders his financial plot in realistic terms and advances a trenchant critique of the interestedness of that portion of society normally represented by his contemporaries as outside, above, or at worst only victimized by the frenzy of commercial speculation.

North's efforts to establish the realism of his financial plot extend to his parodic re-presentation of the rhetorical forms of speculative puffery directed at the investing public in the 1840s, as well as his specific allusions to the railway mania of 1845–7. After his initial meeting with Grey, Darian carries away a "gold-lettered handbill" promoting the new free-trade in souls.[67] This advertisement promises that the new soul agency enjoys "CAPITAL UNLIMITED" and features a number of what Mary Poovey labels "front-sheeters," defined as "prominent men who might—or might not—have agreed to serve as the company's directors."[68] These include the then-secret author of *Vestiges of the Natural History of Creation* (Robert Chambers) as actuary, Theophrastus Donamy as company phrenologist, Dr Paracelsus Wriggledum as physician and mesmerist, and others. The prospectus goes on to syllogistically rationalize its business plan, offering a major premise, "It is a long-established axiom that every man has his price"; a minor premise, "The soul, or galvanic mainspring of the human machine, regulates all its movements"; and a conclusion, "Therefore everything a man does for money, or other payment, is a sale or mortgage of his soul to another person." On the basis of this conclusion the company promises "to facilitate those negotiations which, in every civilised community, must constantly occur . . . from the purchase of a young wife for an old *roué*, to that of a ministerial or opposition majority." Such language would have been familiar to North's contemporaries from the report of the 1844 Select Committee on Joint-Stock Companies, as well as from the "frenzy . . . of fraudulent practices" that accompanied the subsequent railway mania precipitated by George Hudson.[69] Indeed, Grey's "fat friend, Robert Russel Brown," is described as "an embryo George Mudson of the soul-market. They called him Lucifer Brown afterwards, just as Mudson was nicknamed the Iron Czar" (86).

Even the presence of the "Supreme Illuminati," which may strike twenty-first century readers as ridiculous or fanciful, should be read as an index of North's effort to render his financial plot familiar and believable to his nineteenth-century contemporaries. As J. M. Roberts observes, "For about a century and a half large numbers of intelligent Europeans believed that much of what was happening in the world around them only happened because secret societies planned it so . . . More believed such nonsense, probably, between 1815 and 1914 than at any other time."[70] Building upon Roberts, I have argued at length elsewhere that, particularly during times of political crises like those of 1848, this belief manifested through a widespread rhetoric of secrecy that invoked conspiratorial groups like the Illuminati to explain the meaning of contemporary events.[71] Numerous other writers had already capitalized upon this pervasive belief in the influence of secret societies over public affairs, a fact that North acknowledges in a brief allusion to Edward Bulwer(-Lytton)'s *Zanoni* (1842), which imagines a role for the Rosicrucians in the French Revolution. North is careful to distance the more realistic *City* from this "weird romance," however, just as he elevates Viridor above his no-longer-radical predecessor Bulwer through a paragraph-length apostrophe that includes the question, "'What secret chain debarred thy soul from liberty?'" (178). Once they appear in the flesh, North's Illuminati practice no esoteric mysticism, but instead profess their commitment to "Love" and "Knowledge" and agree to pursue an eight-point plan of practical reforms that includes as its first three items universal suffrage, education, and social welfare (184, 188–9). Hardly outliers on the lunatic fringe, they articulate a version of "the ethos and hopes of intellectual Chartists."[72]

More than just an element of narrative plausibility, the group of Illuminati also offers some of the clearest evidence for that precise version of the status economy most valued in *City*. Given the foregrounded collapse of the financial plot, it almost goes without saying that North will have nothing to do with any form of status grounded in wealth. Neither does he attach any value to status linked to aristocratic birth, derided in the text as "an exploded system," even "a satanic delusion, soon to be dissipated by the breath of liberty and reason" (117, 241). Part of the problem with aristocratic birth as a basis for status is the readiness with which rank and titles can be commodified:

> One set of ingenious rascals had started an office as agents to all kings in Europe for the sale of titles. Patents of nobility were growing as common, and about as valuable, as protested bills in the market. Pedigrees were to be had with them, if required; and men sold their ancestors and proclaimed themselves bastards, with the same coolness shewn in saddling their children with debt, to relieve themselves from taxation. (225)

This same readiness to become the object of a commercial juggle is only one of the bases for North's contempt of some of the traditional professions. For instance, the law is derided as full of "conceit, arrogance, and toadying snobbism . . . a capital nuisance to get rid of," whereas the clergy are dismissed as "trained professors of . . . the mechanical exhibitions of priestcraft" (55, 185). Thus is status on the basis of "occupational prestige" greatly curtailed.

Instead, North advocates for a less quantifiable but for him no less certain foundation for status in the realm of spirit and the possession of genius. Reflecting upon Grey's ready obsequiousness by the end of his early interview with Darian, the narrator remarks, "There is a spiritual as a social scale of infinite gradations. A spirit of the secondary must bend to a spirit of the primary order" (22). Such primary spirits, for North, are distinguishable by their "individual genius and individual exertion, the principal fountain of all general improvement" (50); later, Viridor similarly tells his fellow Illuminati, "All progress originates in individual genius" (186). The particular variety of individual genius especially worthy of status for North is that possessed by "literary men," who combine talent with generosity, or, in the terms of Viridor's above-mentioned Illuminist platform, "Knowledge" with "Love":

> I know at this present moment at least a dozen men with whom I scarcely share an opinion, who would if requisite divide their last guinea with me as a matter of course, and without even the notion that they were exercising more than ordinary liberality. I do not know one man of any other profession on whom I could reckon with certainty even in the most extreme case of emergency. (30)

Fictional evidence for the versatile excellence of literary men emerges from Darian's military experience of the Hungarian revolution, during which his best officers had come from their ranks, whereas Viridor's equally fictitious participation in the revolution in France cites the historical example of Lamartine to support the same point (60, 84). At the climax of the financial plot, the writers' strike inspired by Viridor and his Illuminati, these literary professionals assert their own rights to social status in uncompromising terms: "Our names to our articles, the position in society which our respective talents entitle us, the political independence and influence which our reputation must secure us. Keep your gold, squeeze more from our brains, if it please you, but leave us our dignity as men" (239). Ultimately, rather than appealing to the more traditional and more easily verifiable forms of status identified by Weber, North echoes Shelley in asserting his poets as the conquerors of the market and the now-acknowledged legislators of the world.

"Away with all temporising"[73]

This Shelleyan solution to the problem of unlimited financial speculation compounds the unusual nature of North's fictional critique of England's ironically titled "golden age," a critique already distinctive in its length, its literalness, and its narrative centrality. If possible, the roughly one half of the book not devoted to the financial plot presents even more challenges for readers accustomed to the formal conventions of the mid-century novel. There are at least a half-dozen additional plots, all at best only loosely connected to the machinations of the soul market; several kinds of paratexts, including a large number of authorial footnotes; and a range of extraordinarily high-profile asides on a variety of topics, ultimately eroding the distinction between author and narrator while meditating anxiously about the process of writing and publishing itself. Early reviewers noted this violation of fictional decorum right away, with the bemused reader for *Tait's Edinburgh Magazine* calling *City* "a very strange production" and the slightly more sympathetic writer for the *Westminster and Foreign Quarterly Review* recommending "careful revision and unsparing excision" to arrive at "a useful auxiliary to the cause of the people."[74] *City*'s more recent critics have voiced similar concerns, with Stern unsure "that this is a 'novel' at all" (47), Scott prepared to see it as "a romance, or political fantasia, as well as a scathing political satire" (8), and Lamouria observing that "*City* often reads less like a mid-century novel than a *bricolage* of various genres of writing packaged in a three-volume format."[75] "Packaged" is the key word here, since although *City* is ostensibly divided into three "books," these are of such noticeably different sizes that it would probably be more accurate to read the text as an unbalanced one-volume work.[76]

It is as if in excoriating the free market for over-reaching, North cannot avoid producing a book that stages a generic revolt while it describes a financial and political revolution.

The two male characters who alternate in serving as the narrative's protagonist, Darian and Viridor, each also provide the point of focalization in three secondary plotlines. Immediately after Darian's first, anonymous meeting with Grey, the narrator devotes a chapter to "recounting the facts in their naked simplicity" surrounding the "extraordinary misfortunes of that famous race," the St. Georges (24). A fantastical inheritance plot in miniature ensues, including romantic and political entanglements with the Russian court, a deadly Anatolian plague, and the unwavering devotion of a family servant; all merely lay the groundwork for Darian's original estrangement from his father and subsequent assumption of the ducal title. Three chapters later, Darian narrates his own personal history to Viridor, drawing attention to the similarities in their experience "at school together" and later as dissatisfied law students (55). What appears on its way to becoming a small bildungsroman pivots, once Darian's political radicalism results in his estrangement from his family, into an historical adventure plot as Darian serves as an officer in the Hungarian army seeking political independence from the Austrian empire during the European revolutions of 1848. This plot culminates with the chance meeting of Darian and a loyal family retainer, Thomas Stanley, come to tell him of his waiting inheritance; at the same time, the Austrian troops arrive at their location intending publicly to flog, likely to death, "the famous Basiline, Countess of Arpath," Hungarian poet and revolutionary (67). Darian rescues Basiline, Stanley is killed, Hungarian reinforcements arrive, and the Austrians are driven from the field, with Darian himself whipping the Austrian general during the retreat. Implied at this "crisis in Darian's narrative" is a third, romantic plot featuring Darian and Basiline, the details of which are left to an imagination guided by their shared "attitude and expression . . . of a love without drawback, the sublime adoration of a woman for her hero, and a lover for his mistress" (68).

As *City* progresses from its first to its second volume, Viridor begins to eclipse Darian both in the central financial plot and in the number of secondary plots with which he is associated. Viridor's own historical adventure plot occurred in "Paris, amid the vortex of its Revolution, and at the right hand of that hero of modern days, Lamartine," the specifics only implied by the contours of Darian's first-person narrative and by a note inserted into the background provided about Viridor's somewhat more realistic struggles with his own overbearing father (57). The reader receives a much fuller account of Viridor's experience of romance, however, in the form of a secondary domestic plot that stretches across three different chapters. Inspired by the attachment of Darian and Basiline, whom he thought of "as of a beautiful type, of something he longed for, yet despaired of finding," Viridor falls in love with seventeen-year-old Grace Morton (126). In their chance first meeting in Regent's Park, Viridor had rescued "this fair child of poverty and obscurity" from an overly aggressive cow (135). Flouting convention, they later meet in his chambers for tea, and Viridor subsequently brings Grace as his date to the party that is the penultimate stage of his Illuminati-supported revolution. The domestic plot actually supplies the final incident in *City*, when, after the revolution has been accomplished, Viridor returns to his apartment to find the exhausted and anxious Grace waiting for him and proposes to her. This same apartment also serves as the site of Viridor's third ancillary plotline, a locked room mystery in which he discovers that the former inhabitant of his chambers, a destitute inventor, has been living secretly in an only apparently locked "large lumber-closet in the bed-room" (215). True to his "sense of justice to the poor," he offers the stranger assistance, and later arranges for his presence at the same leveling party to which he escorts Grace (219).

Although they either provide a certain background coloring for or intersect at the level of incident with the rise and fall of the free market in souls, these ancillary plots do not function as they should in a more typical Victorian multiplot novel. That is, through the unraveling of seemingly unrelated events they do not provide a new vantage from which to discern aspects of the central story, developing patterns of imagery or conceptual structures that are only implied. Even the conflation of the two male revolutionaries that they encourage does not result in a surprising and heuristically productive motif of doubling – a metaphor at the level of character practiced with such aplomb in the novels of Dickens, for instance – because these two very similar men are introduced as allies and work in concert throughout the book for the same ends. Thematically, the fact that both Darian and Viridor rebel against overbearing fathers on their paths to becoming political revolutionaries on the Continent in 1848 implies that their slightly later cooperative campaign against the soul market may be an extension of their struggle against patriarchal authority; the fact that the collapse of the market leads directly to the fall of the government initially appears to support such a reading.

However, Darian, Viridor, and their Illuminati allies succeed in large part because of the financial backing of the St. George family fortune, which bankrolls Darian's initial visit to Grey's office, his speculative inflation of the value of Viridor's soul, the Great Exposition of the Souls of All Nations, the leveling party, and even the journalism strike. Moreover, the free market in souls, itself, represents a significant challenge to traditional patriarchal authority, in that it converts the status economy of aristocratic pedigree into the market economy of souls and titles for sale to the highest bidder. Fully realized, Grey's system supplants existing patriarchal arrangements as or more effectively than a political revolution. Thus, by the end of *City* one form of anti-patriarchy has successfully overthrown another, thereby precipitating the fall of a ministry led by the Whigs. Adding romantic entanglements and destitute former lodgers does not lend additional clarity to the matter, and no doubt contributed to the original reviewers' sense of the book's strangeness.

Also strange are the quantity and variety of *City*'s paratexts, any one of which might not disturb readers' sense of generic fitness but which together estrange the text far into the margins of the mid-century novel. Moreover, several of the individual paratexts are, themselves, overabundant in content, further reproducing within the material object of the book itself the central characteristic of its fictionalized free market, monstrous inclusiveness. Thus, the overpopulated frontispiece, which appears to represent the dreams of its author, who reclines in the lower left corner, features no less than three dozen individual human and humanlike figures. It may be too much to read this etching as either a symptom of North's "megalomania" or an allusive nod to "Hindu iconography," but it is certainly the case that the proliferation of hyperactive men and man-like creatures contributes to a sense of "eroding boundaries," even "chaos" within this preliminary image.[77] The title page is similarly crowded, providing notice of the book's main title, alternate title, and subtitle; juxtaposing the proverbial "Every man has his price" with the biblical "What shall it profit a man if he gain the whole world and lose his own soul" (Mark 8:36); credentialing North using three of his prior publications; advertising F. H. T. Bellew's "four highly finished etchings," a number which includes the frontispiece; and identifying the publisher. A dedication page follows that includes four different typefaces, and that in its conflation of "living men of letters" with "fellow soldiers in the war of liberty" hints at that version of the status economy to be championed in the fiction to come. Before the narrative proper appears, however, another paratext presents, in the form of a sixteen-stanza poetic prologue written by North and featuring the Shelleyesque allegorical figures of "Love" and Freedom" conquering the "burning, savage lust of gold . . . That overspreads the shuddering globe" (xii, x).

Nineteenth-century readers who persevered through this initial crowd of paratextual materials would have found their capacity for "ironic credulity," based upon their experientially-conditioned sense of the text's "fictionality," tested repeatedly by the inclusion of authorial footnotes.[78] *City* features thirteen such notes distributed throughout the narrative, with functions that include the identification of the primary source for an allusion featured in the main text, the amplification of an attack on a writer or politician made in the main text, the statement of authorial opinion about a variety of subjects, and the revelation of autobiographical and often self-aggrandizing details of North's own life.[79] Although notes of the first type appear in many nineteenth-century novels and need not interfere with readers' judgments of plausibility, only two of North's thirteen notes perform a solely identificatory function. The remaining eleven push insistently at the generic boundaries between the novel, the manifesto, and the memoir. Thus, in the first chapter devoted to Viridor's relationship with Grace Morton, the following brief poetic excerpt is offered to explain Viridor's despair at witnessing Darian and Basiline's love while enjoying no romantic attachment of his own:

> "From Paradise an outcast
> Who weeping sits at the forbidden gates." (123)

A multifunctional footnote attached to these lines begins by identifying the source of this quote as Alphonse de Lamartine's *Poetic Meditations*. The note then reveals that the translation is the author's own, a "true labour of love" for which he gained "neither money nor fame" but which did earn him "a letter of exquisite delicacy" from Lamartine himself (123). In fact, Lamartine's *Poetic Meditations* is featured on the title page of *City* as one of North's prior publications, each of which appears at least once in the book's footnotes. The note then proceeds to make an aesthetic judgment of Lamartine as the equal, at least, of Tennyson, before taking a final swipe at the reviewers who "scorned" North's translated volume (123). No portion of this note is necessary to understand Viridor's emotional state, although it is possible to read in this escalation from information to autobiography to aesthetics an appeal to status grounded in genius.

The risk is that the proof of genius resides in particular cases, and that if the reader does not admit the validity of these cases – because, for instance, the most proximate genius in question disrupts the fictionality of his own narrative to indulge in self-interested attacks on past reviewers – then the larger status economy of genius is, itself, compromised.

Another composite note, this one inserted at the climax of the financial plot, illustrates even more pointedly how North's predilection for expansive paratexts can imperil both the fictionality and the implied argument of *City*. Refusing the material inducements offered by newspaper owners to encourage them to return to work without claiming authorship of their articles, the striking journalists cite among the inequities of anonymous publication the ease with which individual writers "may at any moment be cast aside like worn out gloves by our masters, and in case of distress have not even a claim upon that last of all resources of literary desperation" (239). A lengthy footnote, carrying over onto the next page, begins by identifying this "last of all resources" as the Literary Fund. Shifting to the first person and growing overtly autobiographical, North then asserts, somewhat disingenuously given his connection to *The Puppet Show*, that he "never yet had any connexion whatever with any newspaper" but that he is nevertheless "firmly persuaded that the anonymous system is utterly unworthy of an age of enlightenment and honesty" (239). He then holds himself up as an example of forthrightness, reminding readers of his publication of *Anti-Coningsby*, revealing his instruction to his publisher to release his name and address upon demand, and recounting his behavior at a private party at which "I caused myself to be pointed out to the Young England leader, that he might have every opportunity of demanding satisfaction of any kind he pleased" (240). Dismissing dueling as an "insanity" preferable only to Disraeli's implied "cowardice" at failing to acknowledge his offer, North concludes by citing Bulwer Lytton as an authority on the perniciousness of anonymous publication and promising, "I will never cease to denounce it, whilst I can find a publisher, or pay a printer, to give my thoughts to the public" (240). Another appeal to by serving as a demonstration of (alleged) genius, this footnote conflates disinterestedness with inexperience, moral scrupulousness with self-aggrandizement, and modern middle-class notions of gentlemanliness with outmoded and even rakish standards of gentility, all while deferring the narrative exposure of Darian and Viridor as the prime movers behind the strike. Moreover, the final promissory declaration so disregards the conventions of the mid-century novel that it supplants the simple past of fiction with the future imperative of polemic, even as it eschews the partial anonymity provided by a narrator in favor of the unfiltered convictions of an author.

This same impulse to dispense with anonymity of any sort, including that provided by a third-person narrator, appears throughout the main text of *City* as well. On the one hand, this textual peculiarity bespeaks North's intense confidence in his own personal genius and in the ready transferability of genius from one field to another.[80] Thus, North employs unfiltered second-person address to speak directly to "my dear brother literati" about their role as "the defenders of the *people*, which we, and we only, represent, in this age of transitions?" (98); to "Young England" to plead that its members "give me a little corner of your hearts; believe in my sincerity, even should you deride my pretensions" (120–1); and to "my dear brother Fire-worshippers" to caution them against "falling in love just at present" (122). In the midst of both the main and secondary plots he also contrives space for first-person asides on topics as diverse as the possibility of high quality and affordable home cooking (51–2); the present subdivision of society in four classes, Aristocrats, Plutocrats, Democrats, and Somnocrats (110–20); the appropriate representational aspirations of visual art, somewhat surprisingly exemplified in the work of popular illustrators such as John Leech, Hablot Brown (Phiz), and Richard Doyle (132–3); and the desirability of a monetary policy that dispenses with the gold standard in favor of "notes issued on the security of land, and payable as taxes, government salaries, &c." (227–8).[81] Even a Victorian sage like Carlyle or Ruskin, writing in nonfiction prose, would be hard-pressed to keep up with North's breathless range.

On the other hand, this persistent preference for direct authorial address also produces, especially late in the book, revealing moments of meta-narrative anxiety about the sufficiency of *City*'s own opposition to the golden juggle of the market. The problem is one of both form and audience. Acknowledging the former, North struggles to classify

> this volcanic eruption of my soul, speech in the spiritual parliament of thought, sarcastic *repartee* to liars social, liars political, liars dialectic, analytic, and synthetic,—this mythical history, magnetic revelation, dream of poetic vanity, incomprehensible cartoon, or whatever else it turn out to be in the eyes of men or angels,

before he settles, finally, for the startlingly pedestrian "this volume, bound and illustrated, and to be had at circulating libraries" (223). That is, North finds himself unable to escape the language of the market to describe the product of his soul. Additionally, in recognizing that the primary means for distributing *City* lay with the circulating libraries, he is forced to acknowledge that genius must abase itself before the censorious purchasing power of Mudie's and other, smaller operations. Even if picked up by circulating libraries, this uncompromising text still requires an audience to acknowledge its status as a work of genius, and North has difficulty imagining qualified readers. Ultimately, he pins his hopes on "those only whose hearts beat in harmony with my own," hoping that they will overcome their natural dread of "even an imperfect advocacy of their principles" and give him some "consideration for having so rudely fulfilled a task which no other man has had the audacity to attempt" (224). Although North quickly recovers his bravado, defying his critics and launching into the final spasmodic excesses of the soul market, the vulnerability of *City* to normative standards of genre, propriety, and commodification remains. In his desire to beat the market at its own game, by showing that genius can encompass absolutely everything, North cannot help worrying that he has made his book unsalable.

"Pen! pen! cease thy digressive mania"[82]

As it turned out, North's concerns were justified. Not only was *City* not picked up by Mudie's, according to one account not a single copy of the book was sold.[83] Which fact may make it seem "digressive," perhaps even a bit perverse, to assert that North's admittedly problematic *Romance of the "Golden" Age* musters a productive challenge to the form of the mid-Victorian novel. And yet, with respect to other financial fiction, *City* reveals the unrealized potential of an economic plot allowed to take center stage: most notably, financial speculation by itself has the power to overdetermine narrative every bit as much as domestic imperatives; at the same time, money power can stand alone as a social problem every bit as much in need of solution as factory reform or the New Poor Law; and finally, strict realistic fidelity to the imperatives of a market economy can lead to almost fantastically inevitable social transformation. Methodologically, North's productively idiosyncratic approach to the subgenre also reinforces the heuristic value of sociological theory to those invested in the period's novels of economic critique. In particular, Weber's attentiveness to the coextensive and competitive institutional, legal, and social structures within capitalist economies reveals the unexpected affiliations created when individual novelists proffer fiction as a morally preferable alternative to financial speculation, one capable of achieving greater individual autonomy, collective equity, and formal rationality than the fluctuations of an unfettered free market.

Considered in a broader generic context, *City* radically challenges a number of the supposedly natural features of the Victorian novel. Its myriad paratexts expose both the market-driven puffery of novelistic front matter and the narrow commitment to facticity that could underwrite an unself-conscious approach to fictional realism. In addition, its unbalanced distribution of plot and incident across three "volumes" of dramatically unequal size exposes the artificial hegemony of the three-decker format at mid-century, well before that format's late-century decline. Moreover, its episodic, heterogeneous, and overtly politicized narrative retreats away from the tightly plotted world of domestic fiction and towards an Early Modern and soon-to-be Modernist fictional aesthetic grounded in romance, essay, and satire. That, writing in 1850, North could imagine a return to these antecedent forms suggests, at the very least, that the "conventional necessity" governing more recognizable mid-century fictions may have been insufficient for grappling with the dramatic effects of the nineteenth-century scramble for wealth upon the updated narratives of epistemology and social categorization that, according to Michael McKeon, prompted the emergence of the novel in the first place.[84]

Notes

1. In seeking to understand and briefly reconstruct the contours of Victorian finance, including the many ways by which speculators could be separated from their money in fact and fiction, I am especially indebted to Edward Chancellor's *Devil Take the Hindmost*, Paul Delany's *Literature, Money, and the Market*, Gail Turley Houston's *From Dickens to Dracula*, Jeff Nunokawa's *The Afterlife of Property*, Mary Poovey's *The Financial System in Nineteenth-Century Britain*, George Robb's *White-Collar Crime in Modern England*, Norman Russell's *The Novelist and Mammon*, John Vernon's *Money and Fiction*, Tamara S. Wagner's *Financial Speculation in Victorian Fiction*, and Barbara Weiss's *The Hell of the English*.
2. Thomas Carlyle is generally credited with inventing the phrase "cash nexus" in *Chartism* (1839); his pejorative sense of the term certainly had a profound effect on later Victorian novelists and social theorists.

3. On the Mississippi Bubble, see Chancellor, 60–1; and Wagner, *Financial Speculation*, 21–2.
4. On the South Sea Bubble, see Chancellor, 58–95; Robb, 13–14; Russell, 27–9; and Wagner, *Financial Speculation*, 22–3.
5. Chancellor, 77. In a similar nod to the widespread effects of the collapse of the South Sea Bubble, Robb notes the "inevitable crash brought ruin to thousands of humble investors as well as a number of prominent merchants and tradesmen" (14).
6. As Anna Kornbluh notes, from "the 1830s to the 1880s, crises were rampant and recurrent. Financialization developed from rapidly paced legal innovation . . . Each new act drew fierce contest, followed by yet another large-scale crisis" (*Realizing Capital*, 3). The notable regularity of these boom/bust cycles prompted various explanations from nineteenth-century economic writers and theorists, including S. J. Lloyd, Lord Overstone, J. S. Mill, Walter Bagehot, W. S. Jevons, and, eventually, Clémont Jugler, for whom the "Jugler cycle" is named (see Chancellor, 120–1).
7. Russell, 48.
8. The mechanism for such purchases was a futures contract, which is defined with particular cogency by Kornbluh (*Realizing Capital*, 5).
9. On the 1824–6 speculative boom/bust cycle, see Chancellor, 100–121; Poovey, *The Financial System*, 15; Robb, 15; and Russell, 43–8.
10. On the 1840s Railway Mania, see Chancellor, 124–51; Robb, 31–55; and Russell, 163–87.
11. All of the terms appearing in quotes in this passage are succinctly explained by Poovey, *The Financial System*, 18. According to Robb, there was sufficient money to be made in this advertising phase that, for "fraudulent companies, the success of their bill was a thing to be dreaded," and so their early promoters would simply decline to appear before the review committee (36).
12. Robb describes Hudson as the "parvenue *par excellence*" and offers a succinct summary of his numerous dubious financial practices (32). For a more sympathetic account of Hudson, see Russell, who cautions against "the dangers of trying to judge the commercial institutions of the era from an examination of fiction and *belles lettres*" (181).
13. Robb, 31. According to the statistics on bankruptcies, compositions, and assignments for the years 1847, 1848, and 1849 provided in Table 4 of Weiss, over ten thousand individuals were forced to enter into some sort of arrangement with creditors in each of these years immediately following the Railway Mania (179).
14. On Victorian efforts to meaningfully differentiate among investing, speculating, and gambling, see David C. Itzkowitz's "Fair Enterprise or Extravagant Speculation"; Poovey, *The Financial System*, 124; and Wagner, *Financial Speculation*, 8.

15. On financial reforms of the 1850s and 1860s, see Donna Loftus's "Capital and Community" and Weiss, 137–9; both highlight the moral objections raised against limited liability's apparent legitimation of the absence of personal responsibility in financial matters.
16. On the failure of Strahan, Paul and Bates, see Robb, 60–1; and Russell, 70–2.
17. On John Sadleir and the failure of Tipperary Bank, see Chancellor, 147; Robb, 61–2; Russell, 135–7; and Weiss, 141–2.
18. On the failure of the Royal British Bank, see Robb, 62–3.
19. Russell, 140.
20. Robb, 71.
21. On Scott's rather sad story, see Chancellor, 112–13; and Weiss, 15.
22. Depending upon one's ideological convictions, both the origin and the employment of wealth might also be problematic, especially if the money involved could be tied to the global institution of slavery. For efforts by Quakers on both side of the Atlantic to enact their abolitionist commitments through boycotts of consumer products produced by slave labor, for instance, see Julie L. Holcomb, *Moral Commerce*.
23. Weiss, 15.
24. Described by Russell as "the most gigantic and impudent insurance fraud ever perpetrated" (86), the Independent and West Middlesex Fire and Life Assurance Company was still in the news in 1841, when the *Examiner* featured a report in its "Police" section on January 24 recounting the flight of the company's directors from their offices on Portman Square with "upwards of £98,000 of annuities, cash paid down to them in sundry sums by the victims" (59). For more on Thackeray's fictionalization of the Independent and West Middlesex, see Russell, 90–3.
25. William Makepeace Thackeray, *The History of Samuel Titmarsh and the Great Hoggarty Diamond*, 159–60.
26. Like the commissioner, Sam's mother also reflects that "she and I [Sam] too were justly punished for worshipping the Mammon of unrighteousness, and forgetting our natural feelings for the sake of my aunt's paltry lucre" (Thackeray, 181).
27. The novel's final paragraph reveals that while Sam's experience may be the source of his *History*, he is not its author. The task of actually writing and publishing the story has fallen to his cousin Michael, a professional literary man whose role remains understated in the narrative but important to the argument I am making here about novelists' efforts to construct a definition of middle-class status warranted through negative assertions of value, in this case the explicit rejection of wealth and the implicit rejection of birth, both represented by Uncle Hoggarty's diamond.

28. Chancellor, for example, cites MacKay's *Memoirs* as a source for his own approach to the "history of speculation" as more than just "a description of economic affairs" but also "something of a social history . . . Above all, I hope to have retained some of MacKay's enthusiasm so that the reader will come to agree with his observation that the 'subject [of speculation] is capable of inspiring as much interest as even a novelist can desire'" (xiv).
29. Charles Dickens, *Dombey and Son*, 2.
30. Weiss, 118; Dickens, *Dombey and Son*, 3. For Weiss's full, predominantly religious reading of the novel, see *The Hell of the English*, 114–26.
31. "In the person of Mr Dombey Dickens is concerned not with a bona fide portrait of a merchant, but with the soul-sickness of a man made arrogant by wealth. Despite the title of the book, which is ostensibly the name of a firm, *Dombey and Son* is essentially a domestic novel" (Russell, 198). What connects the economic with the domestic in the novel, according to Jeff Nunokawa, is their mutual imbrication of property, secrecy, and Orientalism; see his chapter-length reading of *Dombey and Son* in *The Afterlife of Property*, 40–76.
32. Dickens, *Dombey and Son*, 98.
33. Ibid. 99–100.
34. Ibid. 289, emphasis in original.
35. Ibid. 272.
36. Ibid. 704.
37. Ibid. 890.
38. Ibid. 925.
39. As Wagner observes, the perilous softness of the cash "underpins the central madhouse narrative and links it to the nautical, suburban, and romance plots" (*Financial Speculation*, 120). For a full-length reading of *Hard Cash* as a novel of financial speculation, see Wagner, *Financial Speculation*, 113–21. For a less connected set of nevertheless relevant reflections, see also Russell, 57–8, 82–3, and 175–6.
40. Charles Reade, *Hard Cash*, 91.
41. Ibid. 91.
42. Both the fiduciary origin of and the piratical threat to Dodd's money should be read in light of mid-Victorian England's horrified fascination with India and the recently suppressed rebellion of 1857–8, most commonly known in Britain as the Indian Mutiny, as well as with Malay piracy. On Reade's willingness to capitalize upon his contemporaries' racialized interest in South Asia, see Sean Grass, "Piracy, Race and Domestic Peril in *Hard Cash*," esp. pp. 183–4.
43. Reade, 83.
44. Ibid. 100.
45. Ibid. 100–1.
46. Ibid. 103.

47. Richard Hardie's success in Turkish bonds represents only the first step in his financial resurgence. By the end of the novel, his "speculations, especially in land and houses," have yielded a balance of £60,000; however, he is unable to enjoy or even to apprehend his second fortune, as his earlier brush with bankruptcy has left him a monomaniac "writh[ing] under imagined poverty" (Reade, 471, 473).
48. Dickens, *Dombey and Son*, 68–9. This early passage is not without acknowledgments of railways' financial side, however: Dickens notes the as yet limited penetration of "bold speculators," who have thus far only built the Railway Arms tavern and gentrified two established local shops into the Excavators' House of Call and the Railway Eating House (68); additionally, the name of Stagg's Gardens, although attributed by locals to either "a deceased capitalist, one Mr Staggs," or "those rural times when the antlered herd, under the familiar denomination of Staggses, has resorted to its shady precincts," would have reminded contemporary readers of speculators in railway scrip, known as stags (69). Dickens returns to these same precincts in chapter fifteen, recording the complete transformation of the neighborhood into "a vista to the Railway world" dominated by "conquering engines . . . dilating with the secret knowledge of great powers yet unsuspected in them, and strong purposes not yet achieved" (233–4).
49. Ibid. 298.
50. Ibid. 823.
51. Ibid. 886.
52. According to Weiss, the "bankruptcy of Mr Melmotte is a stunning reversal toward which everything in the novel has been building; bankruptcy has become at once the controlling image, theme, structural device, and metaphor in *The Way We Live Now*" (85); for an extended reading of the full novel, see Weiss, 159–72.
53. Itzkowitz, 131; Wagner, *Financial Speculation*, 163; Weiss, 160.
54. Trollope, *The Way We Live Now*, 23. As Russell asserts, "Novelists were quick to condemn the New Man of commerce as unscrupulous, course, bloated, probably dishonest, and given to what Bulwer called 'scarlet vulgarity', and the casual reader of *the Way We Live Now* will find many familiar echoes of this literary tradition" (150); for an extended reading of the financial plots of novel, see Russell 149–62.
55. Acutely aware of the exceptionality of Carbury, Delany asserts that "*The Way We Live Now* is an elegiac novel, a lament for the passing away of the old prestige order where identity depends on one's rank, lineage, and connection with the land" (19); for an extended reading of the full novel, see Delany, 19–32.
56. Trollope, *The Way We Live Now*, 43, 47, 49.
57. Melmotte's initial social rise makes him "meaningful as an instance of business charisma, from the generic stories in which his charismatic

power is generated to the routinized way this power is understood" (Hunt, 95); for an extended reading of the novel, see Hunt, 94–104.
58. Trollope, *The Way We Live Now*, 339, 343.
59. Ibid. 375.
60. Lanya Lamouria, "North's *The City of the Jugglers* (1850) and the European Revolutions of 1848," 18; Rebecca Stern, "*The City of the Jugglers* and the Limits of Victorian Fiction," 50. Mary Poovey provides the authoritative description of the shape of Victorian financial fiction: "The vast majority of British novels published between the late 1840s and the end of the century use financial plots ... as thematically central but formally marginal elements of a narrative system that creates a formal consensus among the novel's variety of events and characters" ("Writing about Finance in Victorian England," 37).
61. Patrick Scott, "Introducing a 'Lost' Victorian Novel: The Elusive William North and *The City of the Jugglers* (1850)," 14. In their contributions to the 2009 issue of *Victorian Newsletter*, both Scott and Lamouria convincingly connect the broader significance of *City* to its commitment to the European revolutions of 1848. Lamouria's original 2009 contribution was much expanded upon in the 2015 article "Financial Revolution." My own interest in the book aligns more closely with that of Stern, who denotes it "a *lumbering limit* case of what Ian Duncan might term the *monstrous novel*, pressing as it does at all the capacities of taxonomy" (48).
62. Review of *The Imposter; or, Born with a Conscience*, 576; Allan Life and Page Life, "North versus North: William North (1825–1854) in Light of New Documentation," 68.
63. William North, *The City of the Jugglers*, 8. Hereafter cited parenthetically in the text.
64. North's rhetoric concerning slavery in the novel ranges from the pejorative notice of Grey's final emigration and career to the more problematic description of white authors and editors as the "slaves" of their periodicals' owners. In thus appropriating the language of violent human bondage and trafficking to mid-century English labor conditions, North was certainly not alone – and he does not go to bigoted extremes that Carlyle would in his depiction of Quashee in his "Occasional Discourse" (1853) – but his willingness to link the two may still strike modern readers as self-serving and woefully ignorant at best.
65. The novel reiterates this rejection later when Darian and Viridor's fellow revolutionaries arrive at "analyses of the various social and communist theories prevalent in France and Germany, and resolutions as to their hostility to all real liberty" (193).
66. Many of Weber's definitional statements about market and status economies from *Economy and Society* are also reproduced in S. N. Eisenstadt's selected edition *On Charisma and Institution Building* (see esp. 175–8, 206–7).

67. All quotations from the prospectus appear on pp. 40–1.
68. Poovey, *Financial System*, 18.
69. Ibid. 18.
70. J. M. Roberts, *The Mythology of the Secret Societies*, 102.
71. See my *Plots of Opportunity*. Even North's revolutionaries employ the rhetoric of conspiracy to explain their own marginalized role in society: for instance, Viridor "saw himself, and others like him, men of thought and action, of power to conceive and realise the desires that burned within the age, excluded by a brute-force tyranny, an idle subterfuge, *a legalised conspiracy of orthodox social banditti*, from all part and share in the direction of the community to which he belonged" (179, emphasis added).
72. Scott, 14.
73. North, 179.
74. "The City of the Jugglers; or, Free-trade in Souls," *Tait's Edinburgh Magazine*, 453; "The City of the Jugglers; or, Free-trade in Souls," *Westminster and Foreign Quarterly Review*, 267. These two reviews are additions to the materials included in the "Preliminary Checklist" compiled by Page Life, Patrick Scott, and Allan Life for the 2009 special issue of *Victorian Newsletter*.
75. Stern, 47; Scott, 8; Lamouria, "North's *The City of the Jugglers*," 17.
76. *The City of the Jugglers* was, in fact, originally offered for sale as a single volume priced at 10s6p.
77. Life and Life, 84–6.
78. Both "ironic credulity" and "fictionality" are terms deployed by Catherine Gallagher to explain the reading experience fostered by the realist novel, which seeks "to suspend the reader's disbelief, as an element is suspended in a solution that it thoroughly permeates. Disbelief is thus the condition of fictionality, prompting judgments, not about the story's reality, but about its *believability*, its plausibility" ("The Rise of Fictionality," 346, emphasis in original).
79. Notes appear on pages 27, 58, 86, 93, 97, 112, 117, 123, 147, 175, 196–7, 239–40, and 243, and are as evenly distributed between the main financial plot and the secondary plots as an odd number will permit.
80. Life and Life describe North's writing as characterized by the "glorification of the inspired amateur" informed by his "conviction that genius in one endeavor could flourish elsewhere" (65, 81).
81. In this last aside, North demonstrates his awareness of the wider fascination with England's increasingly complex credit economy, a topic that Wagner identifies as central to Victorian financial fiction:

> The majority of Victorians indisputably viewed the representational, or fictitious, value of paper currencies with both suspicion and a sense of enthrallment. They created and consolidated what were to become the prevailing

moral accounts of capitalism's impact on literature. An ongoing controversy on the commodification of popular fiction made sure that identification of these different papers remained central even after paper money had long become part and parcel of everyday life. (*Financial Speculation*, 11)

82. This self-referential command appears in a parenthetical early in book two (148).
83. Scott, 7. The commercial failure of *City* meant that North, rather than ascending to the dizzying heights of Shelleyan legislator of the world that he imagined for Viridor, was forced to seek a fresh start in America, like Grey. He did not become a slave trader, however, but instead worked intermittently within New York's bohemian arts community before dying by suicide in 1854. On North's career in American, see Whitley and Weidman.
84. The phrase is North's own, and appears in his abruptly unconventional announcement of the end of *City*: "This is the beginning of the history I have hoped would find some few kindred souls to sympathise with its mysteries. The beginning, did I say? Yes, the beginning, indeed; however contradictory may seem the conventional necessity which compels me, at the same moment, to acknowledge with regret that it is THE END" (250).

Chapter 3

The Violence at the Heart of the Social Problem Novel

Among the ways in which North's *City of the Jugglers* refuses to conform to the expectations of period fiction is its approbation of an escalating series of collective actions by the citizens of London. Easiest for its imagined nineteenth-century readers, among them fellow journalists and novelists, to accept, perhaps, would have been the "glorious conspiracy of talent against capital" engineered by Viridor and Darian at their unstratified social gala (240). The resulting unanimous strike by the metropolis's professional "journalists of all grades, editors, sub-editors, compilers, financiers, reporters, and even penny-a-liners," brings all London business to a halt for a full day before "revolutioniz[ing]" every newspaper and journal in the capital except the "leviathan *Timeserver* [which] began gradually to diminish" (238, 241, 241). Viridor's successful election to parliament occurs one month after the subsequent "great political battle . . . between the House of Commons and the Press" has forced the fall of the government, and, although it remains within the franchise limits set by the First Reform Act, his victory is, itself, a sign of the strength of the people (241). Even though "every five-pound note was in favour of the Plutocrat," and Viridor's campaign refuses to bribe his unspecified constituency's electors, he wins "by a majority of nine, the number of the muses" (242). The evening after Viridor's election witnesses a general rising of London's population, during which "the mob . . . joined, either openly or secretly . . . [by] the greater number of the middle classes . . . rushed and surged, and recoiled, in the principal thoroughfares of the capital" (244). Although Viridor and Darian rescue the Soul Agent from incipient lynching, pacify the crowd, and avert a violent overnight revolution – Grey's financial backer, Brown, does have "the misfortune to the hanged from a lamp-post on Blackfriars Bridge" (247) – the novel emphatically reserves a place for collective action by the nation's un- and under-enfranchised majority. The "violent opposition" raised in Parliament to Viridor's bill for universal male suffrage is overcome with help from the "choral eloquence" of fifty thousand supporters stationed outside Westminster Hall (247). In thus narrating without repudiating the united force – whether moral, physical, or simply declamatory – of London's and, extended by statute, the nation's millions, *The City of the Jugglers* breaks ranks with most mid-Victorian fiction, which often grounds its legitimation of the middle classes in condemnation of coordinated working-class agency.[1]

On one level, the consistency with which period novels remain skeptical if not outright hostile toward the collective actions of their own working-class characters reflects the discursive legacy of the debate surrounding the First Reform Bill. In addition to serving as the rhetorical context within which the middle classes secured their own political recognition, this prolonged and highly public conversation established the parameters of what Chris Vanden Bossche, in *Reform Acts*, denominates "social agency," a category of specifically public activity whose normative value stretches into the 1860s. "Both the proponents of the Reform Bill and the Chartists," Vanden Bossche writes,

> defined the social agent as a political constituency and action as electing legislators and legislating . . . This discourse marked the dividing line between reform and revolution in terms of whether a particular action was mandated by, or a threat to, the constitution. Similarly, it defined those who possessed social agency as members of a constituency whose position in the social structure ensured that they would act in accord with the constitution.[2]

Initially concerned to explain how Chartism, in both its moral- and physical-force iterations, ran afoul of such "parliamentary discourse" – which marginalized the working classes as either already indirectly represented by or in revolutionary, unconstitutional competition with the aristocracy and/or the middle classes – Vanden Bossche reinterprets a substantial number of social-problem novels as concerned not merely with industrialization but also with the political implications and exclusions of franchise reform.[3] Pithy rereadings of both lesser-known works by Pierce Egan, Harrison Ainsworth, R. S. Surtees, and Thomas Martin Wheeler, and more canonical novels by Charles Dickens, Benjamin Disraeli, Charles Kingsley, Elizabeth Gaskell, and George Eliot trace the class-bound imbrications of enfranchisement and disinterestedness in the period's political fiction, which overwhelmingly rejected collective articulations of moral-force debate and examples of physical-force resistance as equally unacceptable under England's unwritten constitution. Although individual working-class characters might be represented sympathetically, collectives of working-class bodies were overwhelmingly associated with mobs, riots, and other revolutionary disruptions of middle-class characters' social structures.

At the root of middle-class writers' and readers' problem with working-class collectives was the sheer number of potentially disaffected bodies that might combine together. When it expanded the franchise to all those meeting the £10 minimum threshold and in so doing helped to define the lower limits of the middle class, the First Reform Act also statutorily excluded just over 80% of the adult male population from direct participation in England's political process.[4] The rapid urban growth brought about by widespread implementation of the factory system in the north and the explosion of casual trades in and around London then concentrated the majority of England's unenfranchised in the new industrial cities (Manchester, Birmingham, Leeds, et. al.) and the capital.[5] Now city-dwellers, their potentially overwhelming numbers were neither fully confined by the slums (such as Angel Meadow in Manchester, Hockley in Birmingham, Tindall's Yard in Leeds, and Seven Dials, St. Giles, and Jacob's Island in London) dedicated to housing them, nor fully controlled by the statutes (among them, the Metropolitan Police Act, County Borough Police Act, and New Poor Law) passed to surveil and discipline them, nor fully contented by the sanitary reforms and private philanthropic endeavors undertaken to ameliorate their lot.[6] In response to often appalling living and working conditions and motivated in part by an always "potentially radical political culture grounded in opposition to the those with economic power," workers developed a "general sense of cooperation, of mutuality, seen for example in the Friendly Societies for mutual benefit and care" that stood in sharp contrast to the liberal individualism of the middle classes.[7] That they greatly outnumbered these more affluent, politically enfranchised urban neighbors – some of whom were also their unloved employers – remained an anxiety-producing demographic fact of Victorian life.

Earlier decades, when many of those currently living in urban slums had instead resided in less densely populated textile and agricultural districts, provided ample evidence for the violence that could break out when the poor coordinated their expressions of discontent. Two movements in particular, both ostensibly led by mythic figures devoted to reasserting workers' traditional rights in the face of technological change and economic dislocation, required domestic military deployments to pacify. Operating in the north of England between 1811 and 1817, various groups of Luddites in the east Midlands, Yorkshire, and Lancashire combined industrial sabotage – breaking stocking frames, shearing frames, finishing machines, and steam looms that threatened "full fashioned work at the old fashion's price . . . established by Custom and Law" – with parliamentary petitions to reinstate paternalistic legislation governing trade practices and wages.[8] Parliament responded by reclassifying machine-breaking as a capital offense in 1812 and the government deployed more troops to guard textile mills and prosecute General Ludd's "army of redressers" than were then in the field against Napoleon.[9] Use of horse-powered threshing machines in agricultural districts during a period of low wages, widespread unemployment, and poor harvests precipitated similar acts of social disturbance in England's south and east in 1830. Followers of "Captain Swing" sent threatening letters to magistrates, large landowners, parish clerks, and Poor Law officials asserting the longstanding practice of allowing the rural poor to graze their livestock on common land, demanding an increase in laborers' wages, and protesting against the tithe collected by the parish under the unreformed Poor Law. They also organized public protests to destroy or dismantle the offending machinery and burned hayricks, farm buildings, and tithe granaries. Once again, the government response was harsh, with local magistrates replaced by special committees of judges who ultimately sentenced nineteen persons to death, over 500 to transportation, and over 600 to jail terms of varying lengths for their roles in what came to be known as the Swing Riots. The longer-term parliamentary response also included passage of the much-maligned New Poor Law that featured so prominently in nineteenth-century orphan narratives.[10]

In the years leading up to the time of Captain Swing, Parliament had actually begun to repeal some of the more obviously repressive legislation that had grown up in response to past examples of civil unrest, including the Combination Acts 1824–5, the Test and Corporations Act 1828, and many of the civil disabilities attached to Roman Catholicism in England since the time of the Elizabeth I (1829). This process of legislative liberalization both raised public expectations of franchise reform and permitted the legal growth of trade unionism. After the Whig government failed to pass their bill for reform through the House of Lords in October 1831, riots erupted in urban centers, including Bristol and Nottingham. Lord Grey resigned as Prime Minister on 9 May 1832, precipitating the "days of May," a proto-revolutionary ferment of torchlight demonstrations, public meetings, and property destruction. Leading the public pressure for reform – ultimately achieved only after Grey was reappointed and King William IV threatened to pack the House of Lords with new peers friendly to Grey's bill – was the Birmingham Political Union, whose combined working- and middle-class membership mobilized reform-friendly crowds in the hundreds of thousands. Although historians remain divided about the revolutionary potential of the days of May, contemporaries were deeply shaken by the sight of so many members of the urban working class turned out in support of a common cause. As, throughout the 1830s, many of these same workers joined newly legalized trade unions, reports of the ritualized violence of their initiation ceremonies and news of the actual violence that sometimes occurred during strikes appeared to confirm middle-class Victorians' fears about the dangers of working-class combinations. With their "*insignia* of terror," ceremonials borrowing from Christian liturgical and freemasonic forms, and "imprecatory" oaths, union initiations received sensationalized attention in *The Annual Register*'s summary of the 1838 House of Commons *Report of the Select Committee on Combinations*.[11] Also featured in the report were instances of vitriol burning, assaults on strike-breaking "nobs," and acts of arson. In addition, union-related murders received widespread media coverage, including the 1831 shooting death of Manchester industrialist Thomas Ashton and the myriad violence surrounding the 1837 strike of the Glasgow Spinners Union, culminating in the murder-for-hire of John Smith in Anderston.

In January of 1838, five members of the Glasgow Spinners Union were tried for murder, arson, assault, and other crimes before the High Court of the Justiciary in Edinburgh. In May of that same year, the London Working Men's Association published the "People's Charter," which famously prescribed six points of electoral and parliamentary reform. At a mass meeting in Birmingham in August, the Charter emerged yoked to a plan proposed by the revived Birmingham Political Union for the presentation of a petition to Parliament demanding universal male suffrage. At subsequent demonstrations with attendances sometimes eclipsing 100,000 persons, the Chartists elected members of a national convention to coordinate the petition, which was first presented to Parliament in May 1839, accompanied by over one million signatures. After Parliament voted, on 12 July, not to consider the petition, civil disturbances erupted, including a clash with the army in Newcastle, the so-called Bull Ring riots in

Birmingham, and, in November, the Newport Rising, which ended in armed conflict between the roughly 10,000 men led by John Frost and soldiers from the 45th Regiment of Foot guarding Chartist prisoners held at the Westgate Hotel.[12] Further Chartist conventions and parliamentary petitions followed in 1842 and 1848, as did more violent demonstrations, most notably a series of strikes in Manchester and the surrounding areas of Lancashire and Staffordshire that came to be known as the Plug Plot Riots of 1842. Outside of the Chartists' own newspapers – that is, the *Northern Star, The Charter, The Southern Star, The Poor Man's Guardian,* and *The Chartist Circular* – both moral-force efforts at parliamentary persuasion and physical-force confrontations such as those at Newport and Manchester were met with hostility in British press reports, which "played up their unruliness, [and] fed middle-class apprehension about the potential for violence inherent within the working classes."[13] Ultimately, the sheer numerical presence, political goals, and shifting tactics of Chartism dramatically raised the stakes of allowing collective force, whether "moral" or "physical," to serve as a path to social legitimacy.

A number of factors – the collapse of Chartism as a national movement after 1848 among them – ushered in a period of generally increased prosperity and relative social calm in the 1850s and 1860s. Even during this "age of equipoise," however, the numerical preponderance of England's laboring classes remained a potential threat to middle-class hegemony.[14] This threat manifested economically in what labor historians Sidney and Beatrice Webb first coined "New Model" unions in their *History of Trade Unionism* (1894). Composed of skilled artisans organized on a national scale, groups such as the Amalgamated Society of Engineers (founded 1851) and the Amalgamated Society of Carpenters and Joiners (founded 1860) preferred to negotiate with employers over hours, working conditions, and wages, but their members were occasionally involved in lockouts and strikes, including the national lockout of ASE members by employers in 1852, and the more successful Stonemason's strike of 1859, which contributed to the foundation of ASCJ. After a decline in union membership and influence in the decade following the Glasgow Spinners trial, trade unions also returned to the industrial north. In 1853, weavers in Preston demanded a ten percent increase in wages and, when they were refused, they began a series of selective strikes at individual mills. Mill owners responded by shuttering all of their factories, leaving over 15,000 textile workers out of work. Supported by voluntary subscriptions from other unions, the Preston weavers remained on strike for 37 weeks at a total cost to the working classes estimated by *The Annual Register* to exceed £500,000.[15] Although unsuccessful, the Preston strike was an impressive mobilization of resolve and resources only made possible by the coordination of large numbers of workers for the better part of a year.[16]

In the 1860s, pressure began to build for further electoral reform to allow at least a percentage of these workers to vote. In 1865, a group of trade unionists and former Chartists led by George Howell – a "New Model" union member of the Operative Bricklayers' Society – and other figures from the London Trades Council – of which Howell was secretary – formed the National Reform League, a working-class political pressure group dedicated to extending the franchise. After the failure of Gladstone's Reform Bill in March 1866, the National Reform League organized several large demonstrations, including in Trafalgar Square on 29 June and in Hyde Park on 23 July. At the latter, in an act of physical force reminiscent of Manchester or Newport in the 1840s, an estimated 200,000 working-class protestors broke through railings and police lines to assemble under the Reformers' Tree in the northeast quadrant of the park. Mass meetings continued, among them another in Hyde Park on 6 May 1867, until the passage of the Disraeli's Second Reform Act 1867 slightly more than doubled the size of the electorate.[17] It did not assuage many prominent members of the middle class that they could now be outnumbered at the polls by newly legitimated working-class voters who had shown themselves still capable of physical force.

The Violence of Fictional Collectives

Given the fundamental ideological conflict between middle-class competitive individualism and working-class cooperativism, one should expect distrust of collective action by England's less affluent citizens to appear in a wide range of the fiction written to articulate Victorian writers' and readers' status anxieties. However, one subgenre of the nineteenth-century novel is particularly attuned to the sociohistorical problems and situations sketched above: namely, the industrial novel. This chapter will survey several representative examples of this mid-century form, including Charles Dickens's *Barnaby Rudge* (1841), Charlotte Brontë's *Shirley* (1849), Charles Kingsley's *Alton Locke* (1850), and Elizabeth Gaskell's *North and South* (1855), before devoting prolonged attention to what is generally agreed to be the subgenre's final major iteration, George Eliot's *Felix Holt: The Radical* (1866). In addition to their shared investment in England's industrial and political history, what these novels have in common is a repudiation of force, especially when exercised by the numerical majority, as a basis for social dominance and legitimate status. Whether or not they uncritically embrace atomistic liberalism, these texts consistently ground their characters' deserts in their rejection of the violent agency of working-class crowds and riotous, even revolutionary, mobs.

Although the novelist's intent, as stated in the preface, may have been to expose how "what we falsely call a religious cry is easily raised by men who have no religion," *Barnaby Rudge* also "teach[es] a good lesson" about the anti-social potential for violence of the working-class crowd.[18] Written in the immediate aftermath of the Glasgow Spinners trial, the publication of the *Report of the Select Committee on Combinations*, and the rejection of the initial Chartist petition, the novel first appeared in the pages of Dickens's weekly periodical *Master Humphrey's Clock* between February and November of 1841.[19] It somewhat incongruously includes highly topical references to contemporary trade union activity within its narrative timeframe, which Dickens divides slightly unevenly between 1774–75 (chapters 1–32) and 1780 (chapters 33–79). These dates allow him to fictionally recount the events leading up to and the actual outbreak of the anti-Catholic Gordon Riots.

Barnaby Rudge thus contains two cautionary examples of dangerous collectives that result in large-scale social violence: the quasi-trade-union conspiracy of apprentices; and the Protestant Association, which had itself recently been reconstituted in response to the passage of the Catholic Emancipation Act 1829. Led by that "curiosity of littleness," Sim Tappertit, the 'Prentice Knights are an anachronistic, even "burlesque" addition to the novel's late-eighteenth-century setting.[20] For readers primed by recent exposés of violent unionism, however, they would have seemed a familiar component of industrial life: Dickens includes an initiation ceremony that both parodies *The Annual Register*'s foregrounding of "*insignia* of terror" – represented in the novel by a "blunderbuss," a "saber," and "a couple of skulls" – and features a particularly anti-social oath sworn by new members in opposition to the "Lord Mayor, sword-bearer, and chaplain," "sheriffs," and "court of aldermen" of London.[21] These civil authorities remain threatened by only rhetorical violence in 1775, when the energies of the 'Prentice Knights and the "master spirit at their head" remain focused on the alleged abuses of their vocational masters and, in Sim's case, the attractions of Dolly, his own master Gabriel Varden's daughter.[22]

In 1780, however, the now-renamed United Bulldogs play a prominent role in the Gordon Riots. Sim, the newly initiated Hugh, their unwitting confederate Barnaby Rudge, and their executioner-affiliate Dennis the Hangman each lead companies of working-class men in the streets of London "as if the city were invaded by a foreign army."[23] They, in concert with the "forty thousand strong" members of the Protestant Association, ultimately besiege Parliament, fight in the streets with the Horse Guards, destroy a number of Roman Catholic churches, and succeed in forcing the doors of Newgate Prison.[24] From a campaign against "Popery," the riots quickly escalate to a war against "Property," with Hugh even declaring himself ready to "'set a lighted torch to the King's throne itself!'"[25] Easily swayed by Lord George Gordon's public orations and Sir John Chester's private machinations, London's laboring men, once combined together, metastasize into a mob capable of destroying the institutions and symbols of social domination, even if that means killing themselves in the process. In addition to their willingness to "perish in the fire themselves" during the assault on Newgate Prison, the rioters also ascend to "a worse spectacle than this—worse by far than fire and smoke, or even the rabble's unappeasable and maniac rage" once the destruction reaches a warehouse filled with liquor.[26] Dickens's penchant for the grotesque slides into horror as he describes what ensues:

> The gutters of the street, and every crack and fissure in the stones, ran with scorching spirit, which being dammed up by busy hands, overflowed the road and pavement, and formed a great pool, into which the people dropped down dead by dozens. They lay in heaps all round this fearful pond, husbands and wives, fathers and sons, mothers and daughters, women with children in their arms and babies at their breasts, and drank until they died. While some stooped with their lips to the brink and never raised their heads again, others sprang up from their fiery draught, and danced, half in mad triumph, and half in the agony of suffocation, until they fell, and steeped their corpses in the liquor that had killed them.[27]

Intemperate consumers of ill-gotten spirits, members of the mob become that which they imbibe, their descent into violence stripping them of both life and discrete identity.

Whereas the prime movers in Dickens's reconstruction of the Gordon riots are motivated by lust (Sim), greed (Hugh), jealousy

(Sir John), blood-thirstiness (Dennis), denominational chauvinism (Gordon), and even disabling misunderstanding (Barnaby), the wellspring of social unrest in Charlotte Brontë's *Shirley* is the much simpler absence of bread. In the words of Brontë's model textile worker, the "hard-favoured, but modest and manly-looking" William Farren, "I know it isn't right for poor folks to starve."[28] Set during the early years of Yorkshire Luddism (1811–12), *Shirley* undermines force as a basis for social legitimacy on both a parodic and a more serious level. Tongue firmly in cheek, the narrator recounts a comically martial encounter between the novel's central Establishment figure, Reverend Matthew Helstone, leading his flock of Sunday school children to an outdoor feast and an agglomeration of "Dissenting and Methodist schools, the Baptists, Independents, and Wesleyans, joined in unholy alliance" to impede their passage.[29] First drowning out their opponents' "most dolorous of canticles" with a rousing chorus of "Rule, Britannia," the Establishment party then march through their denominational opponents, "Helstone and Miss Keeldare . . . the one with his cane, the other with her parasol," keeping their charges in time and formation.[30] Although victorious, they also appear somewhat ridiculous, and it would be difficult to read these opening paragraphs of "The School Feast" as legitimating so much as amicably laughing at Helstone's somewhat tyrannical authority over his household and congregation.

Much more soberly, the novel also includes three instances of violence by the unemployed and working-class masses, all focalized through the consciousnesses of middle-class characters.[31] The first is represented after the fact through a letter addressed "To the Divil of Hollow's-miln" and described by the narrator as "very peculiar" and in need of translation "into legible English."[32] Thus translated, the letter recounts the destruction of manufacturer Robert Moore's new frames and shears and the forcible detainment of the men sent to bring them. What readers perceive for themselves in this initial episode is Moore's love for his machines, called later in the narrative his "grim, metal darlings," and from this perception they are invited to wonder "How did the catastrophe affect him?" rather than to consider what circumstances have driven his workers to such extremes.[33] The second, larger violent episode is the night-time attack on Hollow's Mill itself by the main body of Luddite workmen. Witnessed at night from a distance by landowner Shirley Keeldar – she of the martial umbrella – and rector's daughter Caroline Helstone, the assault on the mill appears in the narrative as an inchoate aural experience that leaves the workers literally unseen once collected together; only

Moore's voice, calmly deploying his men in response to the workers' violence, is clearly discernible.[34] The third case of violence – the attempted assassination of Moore – is an individual not a collective act, but its working-class perpetrator, antinomian weaver Michael Hartley, is represented as mentally unstable and inspired to act by the broader atmosphere of Luddite unrest. Once again, the event itself is narrated indirectly, this time after the fact by Moore's fellow mill-owner Hiram Yorke, who, while present during the act only heard the gunshot and saw Moore fall from his horse.

Begun in the second half of 1848 and published the following year, *Shirley* is generally taken by critics as a repudiation of Chartism, represented indirectly in the novel by the "riotous mob" of Moore's machine-breaking former workers.[35] In thus transferring middle-class anxieties about the potential for working-class social revolution from the 1840s to the 1810s, rendering the collective exertions of Moore's workers as overheard acts of faceless and irrational violence, and reducing Luddism to a matter of bread, Brontë allows for the growth of individual sympathy between Caroline Helstone and William Farren, endorses the "Extravagant day-dreams" for local industrial development proposed by Robert Moore, and supports the liberal paternalism that was cited in the 1840s as obviating the need for electoral and parliamentary reform.[36] Crucially, this essentially middle-class political position is grounded in the narrative rejection of working-class force, figured as collective violence in *Shirley*.

Chartism appears much more directly in Kingsley's *Alton Locke*, wherein the titular Alton finally gains legitimacy by confessing, judging, and ultimately renouncing his earlier affiliations with Chartism and embracing the more quietist reformism of middle-class authors like Kingsley. The first-person narrative of a "Cockney among Cockneys," the novel takes place during the years between the second and third Chartist petitions and is concerned to expose the abuses inherent in what Kingsley, writing as "Parson Lot," had earlier denominated *Cheap Clothes and Nasty*.[37] It also directs readers to acknowledge the "ugly and unmeaning remnant of obsolete fashion" at Cambridge, the dire straits of agricultural laborers, and the overwhelming force of circumstances besetting those who, like the title character, find themselves caught between the worlds of working-class labor and middle- and upper-class culture.[38] Throughout, *Alton Locke* also maintains a consistent repudiation of force as a basis for social legitimacy. For instance, although the annual Cambridge boat races inspire Alton to be "as proud of the gallant young fellows as if they had been my brothers," the "heavy blow from behind" he receives from a young lord when he fails to keep up with the movement of the spectators does little to secure either the protagonist's or the reader's sympathy for the university's "cursed aristocrats."[39] The majority of the illicit force in the novel, however, is associated with Alton's work among the London Chartists, whose moral-force arguments in favor of reforms are continuously implicated in threats of physical-force violence.

Alton's first introduction to the cause comes with this possibility always already present. Demurring initially against "being mixed up in conspiracy—perhaps, in revolt and bloodshed," Alton is persuaded to attend a Chartist meeting by his fellow tailor, John Crossthwaite, who declares, "'What have the six points, right or wrong, to do with the question of whether they can be obtained by moral force, and the pressure of opinion alone, or require what we call ulterior measures to get them carried?'"[40] Somewhat later, Alton begins to write for *The Weekly Warwhoop*, a Chartist newspaper whose belligerent moniker reflects both the "perennial hurricane of plotting, railing, sneering, and bombast" of its editor, Mr O'Flynn, and the characterological effects that hack work have upon Alton himself, who becomes "flippant and bitter . . . cynical, fierce, reckless."[41] O'Flynn's discovery that Alton has apostatized "for filthy lucre" by publishing a volume of poetry expurgated of its political content leads him to abuse his former employee in print, marshalling all of his verbal vitriol to make Alton "an outcast for the People's Cause."[42] Anxious to regain Crossthwaite's respect, at least, Alton volunteers to recruit new supporters at a prospective "rising down in the country."[43] Unfortunately underestimating his ability to control "the spirit of mad aimless riot" among his rural listeners, as well as his own reaction to their abject distress, Alton bids them to "demand your share of . . . the fruit of your own industry.'"[44] The laborers respond to his moral-force exhortation with physical-force violence, looting and burning a nearby farm.[45] After serving a three-year prison sentence for his part in the riot, Alton returns to London just in time for the European revolutions of 1848, the failed presentation of the third Chartist petition, and, in chapter 33, "A Patriot's Reward," an only-just averted descent from "ulterior measures" to a criminal and anti-social conspiracy. Subsequently converted from Chartism to Christian Socialism by pious philanthropist Eleanor, Lady Ellerton, Alton emigrates to Texas. While on the journey, and at Eleanor's behest, he writes "an honest history of [his] life; extenuating nothing, exaggerating nothing"; in other words, he writes *Alton Locke*, which by virtue of this final narrative framing becomes its own repudiation of force at the level of form.[46] Alton finally gains legitimacy, then, but only at the expense of estranging himself from his former associates and opinions and becoming a mouthpiece for Kingsley's middle-class and decidedly moderate Christian Socialism.[47]

Written as cooperatives initiated by the Christian Socialists had begun to fail and Chartism had been replaced by a resurgent and increasingly national, as opposed to local, unionism, Gaskell's *North and South* adopts a more nuanced approach to the issue of force. Brute violence, whether enacted by upper-, middle-, or working-class characters, is consistently condemned by the novel. Thus, Gaskell's protagonist, Margaret Hale, judges that her brother, Frederick, acted rightly in mutinying aboard *The Russell*, because the captain's autocratic threat to flog his men had prompted one to die in an avoidable accident: "'Loyalty and obedience to wisdom and justice are fine,' she declares, "'but it is still finer to defy arbitrary power, unjustly and cruelly used—not on behalf of ourselves, but on behalf of others more helpless.'"[48] Reflecting a similar distrust of bellicose authority, the novel allows the middle-class matriarch Mrs Thornton to undermine the legitimacy of her own past willingness to drop stones on the heads of strikers by having her admit that she fainted before being able to do so.[49] And Margaret herself pacifies the grief-induced violence of Nicholas Higgins, whom she prevents from seeking solace in gin after learning of the death of his daughter Bessy. Even though he has already struck his own daughter Mary when she seeks to prevent his departure, Higgins is "daunted and awed" by Margaret's "severe calm," with which she ultimately induces him to pay his last respects to Bessy's corpse before accompanying her to her own house for tea with her minister-father.[50] The most dramatic instance of collective violence and its resistance in *North and South* occurs during a prolonged strike at Thornton's Mill. Learning that Irish laborers have been brought in to work the looms, the workers coalesce into an "unseen, maddened crowd" that, at the sight of Thornton, utters a collective "yell,—to call it not human is nothing,—it was as the demoniac desire of some terrible wild beast for the food that is withheld from his ravening."[51] When Margaret interposes herself between the crowd and Thornton, she prompts a momentary lull before being struck by a stone; her injury impels Thornton to defy the crowd, which breaks before his "unchanging attitude" and "defiant eyes."[52]

Although, as in earlier industrial novels, *North and South* features a destructive and dangerous working-class riot, both narratively and ideologically it treats this incident somewhat differently from its predecessors. Unlike *Barnaby Rudge*, *Alton Locke*, and to a lesser extent *Shirley*, which locate their mob scenes quite late in their respective stories, Gaskell's novel gets its riot out of the way in chapter twenty-two out of fifty-two, demoting it from the climax to just another moment of rising action. Moreover, whereas in many earlier examples of the subgenre collective violence and trade unionism are mutually imbricated, in *North and South* the riot occurs despite the best efforts of Higgins and other members of the union's governing body, who are determined, according to Bessy, to have no "'going against the law of the land . . . the Committee charged all members o' th' Union to lie down and die, if need were, without striking a blow; and then they reckoned they were sure o' carrying th' public with them.'"[53] Reflective of the new, more pacific nature of the ASE lockout and the Preston strike, Gaskell's distancing of the Milton Committee from the riot does not absolve the union of the use of illicit force, however. John Boucher, one of the union's rank-and-file at the forefront of the riot, first accuses Higgins and his fellow committee leaders of being "'a worser tyrant than e'er th' masters were . . . yo've no more pity for a man than a wild hunger-maddened wolf.'"[54] His accusations are corroborated by Higgins nine chapters later, when, in response to Margaret's ingenuous questioning, he reveals that the union has graduated from physical to social violence – in the form of the complete isolation of and noninteraction with nonmembers – to enforce its domination among the workers. Margaret pronounces such collective anti-sociality "tyranny" and "torture," thereby reinforcing the connection between working-class collectives and still-unacceptable even if tactically updated forms of force.[55]

In being focalized primarily through Margaret, the novel also reinscribes both mill-owner and working-class actions within her south-of-England middle-class perspective. As Rosemarie Bodenheimer notes, this narrative technique subtly aligns *North and South* with the broad "category of middle-class fictions which argue for the identity of interest between workers and owners. That view depends on an acceptance of the liberal principles of economy—the flux of the market according to natural economic laws—whose blows of fortune are seen as affecting workers and manufacturers with equally uncertain results."[56] Both Margaret and her father recognize early on that Milton's constant "antagonism between the employer and the employed" makes little sense in light of the fact that the "two classes [are] dependent on each other in every possible way."[57] Initially unmoved by what he sees as their southern ignorance of England's industrialized north, Thornton eventually comes around to their way of thinking, losing "all sense of resentment in wonder how it was, or could be, that two men like himself and Higgins, living by the same trade, working in their different ways at the same object, could look upon each other's position and duties in so strangely different a way."[58] After his bankruptcy, Thornton is even eager in his next venture to "experiment" with facilitating "personal intercourse" between himself and his employees in order to "'find means and ways of seeing each other, and becoming acquainted with each others' characters and persons, and even tricks of temper and modes of speech. We should understand each other better, and I'll venture to say we should like each other more.'"[59] Although not so sanguine as to believe that this increased social interaction would prevent all future strikes, Thornton does hope it "'may render strikes not the bitter, venomous sources of hatred they have hitherto been.'"[60] Whether Thornton will ever be in a position to implement his plans matters less than Gaskell's readers' being exposed to them at all. The novel, with all of its fictional intercourse between characters of different regions and classes, thereby positions itself as a model capable of defusing illicit forms of force, especially those arising from the combination of working-class bodies.

Immoral Force in *Felix Holt*

As one might expect from Eliot, whose commitment to exhaustive research, meticulous accuracy, and the determinative force of tradition were noted – sometimes even to her detriment, as in reviews of the just-completed *Romola* (1863) – by her contemporaries and have remained a mainstay of her critical reputation, *Felix Holt* positions itself quite self-consciously with respect to its predecessor industrial novels. Although it has, perhaps, the least in common with *Barnaby Rudge*, Eliot's contribution to the subgenre shares Dickens's horror at the prospect of working-class violence once fortified by the overconsumption of alcohol. Adapting the highly effective technique of historical and topographical distancing achieved in *Shirley*, Eliot also sets her narrative of domestic rapprochement and civil unrest slightly more than three decades in the past and well away from any large urban centers. In *Felix Holt*, Eliot also evidently borrows aspects of her title character's social station and climactic life experience from *Alton Locke*, even as she eschews Kingsley's more sanguine panacea of Christian Socialism. And Eliot matches the complexity of Gaskell's more nuanced approach to the problem of force, although rather than relying upon the balm of "mutual intercourse" and shared interests, *Felix Holt* painstakingly counterbalances a social web of individual sympathies, community traditions, and the possibility of cultural development against inappropriate eruptions of antisocial violence, including those mobilized in support of franchise reform.[61]

The psychological and social realism required to render this web both perspicuous and plausible is among Eliot's enduring contributions to the industrial novel, which she elevated to a consistently high level of ethical and aesthetic seriousness. A novel about the nature of representation in all its forms – recall Felix's early description of himself to Rufus Lyon as "'a roughly written page'"[62] – *Felix Holt* unusually, almost anthropologically, directs its narrative attention to all levels of society in Treby Magna, Little Treby, and their environs. For instance, life at Treby Manor encompasses both the well-mannered conversations of the Debarry family and the less elevated interactions of Scales, their house-steward and head-butler; Crowder, their long-term tenant; Brent, their head gardener; and others with Christian, Philip Debarry's "factotum," passing between these two worlds within the household (82). In following Felix's perambulations, the narrative also gains access to Chubb's public house and the working-class miners, stone-cutters, and others laborers of Sproxton who socialize there.[63] Felix, himself, represents what Carolyn Betensky labels an "opportunistic hybrid" of industrial worker and middle-class cultural laborer whose "hybridization allows him to circumvent the anxiety of [working-class] blameworthiness that the subgenre has always struggled to keep down or shed."[64] The novel is similarly ecumenical in its approach to religion, featuring both greater (Augustus Debarry) and lesser (John Lingon) Anglican clergy, alongside the intellectual and doctrinally suspect dissenting minister, Rufus Lyon, as well as diverse and not always theologically discerning members of his congregation. Eliot then traces the "finest threads, such as no eye sees, . . . bound cunningly about the sensitive flesh" of these myriad constituencies, whose social interconnections are sufficiently intricate that "the movement to break them would bring torture" and might even be viewed as "a worse bondage than any fetters" (94). Originally used to describe Mrs Transome's growing subjection to her second son, Harold, this image of invisible entrapment is eminently generalizable to every level of representation in the novel, from the interior life of individuals to the political enfranchisement of entire classes.

That readers come to recognize the degree to which the ties that bind social beings together remain both externally imperceptible and powerfully overdetermining through the thoughts and feeling of characters such as Felix, Mrs Transome, Esther Lyon, even Christian, renders the interior life of individuals of equal significance to the political life of the community. Radicalism in the context of *Felix Holt* is as much about inward revolutions of thought and feeling as it is about who can vote in parliamentary elections.[65] Similarly, status becomes less a matter of family or fortune and more a consequence of education, self-culture, and the development of character. Expressed inwardly in the subtlest of ways and recognizable only in its effects upon others, character also stands diametrically opposed to external forms of violence, which, in keeping with the conventions established by earlier industrial novels, *Felix Holt* figures most overtly in the form of a riot. After establishing the narrative ubiquity and social and ethical perspicacity of Eliot's determinism, this chapter will trace its contributions to the novel's broader diminution of conventional appeals to birth and wealth as warrants for status before reconstructing the repudiation of force that occupies such a central narrative and ethical position in *Felix Holt*.

"Necessity is laid upon me"[66]

With this self-conscious biblical allusion, Eliot's eponymous radical attempts a final answer to his co-protagonist Esther Lyon's heartfelt and "rather frightened" interrogative, "'Why have you made your life so hard then?'" (219). The two are walking out together for the first time in the country immediately surrounding Little Treby, and Esther, who has been smarting under and beginning to reform herself in response to Felix's earlier disapprobation of her "idle fancy and selfish inclination" (104), seeks to understand why, with his obvious accomplishments, Felix chooses not to live "honourably with some employment that presupposes education and refinement" (220). Before arriving at I Corinthians 9:16, Felix recursively returns to a rhetoric of determination to explain his present life: "'I have to *determine* for myself, and not for other men'"; "'It is just because I'm a very ambitious fellow, with very hungry passions, wanting a great deal to satisfy me, that I have chosen to give up what people call worldly good. At least that has been one *determining* reason'"; "'I'm *determined* never to go about making my face simpering or solemn, and telling professional lies for profit; or to get tangled in affairs where I must wink at dishonesty and pocket the proceeds, and justify that knavery as part of a system that I can't alter'" (220, emphasis added). Although these declaratives may initially appear to endorse Felix's freedom of decision and action, they are, themselves, framed in the narrative, on the one hand, "'by conditions that I saw as clearly as I see the bars of this stile. It's a difficult stile too'" (219), and, on the other hand, by the echoes of Saul's providentially irresistible conversion into Paul on the road to Damascus. A determined man, Felix is also overdetermined, his apparent capacity for agency circumscribed by "inherited sorrow" and "some hard entail of suffering" (11). And he is typical rather than unique in this respect, since, according to Eliot's narrator, "there is no private life which has not been determined by a wider public life" (43), and there are few who do not bear "some tragic mark of kinship in the one brief life to the far-stretching life that went before, and to the life that is to come after, such as has raised the pity and terror of men ever since they began to discern between will and destiny" (11).

Notwithstanding the narrator's opening reference to Aristotle's *Poetics* and Esther's later perception of "an unidentified sense of Nemesis," that which curtails characters' unlimited exercise of will in *Felix Holt* is not metaphysical but social (303).[67] Put another way, the "mighty resistless destiny" that exerts the "hard pressure of our common lot" originates not from the gods but from "the acts of other men as well as our own" (385). This principle helps to explain Eliot's meticulous style of narration, since only by reconstructing the accumulated minutia of individual intentions and actions can she establish the plausibility of the limitations placed on her characters. It also renders her determinism "positive," even "positivist," in the nineteenth-century sense of being grounded in observable experience, the instances of which can be painstakingly assembled into inductive generalizations from which one can then predict likely future outcomes with apparently scientific rigor.[68] Such dialectical tacking between individual observation and collective generalization appears throughout *Felix Holt*, perhaps nowhere as clearly as in the narrator's gloss of Matthew Jermyn's ill-considered attempt to persuade Mrs Transome to reveal "the whole truth" to Harold before the latter's Chancery suit can expose the former to professional ruin:

> That a man with so much sharpness, with so much suavity at his command—a man who piqued himself on his persuasiveness towards women—should behave just as Jermyn did on this occasion, would be surprising, but for the constant experience that temper and selfish insensibility will defeat excellent gifts—will make a sensible person shout when shouting is out of place, and will make a polished man rude when his polish might be of eminent use to him. (335)

Here, Jermyn's particular self-defeating behavior, his rapid transition from a "soft and deferential air" to a tone of "reproach" that rapidly intensifies to "a climax, like other self-justifiers" to "a slight laugh of scorn" to self-interested special pleading to, incongruously, "the air of one who thought he had prepared the way for an understanding" (333–5), is both evidence for and explained by a broader generalization concerning the self-destructive interactions of temper and talent. This generalization is itself phrased in such a way as to allow readers to supply their own remembered instances of inopportune boorishness, subsequent examples of which, Eliot's narrator implies, will be witnessed again. That Jermyn and Mrs Transome's failed conversation occurs in "the smaller drawing-room at Transome Court," which has been refurbished by Harold into a charmingly affluent setting for "Mrs Transome's own portrait in the evening costume of 1800" (332), subtly reinforces an even more ubiquitous phenomenon: the overdetermining power of the past "acts of other men as well as our own" over present circumstances.

Eliot's positivistic determinism leaves very little room for characters to maneuver even as it magnifies the moral significance of their minutest acts at both the individual and social level.[69] Thus, Esther's seemingly inconsequential decision to wait up for her father and retrieve his porridge rather than allowing Lyddy to do so constitutes a new "epoch" in their relationship (129), one in which she next overcomes her former reluctance "even to touch his cloth garments . . . to correct his toilette, and use a brush for him" (167), until, having established by these new acts a different horizon of possibilities for herself and her father, "the affectionateness that was in her flowed so pleasantly, as she saw how much her father was moved by what he thought a great act of tenderness, that she quite longed to repeat it" (167). Conversely, Jermyn's repeated pattern of relatively petty professional transgressions, made for his own benefit and those of the Transomes, ultimately lead him to abet the false incarceration of Maurice Christian Bycliffe, thereby contributing to his premature death; to extract more than his share of revenue from the Transome estate, through both mismanagement of the grounds and loan contracts with himself under the name of his London agent, John Johnson; and even to attempt to blackmail Harold into dropping his legal proceedings. As the narrator explains, habitual action not inborn "rascality" lies at the root of Jermyn's now-criminal liability: "He had had to do many things in law and in daily life which, in the abstract, he would have condemned; and indeed he had never been tempted by them in the abstract. Here, in fact, was the inconvenience; he had sinned for the sake of particular concrete things, and particular concrete consequences were likely to follow" (99).[70] Harold's susceptibility to Jermyn's threat of blackmail rests upon the former's ignorance of the tenuousness of his claim on Transome Court. Eliot supplies the somewhat tedious but necessary explanation of the concepts of "base fee" and "right of remainder" that make this instability legally possible in chapter 29. For those outside the orbit of Eliot's lawyer-friend Frederic Harrison, what matters most about the novel's antecedent inheritance settlement is the way that it establishes an enduring social consequence as a result of the individual actions of John Justus Transome and his prodigal son Thomas. Blithely unconscious of this aspect of his family's past and "trusting in his own skill to shape the success of his own morrows," Harold will be brought up short by "what many yesterdays had determined for him beforehand" (157).

"'If a nag is to throw me, I say, let him have some blood'"[71]

Of course, Harold's most dramatic disappointment concerns his discovery that his true patrimony has nothing to do with the prodigality of Thomas Transome. Having just concluded a private meeting of local worthies at the White Hart dedicated to obtaining leniency for Felix, Harold is confronted by Jermyn, whose dramatic revelation, "'*I am your father*,'" is confirmed in one of the room's many mirrors: "As Harold heard the last terrible words he started at a leaping throb that went through him, and in the start turned his eyes away from Jermyn's face. He turned them on the same face in the glass with his own beside it, and saw the hated fatherhood reasserted" (381, emphasis in original). Although there is some consolation to be enjoyed from the fact that Sir Maximus Debarry immediately still acknowledges him, and not Jermyn, as deserving a place in the White Hart – on his mother's side, he does still possess the "good, rich, old Tory blood" of the Lingons (170) – Harold, himself, feels that "the circumstances of his birth were such as to warrant any man in regarding his character of gentleman with ready suspicion" (382). And Harold's uncertainty about the status he enjoys as a result of his bastardy is symptomatic of the novel's broader dismantling of the link between consanguinity and social worth.

Although numerous characters, from Wace the brewer to Harold's maternal uncle Jack, affirm their faith in "blood," the novel's most vocal advocate on behalf of the legitimating power of birth is Mrs Transome. Proselytizing to Esther after the latter's move to Transome Court, she provides "an explanation of the various quarterings, which proved that the Lingon blood had been continuously enriched . . . [G]enealogies entered into her stock of ideas, and her talk on such subjects was as necessary as the notes of the linnet or the blackbird. She had no ultimate analysis of things that went beyond blood and family" (318). This almost-compulsive idée-fixe persists despite "certain deeds of her own life [that] had been in fatal inconsistency with it" and the inevitable conclusions about Harold's own deserts that might be drawn from it (318). Somewhat counter-intuitively, Mrs Transome's "analysis of things" is further weakened by Felix, whose own faith in a very differently inflected notion of "blood" renders the connection between birth and station in much less exclusive terms: also proselytizing to Esther, Felix explains, "'I have the blood of a line of handicraftsmen in my veins, and I want to stand up for the lot of the handicraftsman as a good lot, in which a man may be better trained to all the best functions of his nature than if he belonged to the grimacing set who have visiting-cards, and are proud to be thought richer than their neighbours'" (223).[72] Felix's pride in his vocational heritage might not practically threaten the social system that allows those with "continuously enriched" blood to remain at its peak, but it conceptually undermines the warrant legitimating their elitism. Having heard both characters' positions, Esther immediately recognizes that the "[g]limpses of the Lingon heraldy" afforded to her by Mrs Transome "would cease to be succulent themes of converse or meditation" before long, and that they might be insufficient even now for their advocate to avoid feeling "a vacuum in spite of them" (318).[73]

Esther is not even aware, at this point in the story, of the ease with which the system of status constructed on the basis of birth can be manipulated by unscrupulous individuals. Jermyn's legal maneuvering on behalf of the Transomes, which has included his discovery and suppression of the legal significance of Tommy Trounsem, was originally made possible by a voluntary swap of identities. While imprisoned at Verdun by Napoleon's forces, Maurice Christian Bycliffe and Henry Scaddon agreed to trade monikers so that the true Bycliffe could return to England to stake his claim to the Transome estate. An exchange of "dress, luggage, and names," together with a resemblance of "age and figure" were sufficient to cancel out the differences in their respective births to the degree that Jermyn could arrange to have Bycliffe arrested as Scaddon when he threatened Mrs Transome's interests (183). In the years that follow, Scaddon successfully passes himself off as Christian, using the remains of his fellow-prisoner's property to guarantee his claims. Without sufficient funds, Christian cannot ascend the social ladder to elite status, but he does secure himself a comfortable sinecure with Phillip Debarry, whose own gentle birth apparently does not enable him to scent out an imposter.

Even more than these circumstantial examples, however, Eliot's own systematic determinism diminishes the legitimacy of Mrs Transome's and others' rather simplistic faith in the isolated factor of birth. If every private life is, indeed, determined by both a wider public life and the accumulation of choices made by oneself and everyone else over the course of many yesterdays, then the identity of one's father seems much less significant. Certainly, a singular obsession with birth appears antiquated, even quaint, in light of more recent, scientific attempts to measure the effects of social and natural changes on individuals:

> a man of Sir Maximus's rank is like those antediluvian animals whom the system of things condemned to carry such a huge bulk that they really could not inspect their bodily appurtenance, and had no conception of their own tails: their parasites doubtless had a merry time of it, and often did extremely well when the high-bred saurian himself was ill at ease. (82)

Whatever her pretensions, Mrs Transome never implies that her own Lingon blood is richer than that of the Debarrys, whose preeminent status in the neighborhood of Treby Magna remains beyond a doubt. Nevertheless, Eliot's narrator figures the family patriarch, Sir Maximus, as a dinosaur, one large enough to be unaware of the extensions of his own oversized body, much less of the fact that evidence was mounting that saurians like himself had gone extinct long ago.

"All life seemed cheapened"[74]

Sir Maximus's notions of high breeding may be outdated in the 1830s in which the novel is set and even more so in the 1860s in which it was written, but his attitude towards his own wealth confirms him as "a gentleman of the right sort," one willing "to endure some personal inconvenience in order to keep up the institutions of the country"; unafflicted with meanness and actuated by noblesse oblige, he does not value money for its own sake, but rather for its overdetermined social function of allowing him to "do his duty in that station of life—the station of the long-tailed saurian—to which it had pleased Providence to call him" (83). The same level of financial disinterest cannot uniformly be attributed to the novel's middle-class characters. Jermyn, for instance, in addition to accumulating wealth through sharp practice at the expense of the Transome estate, first rises to prominence in Treby Magna through a land development speculation that snares even Sir Maximus. Back when known only as "a young lawyer who came from a distance, knew the dictionary by heart, and was probably the illegitimate son of somebody or other," Jermyn secured sufficient local capital to erect "handsome buildings," print "an excellent guide-book and descriptive cards," and otherwise attempt to exploit "the discovery of a saline spring" into a spa that would draw fashionable and wealthy tourists to the town (40). The spa plan failed, but not before Sir Maximus was convinced by the "too persuasive attorney" to let the buildings on a long lease that was ultimately taken up by a "tape manufacturer," with Jermyn presumably pocketing the agent's fee (41). In the novelistic present, Jermyn, himself, confronts Christian with his fraudulent past while still Henry Scaddon:

> "Your father was a cloth-merchant in London: he died when you were barely of age, leaving an extensive business; before you were five-and-twenty you had run through the greater part of the property, and had compromised your safety by an attempt to defraud your creditors. Subsequently you forged a cheque on your father's elder brother, who had intended to make you his heir." (183)

Both characters' pursuit of wealth at times rises from the merely unscrupulous to the criminal, thereby providing damaging evidence to support the narrator's subsequent diminution of the legitimating value of statutorily defined middle-class wealth: "No system, religious or political, I believe, has laid it down as a principle that all men are alike virtuous, or even that all the people rated for £80 houses are an honour to their species" (301).

Unlike Jermyn or Christian, Harold Transome does not prey upon his neighbors in the accumulation of his wealth. Instead, recognizing that his elder brother Durfey will inherit the family fortune, he leaves home to "get rich somehow," thereby displaying "the energetic will and muscle, the self-confidence, the quick perception, and the narrow imagination which make what is admiringly called the practical mind" most often associated with the entrepreneurial middle class (93). When he returns to Treby Magna both successful in his own right and heir to the Transome estate, his affluence at first secures him status. Scales overweighs his fortune based upon direct and, one senses, somewhat envious observation of the wealth that can be gained through trade – "'knowing what I know, I shouldn't wonder if Transome had as much as five hundred thousand. Bless your soul, sir! People who get their money out of land are as long scraping five pounds together as your trading men are in turning five pounds into a hundred'" (84) – and this inflated amount then spreads through the community, "adding much lustre to [Harold's] opinions in the eyes of Liberals, and compelling even men of the opposite party to admit that it increased his eligibility as a member for North Loamshire" (89). As it turns out, Harold's wealth is sufficient to bear the loss of between eight and nine thousand pounds in the election, but not enough to gain him the parliamentary seat for which he campaigned. With his subsequent attempt to seek financial restitution from Jermyn initially frustrated by the latter's revelations concerning the Transome estate, Harold begins courting Esther, who recognizes "moral mediocrity" in his "practical cleverness" even before he reveals that the wealth he gained abroad remains tainted by association with the slave trade (340).[75]

For the two co-protagonists of *Felix Holt*, the only morally safe approach to the overdetermining power of money lies in its renunciation. Felix has already cast off his wealth, inherited from his entrepreneurial father in the form of three patent medicines – Holt's Cathartic Lozenges, Holt's Restorative Elixir, and Holt's Cancer Cure – that his own subsequent training as an apothecary has revealed are useless at best and dangerous at worst.[76] An unspecified "six weeks' debauchery" living off the sales proceeds of his family's cures has convinced him that a life of "easy pleasure" among the middle classes is not for him, and so he returns to his artisanal roots by becoming a watchmaker. At the beginning of the novel, he has nothing but disdain for the consumptive markers of middle-class status – synecdochally represented by "'a house with a high doorstop and brass knocker'" (55) – and although Esther teaches him to moderate his opinions somewhat, he remains suspicious of the corrupting effects of excess wealth.[77] Esther's own opportunity for renunciation occupies the majority of the novel's second half. When first introduced, she is acutely aware of the "irreconcilableness between the objects of her taste and the conditions of her lot," but Esther learns from both Felix's and Rufus Lyon's example to question the inherent value of wealth as represented by the Transome inheritance (65). Sensing that "somehow or other by this elevation of fortune it seemed that the higher ambition which had begun to spring in her was forever nullified," she renounces her claim on the estate, refuses Harold's offer of marriage, and returns to her father's house hopeful but not certain of marrying Felix (340–1). Crucially, Esther's "deliberate choice" involves a subtler and more social approach to wealth than Felix's earlier extreme reaction: she reserves just enough of the Transome fortune to provide "two pounds a-week" for herself and Felix so that he will not be obliged to work "if sickness came," as well as a "little income" for both Felix's mother and her own adoptive father, enough to permit her "to live as she has been used to live" and to "save him from being dependent when he is no longer able to preach" (395–6).[78] And this more nuanced resolution of the problematic of wealth prompts the community to recognize Esther and, through her Felix, as possessing a rare form of status. Their wedding attracts both "very great people, like Sir Maximus and his family" and tradesmen like Wace, who tells his wife after the ceremony, "'I feel somehow as if I believed more in everything that's good'" (397).

"'The shouting and roaring of rude men is so hideous'"[79]

Spoken in the lull between the morning's "spirited . . . transition from words to deeds" and the late afternoon's escalation to full-scale riot on election day in Treby, this declaration from Esther is a reminder that *Felix Holt, the Radical* is every bit as invested in the diminution of force, especially as represented by social disorder, as its predecessor industrial novels (256). In fact, Eliot locates the final, alcohol-fueled – hence "spirited" in a literal sense – outbreak of public violence at the end of the second volume, thereby granting it a structural prominence in the narrative that, due to subscription services like Mudie's, would only be reinforced by Victorian patterns of novelistic circulation. As Felix recognizes late in volume one, and seeks to curtail early in volume two, the potential for election-day violence has been building since the Transome campaign's early treating of the Sproxton hands at Chubb's pub, the Sugar Loaf. Jermyn's agent, Johnson, encourages the men to show their support for the Radical cause with a "'little rolling in the dust and knocking hats off, a little pelting with soft things that'll stick and not bruise—all that doesn't spoil the fun'" (117). If they do so, Felix later asserts, they will be exercising only a "wicked" sort of "'power to do mischief—to undo what has been done with great expense and labour, to waste and destroy, to be cruel to the weak, to lie and quarrel, and to talk poisonous nonsense. That's the sort of power that ignorant numbers have'" (247). Once "excited with drink," the mass of working men that assembles in Treby on election day proves Felix right, first by bombarding an unpopular magistrate with produce taken from a greengrocer's shop, then by seeking "more effective missiles and weapons" from the neighboring hardware shop, and following this with a general rush upon all shops operated by Tory voters on the town's main street (262). From assault, petty theft, and more general destruction of property, the intoxicated crowd, now a "mob," then threatens the maligned overseer Spratt with bodily harm before marching on Treby Manor with designs on the Debarry's plate, liquor, and, possibly, female members of the household (264). This final assault on domesticity, including the delicately hinted potential for sexual violence, provides indisputable evidence that numerical preponderance and physical force ought never to be mistaken for social legitimacy.

Written in the shadow of the Second Reform Bill and set during the immediately aftermath of the First, the chaos of election day in North Loamshire carries with it overt implications for further expansion of the franchise. Begun in 1865, hence before the mass meetings that became the hallmark of the National Reform League, *Felix Holt* was initially published in June 1866 and appeared in a second edition in December of that year; given these dates, it would have been difficult for readers to avoid comparing the novel's election-day riot with either the Trafalgar Square or the Hyde Park demonstrations orchestrated by England's latter-day Chartists. Relocating the novel's electoral violence within the rhetoric inherited from the 1840s, Vanden Bossche notes that within the "plot structure" of *Felix Holt*, "the innocent or those who resist physical force get caught up in mob violence," thereby implying "that precisely because moral force cannot be effective without physical force one cannot employ it without being involved in the seditious use of force."[80] The fact that Eliot's mob is motivated by little more than "stupid curiosity" and "a mere medley of appetites and confused impressions" (266, 267) does not invalidate this insinuation of seditious unfitness, but rather inscribes their amoral force within what Joseph Butwin denominates a further "vicious circle: extra electoral activity on the part of the unenfranchised is frivolous, and frivolity proves these people unprepared for the franchise."[81] The novel's representation and repudiation of force as a basis for social legitimacy, therefore, comes at a particularly anxious political moment for *Felix Holt*'s middle-class readers, who saw their own numerical preponderance on election day about to be superseded by a mass of new voters willing not just to demonstrate for their rights, but to break through railings and police lines to do so.

However, Eliot's own objections to force extend beyond contemporary political controversies to encompass broader philosophical concerns brought to the fore by her intellectual commitment to determinism.[82] The election-day riot serves as a troubling example of "wider public life" that overdetermines the "private life" of her novel's namesake, in part by offering an outlet for his own, usually tightly controlled, propensity for violence. In his first introduction to Rufus Lyon, Felix candidly admits, "'I'm perhaps a little too fond of banging and smashing,'" and later amplifies this confession when he thinks to himself, "There's some reason in me as long as I keep my temper, but my rash humour is drunkenness without wine" (57, 124).[83] "Felix had a terrible arm: he knew he was dangerous," the narrator states on the morning of nomination day, and although normally "he avoided the conditions that might cause him exasperation, as he would have avoided intoxicating drinks if he had been in danger of intemperance," the ubiquity of electioneering, of sharp practices and false statements during the campaign, and the proximity of Harold's agent Johnson drives him to conclude his impromptu speech about the wicked power of ignorant numbers with an ad hominem which alerts Christian to the identity of Johnson and allows the two to begin pooling their knowledge so as to bring about the Transome inheritance crisis (242). Quite without meaning to and acting at the mercy of his own exasperated predilections under circumstances determined to bring out them out, Felix helps to violently destabilize the social fabric of Treby.[84] During the riot itself, his "terrible arm" is even more literally in evidence when, seeking to prevent events from escalating to the kind of bacchanalian excesses represented in *Barnaby Rudge*, Felix accidentally kills one of the town's regular constables, the "spirited" Tucker, and emerges from the fatal altercation "with the bare sabre in his hand" (265, 266).[85] Already mistaken by "undiscerning eyes" as "a leading spirit of the mob," Felix now appears armed and dangerous even when attempting to mitigate the violent threat to Spratt and reassure the women of Treby Manor, and he is ultimately shot through "the shoulder of the arm that held the naked weapon" (265, 269). Felix's own physical strength and determination to lead the crowd out of mischief are no match for the overdetermining but illegitimate social force contained in the riot, which becomes "that mixture of pushing forward and being pushed forward, which is a brief history of most human things" (267).

It is important to note that the physical confrontations – whether between Felix and Tucker or between the mob and Treby Manor – that dominate the election riot episode are precipitated by earlier verbal altercations between individuals. Indeed, Eliot expands the category of illicit uses of force to include not just acts but words. "'The mind that is too ready at contempt and reprobation,'" Rufus Lyon cautions Felix, is "'as a clenched fist that can give blows, but is shut up from receiving and holding ought that is precious'" (57). The narrator minces fewer words on nomination day, asserting that "wit is a form of force that leaves the limbs at rest" (244). Felix then demonstrates the dangers of wit motivated by contempt when he denounces Johnson, who had, as early as their first meeting at the Sugar Loaf, adroitly "caricatured" Felix's own "serious phrases" in convincing the colliers to make a show of force on the upcoming election day (115). During the riot itself, the many partisan cheers, "sarcasms, and oaths . . . seemed to have the flavour of wit for many hearers" and help to incite to the riot that follows (256). And it is the words "'Let us go to Treby Manor'" that fatally render Felix "powerless" to exercise his "vaguer influence" over the crowd (268). For Eliot, the wrong words at the wrong time are every bit as dangerous as deeds undertaken while intoxicated; both represent force misapplied and sometimes fatally misapprehended as a basis for social authority.

Avoiding "disorder . . . aggravated by obscurity"[86]

In place of the blunter instruments of birth, wealth, and force – whether physical or rhetorical – Eliot suggests that subtler determinants may be more appropriate for an age of "new conditions" precipitating "that higher consciousness which is known to bring higher pains" (41). Affective sympathy, a commitment to education, and a willingness to accept "the minimum of effect, if it's of the sort I care for" rather than "the maximum of effect I don't care for" are the characterological traits held up in *Felix Holt* as appropriate warrants for social worth (363). The individual who exemplifies these traits most consistently is Rufus Lyon, whose strength takes the form of "willing bondage to irremediable weakness" (66). Lyon's example slowly moderates the excesses of Felix's "contempt and reprobation," even as his sartorial shortcomings provide Esther with her first opportunity to practice "acts of tenderness," which, much later in story, enable her to sympathize with and begin to heal the emotional schism between Harold and Mrs Transome. Felix and Esther's growth into full possession of these qualities is the central preoccupation of the novel, with the more visible social events surrounding the election providing opportunities to measure their progress.

In keeping with the principles of Eliot's determinism, even the smallest interactions between Felix and Esther can have unforeseen significant effects on Treby society. Felix's early scolding prompts Esther for "the first time in her life" to feel "seriously shaken in her self-contentment," and her desire to no longer deserve being perceived as "trivial, narrow, selfish" leads her to deepen her intimacy with Lyon, who then shares her mother's story and her own probable parentage with her (106). Once ensconced with the Transomes, Esther, who now possesses "the keen bright eye of a woman when it has once been turned with admiration on what is severely true," is able to see through the allures of Harold's wealth to the "silken bondage" beneath (344, 389). Her increased appreciation for the severely true and her amplified sympathy enables her to testify at the trial, thereby prompting the meeting at the White Hart that secures Felix a reduced sentence, forces Harold's recognition of his own relationship to Jermyn, and leads to "the most serious moment in Harold Transome's life," namely his renunciation of his claims on Esther herself (385). The final resolution of Felix's and Esther's marriage then accomplishes a reunion of all members of the Treby community, even as Esther's small financial provisions for the future lead Felix to imagine setting up "a great library" whose books will be lent to the working-class children and adults whom he hopes to teach (396).[87] "So fast does a little leaven spread within us," the narrator remarks, "so incalculable is the effect of one personality on another," that the minutest developments of the right sort of character may, even should, overdetermine for the better the fate of an entire community (194).

Notes

1. The Victorians' distrust of collective action was, if anything, even stronger in a colonial context, where civil disturbances were likely to be met with both widespread condemnation and overwhelming force, as happened in both Jamaica (1831–2 and 1865) and India (1857–8), to name only two examples.
2. Chris R. Vanden Bossche, *Reform Acts*, 6.
3. Ibid. 32.
4. It was because of the Act's exclusionary results that the "alliance between the bourgeoisie and the people" that had grown up during the

parliamentary debate over Reform, "was dissolved immediately after 1832" (Louis Cazamian, *The Social Novel in England 1830–1850*, 28).
5. According to Carolyn Betensky, "the poor and working classes greatly outnumbered and were perceived increasingly – and . . . with growing panic – to outnumber, the middle classes that dominated them" (*Feeling for the Poor*, 62).
6. On both narrowly legislative and broadly social manifestations of the Victorians' "spirit of reform," see Patrick Brantlinger's *The Spirit of Reform*. According to Brantlinger, "The spirit of reform in the early 1830s involved evangelical and humanitarian protest, the advocacy of limited government to correct social abuses and to refurbish outmoded institutions, and Benthamite and Owenite schemes for improving mankind itself," whereas in the following decade "reform tended to be identified less and less with legislation and with bureaucratic social planning than with voluntary humanitarian activity" (1–2).
7. Herbert Sussman, "Industrial," 252. As Sussman cogently summarizes, "From the bourgeois political standpoint, workers who rejected atomistic competitiveness to join in collective, albeit peaceful, political action . . . became dangerous . . . a source of potential revolution . . . figured in a politically charged vocabulary as a mass . . . the crowd . . . or the mob" ("Industrial," 255).
8. Malcolm I. Thomis, ed., *Luddism in Nottinghamshire*, 2.
9. For fuller accounts of Luddism, see Robert Glen, *Urban Workers in the Industrial Revolution*; Adrian Randall, *Before the Luddites*; and Thomis, *The Luddites*.
10. For a fuller history of England's Swing Riots, see Eric Hobsbawm and George Rude's *Captain Swing*.
11. *The Annual Register, 1838*, 204–5. I have written at length elsewhere about the rhetoric of conspiracy directed at trade unions on the basis of this and similar evidence, as well as about the details of the Glasgow Spinner trial. See Pionke, *Plots of Opportunity*, 22–49.
12. Chartism is well-traveled historical ground. Among the many possible sources, see Malcolm Chase, *Chartism: A New History*; James Epstein and Dorothy Thompson, eds., *The Chartist Experience*; David Goodway, *London Chartism 1838–1848*; David Jones, *Chartism and the Chartists*; John Saville, *1848: The British State and the Chartist Movement*; and Gregory Vargo, *An Underground History of Early Victorian Fiction*. In *Reform Acts*, Vanden Bossche offers a particularly cogent summary of the complex tactical relationship between Chartist strategies of moral-force suasion and physical-force action (21–36).
13. Kate Flint, ed., *The Victorian Novelist*, 5. Numerous critics note the fear engendered by Chartism's naked demonstration of the force of working-class discontent: thus, Brantlinger asserts that the shift in England's "spirit of reform" from legislative intervention to humanitarian voluntarism mentioned above can be attributed to "fear of

Chartism, which put middle-class liberals on the defensive and made them more wary of tampering with the machinery of society than they had been from 1832 to 1836" (2); Betensky similarly refers to the "growing panic" brought on by "the rise of the Chartist movement" (62); Cazamian writes, "Around 1842 poverty reached the proportions of a national affliction . . . This was the time of the second Chartist petition and major industrial troubles. Revolution seemed immanent" (71); Raymond Williams also cites in *Culture and Society* a "*fear of violence* which was widespread among the upper and middle classes . . . fear that the working people might take matters into their own hands was widespread and characteristic" (90, emphasis in original); and Vargo supplies numerical evidence for these broad anxieties in the "800 newsvendors and journalists imprisoned in the war of the unstamped; the 1500 people jailed in the Chartist strike wave of 1842; and the nearly 100,000 police, troops, and special constables mobilized to ensure public order in London in April 1848" (4).
14. W. L. Burn first applied this memorable phrase to the period of relative prosperity and domestic quiescence in *The Age of Equipoise: A Study of the Mid-Victorian Generation*. The exclusions required to maintain Burn's thesis have been criticized by subsequent historians, but the label has persisted, and the book has even recently been reprinted.
15. This figure appears on p. 80 of the Chronicle section of *The Annual Register* for 1854. The definitive history of the Preston Strike remains H. I Dutton and J. E. King, *'Ten Per Cent and No Surrender': The Preston Strike, 1853-54*.
16. Although less organized and of shorter duration, the Sunday Trading Riots, which erupted in Hyde Park in late June and early July 1855 in response to Lord Grosvenor's legislative attempt to interdict shopping and drinking on Sundays by means of the Sunday Trading Bill, also alarmed middle- and upper-class Londoners, many of whom were accosted in their carriages. On the Sunday Trading Riots, see Brian Harrison, "The Sunday Trading Riots of 1855."
17. On the passage of the Second Reform Act, see Robert Saunders, *Democracy and the Vote in British Politics, 1848–1867*.
18. Dickens, *Barnaby Rudge*, 40.
19. John Butt and Kathleen Tillotson dedicate the fourth chapter of *Dickens at Work* to the complete composition and publication history of *Barnaby Rudge*; see 76–89.
20. I have taken the liberty of strategically misquoting Dickens's description of Sim's synecdochal legs, described by the narrator as "curiosities of littleness" (*Barnaby Rudge*, 78); "burlesque" is Thomas Jackson's pejorative for Dickens's deliberately ludicrous depiction of Sim's conspiracy of apprentices (*Charles Dickens*, 28).
21. Dickens, *Barnaby Rudge*, 112–6. Whether Dickens's self-conscious borrowings from contemporary accounts of trade unionism should be

interpreted as an attack, however indirect or analogous, on Chartism is a matter of debate. The topic is discussed at length by Vanden Bossche, who asserts that "Dickens responded not directly to Chartism but rather to the parliamentary discourse that developed in response to it" (61). For Vanden Bossche's extended reading of the novel, see 60–71; for a summary of the debates over the presence or absence of Chartist references in *Barnaby Rudge*, see 214n2.

22. Dickens, *Barnaby Rudge*, 80.
23. Ibid. 464.
24. Ibid. 381.
25. Ibid. 369.
26. Ibid. 550, 611.
27. Ibid. 618.
28. Charlotte Brontë, *Shirley*, 137.
29. Ibid. 304. John Plotz provides a compelling reading of this humorous scene in relation to the nighttime attack on Moore's mill, about which more in a moment (*The Crowd*, 161–3). For his extended reading of the novel's various crowds and their function within the novel's unusually overt reciprocal construction of middle-class domesticity, see 154–93.
30. Brontë, *Shirley*, 304.
31. I have written at length about Brontë's depiction of Yorkshire Luddism in *Shirley*. See Pionke, "Reframing the Luddites."
32. Brontë, *Shirley*, 33.
33. Ibid. 384, 32.
34. According to Plotz, "Robert Moore's function in *Shirley* is to reiterate the necessity of division across the barriers that mark class, vocational, and even dispositional differences: we gentry and industrialists prize solitude, while they, the workers, love their agglomeration, their 'fellow feelings'" (173).
35. Brontë, *Shirley*, 543.
36. Ibid. 645.
37. Charles Kingsley, *Alton Locke*, 21.
38. Kingsley, *Alton Locke*, 132. Given all of these competing imperatives, as Catherine Gallagher observes in *The Industrial Reformation of English Fiction*, "Kingsley's industrial novel, *Alton Locke: Tailor and Poet* (1849), demonstrates just how complicated the issue of freedom is" (89).
39. Kingsley, *Alton Locke*, 135–6.
40. Ibid. 113.
41. Ibid. 190.
42. Ibid. 237, 240.
43. Ibid. 243.
44. Ibid. 259.

45. As Richard Menke, in "Cultural Capital and the Scene of Rioting," notes, "Kingsley does not lose the opportunity of presenting the mob violence that ensues the spectacle that haunted middle- and upper-class response to Chartism" (101).
46. Kingsley, *Alton Locke*, 367.
47. It is in part as a result of Alton's conversion from Chartism to Christian Socialism that Betensky writes that "Charles Kingsley's *Alton Locke* may be read as an extended study of the development of a 'cultured' worker's awareness of his class's and his own preconceptions about the rich" (84).
48. Elizabeth Gaskell, *North and South*, 109.
49. Ibid. 116.
50. Ibid. 220.
51. Ibid. 174, 176.
52. Ibid. 180.
53. Ibid. 199–200. As Vanden Bossche explains, *North and South* "envisions reform of the trade union as integral to the reform of the industrial entrepreneur" even as it "depicts a union leadership committed to moral force yet unable to control their fellow workers' physical-force response to conditions" (176, 178). See 176–88 for an extended discussion of the novel.
54. Gaskell, *North and South*, 155.
55. Ibid. 232.
56. Rosemarie Bodenheimer, "*North and South*: A Permanent State of Change," 290.
57. Gaskell, *North and South*, 119, 118.
58. Ibid. 420.
59. Ibid. 432.
60. Ibid. 432.
61. As the last major industrial novel, *Felix Holt* is frequently measured against its antecedents by critics interested in the development of the subgenre. Raymond Williams provides the foundational example of this historical approach to the form in *Culture & Society* (87–109), with later critics – such as Betensky, Brantlinger, Flint, Gallagher, Lesjak (*Working Fictions*), Vanden Bossche and others – responding to his highly productive model. Eliot's contribution is notably absent from Cazamian's otherwise pioneering sociological account of the English *roman-à-thèse*.
62. George Eliot, *Felix Holt, the Radical*, 52. Hereafter cited parenthetically in the text.
63. Although the novel does not follow Brindle, Dredge, and their fellows back to their place of employment, their narrative presence is sufficiently unusual for Carolyn Lesjak to judge that *Felix Holt* "breaks new ground" in featuring "the newly created phenomena of industrial workers and their labor" (*Working Fictions*, 66)

64. Betensky, 136. Betensky's comparatist appraisal of *Felix Holt* is cast in sociological terms derived at least in part from Bourdieu:

> Before *Felix Holt* social-problem novels featured dominant-class characters who did not care about the dominated-class characters but who came through narrative conversion to care about them (Thornton in *North and South*, Mr Carson in *Mary Barton*, Robert Moore in *Shirley*, Mary Brotherton in *Michael Armstrong*, Louisa and Mr Gradgrind in *Hard Times*). Dominant-class characters could live among the dominated if they presented simulated working-class credentials (Egremont in *Sybil*), or they could maintain a dominated-dominant position so as to mediate between the demands of the opposing classes (Margaret Hale and her father in *North and South*). At the same time working-class characters could adopt or be adopted into a dominant-class cultural milieu by mastering the idiom of the dominated dominant (Alton Locke in Kingsley's novel) or could work their moral excellence to gain fraught and partial entrée into dialogue and commerce with dominant-class characters (Stephen Blackpool in *Hard Times*, Nicholas Higgins in *North and South*). (135–6)

65. This interpenetration of social and characterological concerns has long been recognized by Eliot's critics: thus, David Carroll writes, "At the center of *Felix Holt* is the titular hero engaged in a private and public relationship. He is trying to reform both Esther Lyon and the working class" ("*Felix Holt*: Society as Protagonist," 238–9); similarly, Stefanie Markovits argues that Eliot "shifts the focus from the political revolution implied by the title of the novel to Esther Lyon's 'inward revolution'" (*The Crisis of Action in Nineteenth-Century English Literature*, 89); and, somewhat more pejoratively, Betensky judges that the novel "packages the affective conversion of one middle-class character *as if* the turning of bourgeois feeling were politically radical." (132, emphasis in original).
66. Eliot, *Felix Holt*, 221.
67. Also among the novel's prominent Classical references is the epigraph chosen for chapter 48 – "'Tis law as steadfast, as the throne of Zeus—/ Our days are heritors of days gone by" (382) – taken from Aeschylus's *Agamemnon*. Fred C. Thomson, "The Legal Plot in *Felix Holt*," even identifies this passage as Eliot's most succinct statement of her own determinism and of the novel's most consistent theme, "the motif of inheritance in all its forms" (694).
68. For a recent discussion of Eliot's awareness and fictional incorporation of contemporary social science, including her evolving intellectual relationship with the positivist theories of Auguste Comte, see Scott C. Thompson, "Character and Life."
69. As Stefanie Markovits observes, Eliot "wanted to preserve a sphere for action, in which the will could find free outward expression, but the only sphere she could envision, given her determinism, was tremendously limited" (92).

70. Jermyn's slow descent from philandering to sharp dealing to blackmail provide an especially poignant example of what Thomson summaries as Eliot's deterministic theory of character:

> To George Eliot, character is basically inherited; but character at birth is a morally neutral composite of propensities or tendencies. Environment and experience can variously shape it, encouraging or repressing certain propensities, but not radically change it. By the exercise of moral choice in small matters as well as in great, a person sets in motion a determinism of character (contrapuntal to the external deterministic factors) whereby according to the rectitude of his behavior, which is always to be judged by its consequences to others, he may ascend to nobility or sink to depravity. He must ever beware of habituating himself to wrong-doing, for each mistaken action makes the next one progressively easier to commit, until at last the moral faculties have atrophied. (693–4)

71. Eliot, *Felix Holt*, 179. Spoken by Mr Wace, the brewer, over a market dinner at the Marquis, in support of Harold Transome's candidacy.
72. Felix reinforces this point elsewhere in the novel as well, early on asserting his intention to "stick to the class I belong to" by virtue of patrilineal descent from his father and uncle and aspiring, much later from prison, to convince his "people" – those who share his handicraftsman blood – "'that there's some dignity and happiness for a man other than changing his station'" (55, 363).
73. During a subsequent conversation with Harold, Esther's disenchantment with the attractions of birth-as-status progresses even further as she discerns "that the sense of ranks and degrees has its repulsions corresponding to the repulsions dependent on difference of race and colour" (339); that is to say, that external prejudice and not internal worth may inform such strategies of consanguineous legitimacy. "It is terrible," the narrator writes, "the keen bright eye of a woman when it has once been turned with admiration on what is severely true" (344). Eliot's own "keen bright eye" for her contemporaries' attitudes towards "difference of race and colour" is treated at length by Alicia Carroll in *Dark Smiles*; for Carroll's extended reading of *Felix Holt*, see pp. 65–91.
74. Eliot, *Felix Holt*, 341.
75. In what can best be described as a clumsy proposal, Harold attempts to assure Esther that his feelings for her are entirely new to him by revealing that "'Harry's mother had been a slave—was bought, in fact'" (352). Made in 1832, the same year that parliamentary inquiries into the Baptist War in Jamaica added fresh impetus to outlaw slavery throughout the British empire – a fact to be legislatively if not fully practically accomplished the following year with the passage of the Slavery Abolition Act 1833 – this admission likely would have come as an especial shock to Esther, whose upbringing among Dissenters would have immersed her in the abolitionist cause.

76. As Felix explains to Rufus Lyon, "'I was 'prentice for five miserable years to a stupid brute of a country apothecary—my poor father left money for that—he thought nothing could be finer for me. No matter: I know that the Cathartic Pills are a drastic compound which may be as bad as poison to half the people who swallow them; that the Elixir is an absurd farrago of a dozen incompatible things; and that the Cancer cure might as well be bottled ditch-water'" (53).
77. Noting Esther's moderating effects upon Felix, Betensky asserts that "it's Felix who gets educated about how a middle-class character with 'fine ladylike manners' really can be good" (144).
78. According to Seung-Pon Koo, in "Esther and the Politics of Multiple Tastes in George Eliot's *Felix Holt, the Radical*," Esther's nuanced renunciation "does not completely exclude the value of economic capital" and in so doing "demonstrates the acumen of her economic judgment" as compared with Felix (85).
79. Eliot, *Felix Holt*, 259.
80. Vanden Bossche, 190.
81. Joseph Butwin, "The Pacification of the Crowd," 369. Carolyn Lesjak and Michelle Weinroth come, respectively, to similar conclusions on the basis of a survey of the totality of election-related activity in the novel. According to Lesjak, the early treating scene at the Sugar Loaf demonstrates the workers' lack of "cultural capital to warrant a political right to representation," and this unfitness escalates to a "definitive" and "resounding" refusal of their readiness for enfranchisement once the riot is under way ("A Modern Odyssey," 87). Weinroth similarly asserts that "'Eliot emphatically debunks the electoral process of Treby Magna, portraying its futility in a succession of infelicitous episodes: deflated public speeches at Duffield, heckling and violence on voting day, and the irrational forces fuelling a calamitous riot near Treby Manor" ("Engendering Consent," 21).
82. Although not entirely in agreement with the affective inference of her point, I take the force of Markovits's observation that "as much fear as logic motivated Eliot's beliefs: the risks accompanying any action were tremendous those of political revolution unthinkable" (95).
83. On the morning of nomination day, the narrator goes even further, explaining that the "weak point to which Felix referred was his liability to be carried completely out of his own mastery by indignant anger . . . When once exasperated, the passionateness of his nature threw off the yoke of a long-trained consciousness in which thought and emotion had been more and more completely mingled, and concentrated itself in a rage as ungovernable as that of boyhood" (241).
84. Felix, Rita Bode notes, "is potentially violent toward everyone. His blunt rudeness seems an expression of this violence . . . Felix does not lose control of his passions in the riot, but his 'terrible arm' results in

his murdering Tucker, an act not easily explained away" ("Power and Submission in *Felix Holt, the Radical*," 778).
85. Eliot's repeated use of "spirit" and "spirited" during the riot scene is intended, I think, to indicate that outbreaks of force function just like intoxication, releasing inhibitions that normally act to conserve the social fabric and allowing those drunk on the moment to perform acts which, under calmer circumstances, they would find unthinkable.
86. Eliot, *Felix Holt*, 264.
87. Indeed, Felix admits to Esther that, "'if you take me in that way I shall be forced to be a much better fellow than I ever thought of being'" (396).

Chapter 4

Social Domination, Social Scientific Empiricism, and Novelistic Distrust of the Modern Fact

Eliot was herself convinced by her friend and publisher, John Blackwood, to attempt to act the ameliorating social part of Esther and Felix immediately after the publication of *Felix Holt* and the passage of the Second Reform Act. Heartened by the broad public's positive reception of what he perceived as the novel's fundamentally conservative politics, Blackwood commissioned Eliot to resurrect her protagonist's fictional voice for a nonfictional admonition to England's newest voters.[1] Written in late November and early December of 1867, the resulting "Address to Working Men, by Felix Holt" appeared in the January 1868 number of *Blackwood's Edinburgh Magazine*.[2] Deploying a corporeal metaphor popular among contemporary sociological thinkers, the "Address" advocates for "the care, the precaution, with which we should go about making things better, so that the public order may not be destroyed, so that no fatal shock may be given to this society of ours, this living body in which our lives are bound up."[3] That England's numerical majority, however previously disenfranchised, has been unable or unwilling to cure the social body of "the bad practices, the commercial lying and swindling, the poisonous adulteration of goods, the retail cheating, and the political bribery which are carried on boldly in the midst of us," is a sign, Eliot-cum-Felix asserts, that the nation's new working-class electors may not yet possess "the knowledge, the foresight, the conscience, that will make [them] well-judging and scrupulous in the use of" the vote.[4]

Without these qualities, and denied "by the very fact of our privations" the requisite exposure to Bourdieu's aesthetic objects, these same constituents are likely to undervalue "that treasure of knowledge, science, poetry, refinement of thought, feeling, and manners, great memories and the interpretation of great records, which are carried on from the minds of one generation to the minds of another."[5] Warned away from the exercise of an aesthetic/moral disposition they do not possess, the supposed auditors of Felix's "Address" are advised instead to gain the "practical" knowledge necessary to endure: "It is constantly the task of practical wisdom not to say, 'This is good and I will have it,' but to say, 'This is the less of two unavoidable evils, and I will bear it.'"[6] Concluding with a deterministic warning against the kinds of unintended consequences chronicled at such length in *Felix Holt*, the "Address" warns that, without the ability to "discern between the evils that energy can remove and the evils that patience must bear . . . we can hardly escape acts of fatal rashness and injustice."[7]

Although the self-improving curriculum for the acquisition of "knowledge . . . foresight . . . [and] conscience" is never specified in the "Address," the positivistic roots of Eliot's own determinism suggest that "practical" knowledge would likely include the basic principles of political economy, taught, perhaps, with the aid of Harriet Martineau's *Illustrations of Political Economy* (1832–4), recently reissued in nine volumes by Routledge, Warnes, & Routledge in 1859. It would also require accessibility to rational as opposed to emotional argument, including a willingness to weigh personal pleasures and experiences of pain against the utilitarian greatest happiness for the greatest number, as well as the merits of providing and basing decisions about public policy upon empirical data as represented in government Blue Books and statistical reports. Even with minds largely untouched by the cultural legacy of previous generations and certainly not in possession of any of its artifactual treasures, then, the newly enfranchised might still thereby be rendered docile citizens through a practical education in modern facts.

One might even say, following Mary Poovey, a learned commitment to "Modern Fact," the culturally conditioned faith in the inarguability of numerical representation as transparently meaningful and inherently more plausible than the vagaries of individual experience.[8] Conceptually, of course, political economy, utilitarianism, and even statistics encompass more than just mathematical data; each proffers its own more or less comprehensive theory of both how society works and how best to apprehend its operational efficiency. Moreover, although all rely to varying degrees upon the logical process of deduction, their nineteenth-century practitioners as often competed and disagreed with as reinforced and cooperated with the conclusions of each other. Thus, Benthamite utilitarianism proposed as first principles a calculus of pleasure-seeking and pain-avoidance, along with the rational measure of social utility, that, together, challenged political economy's reduction of humanity to *homo economicus*. Nevertheless, the most influential political economists of the first third of the century were Benthamite radicals, most notably David Ricardo and Nassau Senior. Similarly, the early leaders of Britain's statistical movement at Cambridge – including Richard Jones, T. R. Malthus, Charles Babbage, and William Whewell – were united by their skepticism of political economy's willful avoidance of historical and cultural particularity.[9] Yet, statistics was often conceived and certainly was called upon frequently to serve as "the empirical arm of political economy."[10] It also provided a key source of data for utilitarian reformers, even when the disturbing regularity of those statistics concerning crime rates, births, and suicides, for instance, suggested a dearth of human freedom and hence a formidable barrier to intentionally-directed social improvement.[11]

What could be characterized as the fruitful fractiousness among the principals of these interanimating fields of social thought is one indication that at stake for their largely middle-class, proto-professional advocates was the legitimacy accorded by a robust command of fact in Victorian England. Cultural historians have identified a "great explosion of numbers" in the 1820s and 1830s that accompanied the widespread adoption of industrial production, such that "along with the grand *mélange* of *things* that seemed to flow unchecked out of British factories, a river of knowledge (and questions) about how the world worked coursed through every aspect of Victorian life."[12] Government departments and private associations founded to collect and manage this flood of data provided mathematically inclined members of the middle class with both employment and opportunities to affirmatively assert their own status through the expertise conferred by professional memberships. Among the new institutions created to track the nation's burgeoning amount of social data were the statistical office led first by G. R. Porter at the Board of Trade (founded 1832); the statistical section, F, of the British Association for the Advancement of Science (1833); the Manchester Statistical Society (1833); the Statistical Society of London, founded by the Cambridge group mentioned earlier along with pioneering Belgian statistician Adolphe Quételet (1834); the General Register's Office, created to oversee the expanded census of 1841 and after (1837); and the National Association for the Promotion of Social Sciences (1857).[13] "By mid-Victorian times," Alexander Welsh asserts, "it was taken for granted that any position in public affairs ought to be supported by statistics, reports, press coverage, and expert testimony of various kinds."[14] Those interpreting the statistics, writing the reports, responding to and in many cases providing the press coverage, and offering testimony before parliamentary committees and royal commissions, capitalized upon the "pervasive system of prestige" that had emerged as a consequence of Britain's new knowledge economy.[15] In the words of John Robertson, sub-editor of the *London and Westminster Review* and anonymous author of the 1838 article "Exclusion of Opinions" criticizing the intellectual orientation of the Statistical Society of London, "It is, indeed, truly said, that the spirit of the present age has an evident tendency to confront the figures of speech with the figures of arithmetic, since it is impossible not to observe a growing distrust of mere hypothetical theory and *à priori* assumption."[16]

Robertson's critique was not of statistics in general, but rather of the avowedly apolitical, even anti-ideational stance of the Statistical Society of London in particular; without "opinions," otherwise known as hypotheses or theories, Robertson averred, one is left with mere disconnected factual evidence, and science "is not evidence, but the results of evidence."[17] However, Robertson's was not the only or even the most pressing reason for resisting the blanket authority of fact, especially for middle-class Victorians who were not, themselves, immediately accruing legitimacy on the basis of social scientific expertise. Methodologically, most social investigations were directed at "[p]roducing, processing, and consuming knowledge of how the poor lived," measuring various forms of social deviancy such as crime or suicide, or both.[18] Hence, to be observed by those in command of modern facts was, implicitly, to be labeled by class and pathology; for members of the status-anxious social middle, such an allegation was unacceptable.[19] Medical mapping by sanitary reformers, for instance, challenged "the boundaries of the middle-class and individual self, [which] could only be preserved through a careful policing of the abject and the closure of the boundaries of the body," by moving "away from a model of London as a series of separate parishes or neighborhoods . . . to figure the urban environment, and London in particular, as a body—an organic whole connected by hidden mechanisms of circulation."[20] This may have empowered those medical and statistical professionals who read the new medical maps and contributed to public health, but it also broke down topographical barriers that were simultaneously social bulwarks against the loss of status, even as it labeled every resident of London, regardless of neighborhood, a potential source of social infection. Further concerns arose from the necessary expediency of using partial samples of social data as the basis for general conclusions and policies. As early as 1827, Quételet was forced to reconsider his plans to conduct a partial sampling of Belgium's population in lieu of a full census when met with the then-unanswerable objections of Baron Charles de Keverberg, who noted that the absence of homogeneity among the nation's population, no matter how meticulously subdivided, would result in local variations that could not be accounted for mathematically; taken to its logical endpoint, this critique posited that individuals were too unpredictable to be represented abstractly.[21] Keverberg's point was methodologically relevant not just to inductive fields, here demographic statistics, but also to deductive methods such as political economy and hybrid approaches such as those of the utilitarians, all of whom relied upon impersonal generalizations as warrants for social policy.[22]

In addition to these methodological objections, there were also pressing ideological reasons to question the hegemonic transparency of numerical facts and the emerging disciplines that mobilized them.[23] Both political economy and utilitarianism were susceptible to charges that they lacked sympathy and relied upon dehumanizing models of individual agency: political economy had abandoned Adam Smith's providentialism in favor of simple economic self-interest, whereas first-generation utilitarians conceived of human happiness as mere physical gratification.[24] Hence, when they collaborated to enact social change – such as the New Poor Law, authored by Benthamite radicals Edwick Chadwick and Nassau Senior, grounded in political economists Thomas Malthus's theory of population and David Ricardo's "iron law of wages," and ultimately providing for the incarceration and statistical observation of those found pathological as a result of poverty – they could be accused of being "morally deficient, callously indifferent to the suffering of both the poor and all of those who might be affected by the implementation of the policies they advocated."[25] Also markedly indifferent to the circumstances of individuals, statistics additionally appeared to undermine the possibility of human agency altogether. Large sets of social data showed a distressing, even fatalistic, consistency in a wide range of human behavior, provoking both "a backlash of opposition to statistics and a critical analysis of the nature of statistical reasoning" and eventually inspiring "a wide-ranging revaluation of statistical thought during the late nineteenth century."[26] Finally, developing notions of individuals' right to privacy and the legal redefinition of reputation as property prompted resistance to government-sponsored efforts at data collection, such that those "who could afford to sought shelter from publicity, in the layout of their apartments or in colonizing the suburbs. The middle class protected themselves from view as best they could and strove to keep watch on the servants and the working class."[27] Thus, whether ideologically invested in the affective foundation of human relations, the philosophical necessity of human freedom, or the social and legal protection of privacy – all values affirmed by middle-class Victorians – one might well push back against those forms of "practical" knowledge that dealt in modern facts.

Among those with continued reservations about the claims to knowledge and related assertions of legitimacy made by advocates of political economy, utilitarianism, and statistics were Victorian novelists. Building upon the examples provided by earlier generations of writerly critics and offering more or less realistic fictional models of individual characters with diverse motivations struggling to understand and assert their own capacity for agency in order to achieve affective satisfaction within a complex and at times hostilely overdetermining society, novelists might be seen by their very vocation as inevitably in competition with their social scientific peers.[28] That political economy remained indifferent to imaginative literature, except insofar as it could, like Martineau's *Illustrations*, instruct readers about the far more important matters of wages, rent, production, trade, and the like; and that utilitarianism sometimes displayed outright hostility towards literary and artistic forms of creative representation, as neither rational nor productively contributing to "the greatest good for the greatest number"[29] – with the data from statistics playing a supporting role in both cases – made opposition between fictional and factual forms of social thought almost inevitable.[30]

Victorian Fictions of the Modern Fact

It would, perhaps, be too much to claim that every Victorian novel, by definition, stands opposed to the amalgamation of social thought and quantitative information that I am labeling "fact," but it is certainly the case that many novels of the period contain powerful critiques of the principles and data associated with political economy, utilitarianism, and statistics as bases for social legitimacy. Confining my choices only to the 1850s, the decade in which, according to Porter, the "notion of statistical law achieved its fullest expression in Great Britain,"[31] I shall briefly survey the strategies of resistance to the socially overdetermining power of fact in Charlotte Brontë's *Villette* (1853), Elizabeth Barrett Browning's *Aurora Leigh* (1856), and Anthony Trollope's *The Three Clerks* (1857), before turning to an extended reading of Charles Dickens's *Hard Times* (1854). Varied in style, structure, and both propositional and ideological content, these texts nevertheless offer a shared defense of imaginative writing as a superior mechanism for social analysis and a more legitimate source of social authority than any mere mastery of modern facts.

Set overwhelmingly in Quételet's home country of Belgium, contemptuously rechristened Labassecour [the barnyard] – whose capital city, Brussels, is similarly rendered diminutively as Villette [small town] and whose port city of Ostend appears unappealingly as Boue-marine [sea mud] – Charlotte Brontë's *Villette* ironically represents key components of social status that rely upon the legitimating authority of fact.[32] Whether motivated by Brontë's personally unsatisfying residences in the Pensionnat Heger in 1842 and 1843 or by a more systemic and strategic skepticism of primarily quantitative epistemes, the novel's numerous deflationary incidents can be organized into three broad repudiations of contemporary social scientific approaches. Although infrequent, the novel's depictions of *homo economicus* locate this central heuristic abstraction of political economy outside the pale of both English identity and moral and social acceptability. Thus, the morning after Lucy Snowe lands at Boue-marine, she finds herself at an inn where the waiters and chambermaids evince an uncanny "sagacity . . . in proportioning the accommodation to the guest," each needing only "a moment's calculation" to estimate her "at about the same fractional value" as determined by the relative lightness of her purse.[33] Similarly, once ensconced in the environs of Rue Fossette, Lucy meets and evaluates her fellow teachers, among whom is Mademoiselle St. Pierre, a "prodigal and profligate" Parisienne, "always in debt," and a "cold, callous epicure . . . in all things."[34] In both instances, characters who relate to others on an exclusively pecuniary basis appear interpersonally unappealing and distinctly, pejoratively foreign.

Much more numerous, if never entirely consistent, are instances of Brontë's repeated undermining of "happy," "happiness," and other cognates of the essential metric in utilitarian social prescriptions. Having confessed to Doctor John about her encounter with the ghostly nun, which he believes a "spectral illusion," Lucy is advised to cultivate happiness.[35] She responds acerbically, "What does such advice mean? Happiness is not a potato, to be planted in mould, and tilled with manure."[36] She continues, defining happiness in spiritual terms every bit as much at odds with utilitarian thought as her initial agricultural metaphor: "Happiness is a glory shining far down upon us out of Heaven. She is a divine dew which the soul, on certain of its summer mornings, feels dropping upon it from the amaranth bloom and golden fruitage of Paradise."[37] Somewhat later, Lucy reflects upon the psychological, as opposed to the material basis of happiness, comparing her mental privation at the dearth of correspondence from the Brettons to that of a prisoner who loses their sanity through being held in solitary confinement and dismissing those who think "that physical privations alone merit compassion, and that the rest is a figment."[38] These examples, representative rather than exhaustive, find simplistic and materialistic notions of happiness insufficient to explain the more complex and socially demanding circumstances of even one individual's experience.

Among the complications of Lucy's experience while a resident teacher at the Rue Fossette is being subject to what she terms a "very un-English" system of constant surveillance.[39] Principally "ruled by espionage" with the aid of a "staff of spies," Madame Beck's "strange house, where no corner was sacred from intrusion," evokes the constant state of social observation imagined by contemporary medical mappers, census takers, and professional statisticians.[40] Lucy judges that "keeping girls . . . under a surveillance that left them no moment and no corner for retirement, was not the best way to make them grow up honest and modest women," and that such a comprehensive system of panoptical control risks endowing the observer with "a suspicious nature . . . misled by its own invention," and thus implicitly passes judgment on the most ambitious data collection plans of social statists such as Quételet.[41] She also enjoys her own power to frustrate Madame Beck's designs, feeling a "secret glee" in detecting her employer's attempts to observe her unseen and taking the extraordinary step of hermetically sealing her few letters in a jar which she buries beneath "Methusaleh," the pensionnat garden's venerable pear tree.[42] As narrator, the elder Lucy even self-consciously frustrates readers' efforts to see too much in her story, purposefully hiding the fact that Doctor John is John Graham Bretton, son of her godmother, despite having, as a character, discovered this fact "several chapters back."[43] She similarly delays revealing that Mademoiselle de Bassompierre is their temporary childhood companion Little Polly, and, most famously, she refuses to confirm Monsieur Paul Emanuel's fate at the end of the novel, condescendingly telling readers to "picture union and happy succeeding life" when, in all likelihood, he has drowned.[44] *Villette* thus builds into its very narrative the resistance to excessive observation that Lucy enacts within it, and in so doing mirrors the reactions of many middle-class Victorians to contemporary social scientists who refused to confine their desire for social data to the working classes and other pathological groups.

Although not strictly a novel – instead "a sort of novel-poem," according to its creator[45] – Elizabeth Barrett Browning's *Aurora Leigh* nevertheless mounts a highly novelistic critique of quantitative abstraction and forms of fact with a basis in utilitarianism, statistics, and schematic programs of social engineering. The text repudiates almost immediately the narrow and gendered definitions of usefulness which serve as curricular principles for Aurora's education in England. Aurora's paternal aunt "liked / a general insight into useful facts," and so directs her to learn impractical factoids invented by EBB for their parodic as opposed to pedagogic value.[46] Similarly, because her aunt "misliked women who are frivolous," Aurora receives sanitized instruction in "classic French / (Kept pure of Balzac and neologism)," "a little algebra, a little / of the mathematics," and an "extreme flounce" among "The circle of the sciences."[47] This critique of "use" matures into a rejection of utilitarianism itself, in particular of utilitarianism's dismissal of poets and other writers of imaginative literature as "virtuous liars, dreamers after dark, / Exaggerators of the sun and moon, / And soothsayers in a tea-cup."[48] Relabeling such writers, herself included, the "only speakers of essential truth, / Posed to relative, comparative, / And temporal truths," Aurora also dismisses narrowly utilitarian methods of reading.[49] Instead of "calculating profits, – so much help / By so much reading," which is "ungenerous," readers should "forget ourselves, and plunge / Soul-forward, headlong, into a book's profound" in order to "get the right good from a book."[50] Aurora, and by extension EBB, advocates for a primarily affectual, rather than transactional or quantitatively rational, heuristic, one well suited not just for *Aurora Leigh* but also for much mid-century fiction.

Aurora is beset while growing up not just by her aunt but also by her cousin, Romney Leigh. In addition to serving as her occasional philanthropic antagonist and ultimate love interest, Romney brings Aurora into contact with "mere statistics," initially glossed as the "count of all / The goats whose beards are sprouting down toward hell."[51] Motivated by "the long sum of ill" compiled in the period's many statistical reports to try to ameliorate "general suffering," Romney admonishes Aurora for her, in his view, frivolous authorial ambitions and lack of abstract sympathy.[52] Since Aurora "'could as soon weep for the rule of three / Or compound fractions,'" Romney tells her, "'this same world / Uncomprehended by you must remain / Uninfluenced by you.'"[53] Aurora repudiates his quantitative vision of humanity on several levels, not the least of which is the way that an immersion in statistics can leave one blind to more immediate circumstances:

> You bid a hungry child be satisfied
> With a heritage of many corn-fields: nay,
> He says he's hungry, – he would rather have
> That little barley-cake you keep from him
> While reckoning up his harvests. So with us;[54]

Here, touching the same highly affective chord as "The Cry of the Children" (1843), EBB appeals to readers' emotions through the image of a suffering child, juxtaposing abstract satisfaction with the present – in this case the national production of grain, in the earlier poem the productivity of largely unregulated factories and mines – and concrete evidence of immediate want by an undernourished minor – in this passage a nameless and still-living boy, previously the already dead "little Alice" and her soon-to-follow fellow child-laborers.

Not merely a believer in statistics, Romney is also initially committed to the reorganization of society along the lines suggested by early French social theorists, most prominently Charles Fourier.[55] In fact, he transforms his ancestral property, Leigh Hall, into a phalanstery, only to have it burned to the ground and himself blinded during the fire. It is a measure of Romney's transformation as a character that, after reading Aurora's book (roughly the first four and a half books of *Aurora Leigh* itself), he approvingly recites her much earlier critique of his favorite socialists:

> "It takes a soul,
> To move a body: it takes a high-souled man,
> To move the masses, even to a cleaner stye:
> It takes the ideal, to blow a hair's-breadth off
> The dust of the actual. – Ah, your Fouriers failed,
> Because not poets enough to understand
> That life develops from within."[56]

Having accepted Aurora's premise, that "'poets get directlier at the soul, / Than any of your oeconomists,'" Romney, himself, calls for "'Less mapping out of masses to be saved, / By nations or by sexes. Fourier's void, / And Comte absurd, – and Cabet, puerile.'"[57] *Aurora Leigh* thus dramatizes the power of its own internal synecdoche to repudiate the authority of modern facts, as represented by utility, statistics, and social system-building.

Despite an early, explicit, and decidedly ironic reference to statistics, Anthony Trollope's *The Three Clerks* does not advance the same sort of broad critique of intellectual movements and quantitative disciplines as *Villette* or *Aurora Leigh*.[58] Instead, the novel focuses its disapprobation on a more specific symptom of the mid-Victorian fascination with fact, the introduction of competitive examinations into the Civil Service's process of employment and promotion.[59] Inspired by changes in the Indian Civil Service, which had finally shifted to making appointments based upon the results of competition rather than nomination in 1853, the domestic service's examination system received its warrant from the Northcote-Trevelyan Report of 1854. The Report's authors were Sir Stafford Northcote, former private secretary to William Ewart Gladstone and legal secretary to the Board of Trade, and Charles Edward Trevelyan, veteran of the Indian Civil Service and longtime assistant secretary to the Treasury, with a prefatory letter provided by Benjamin Jowett, who was a commissioner in the Indian Civil Service and a leader in the contemporary process of university reform from Balliol College, Oxford. All three men appear in caricature in *The Three Clerks*: Northcote as Sir Gregory Hardlines, the "insatiable" chief-clerk of Weights and Measures, who "generally succeeded in making every candidate conceive the very lowest opinion of himself and his own capacities before the examination was over"; Trevelyan as Sir Warwick Westend, "a man born to grace, if not his country, at any rate his county; and his conduct was uniformly such as to afford the liveliest satisfaction to his uncles, aunts, and relations in general"; and Jowett as Mr Jobbles, who "was enthusiastically intent on examining the whole adult male population of Great Britain, and had gone so far as to hint that female competitors might, at some future time, be made subject to his all-measuring rule and compass."[60] Between Sir Gregory's hardness, Sir Warwick's dimness, and Mr Jobbles's zealousness for ubiquitous standardization, the new system they devise is, unsurprisingly, entirely deserving of fictional scorn.

Two of Trollope's titular three clerks are tested under the new model of merit-based promotion after the ascension of Hardlines from chief-clerk to commissioner creates an opening in Weights and Measures.[61] Conceding that competitive examinations "at eighteen, twenty, and twenty-two may be very well, and give an interesting stimulus to young men at college," the narrator nevertheless judges them "a fearful thing for a married man with a family . . . to learn that he has again to go through his school tricks, and fill up examination papers, with all his juniors round him using their stoutest efforts to take his promised bread from out of his mouth."[62] The examination itself lasts four days and includes both written questions apparently designed to expose "the blank spots of [each candidate's] mind" and "a certain quantum of Mr Jobbles' *viva voce*."[63] The latter, described by the narrator as "torments," reveals the cruelly ludicrous obsession with quantification that informs the new regime:

> "The planet Jupiter . . . I have no doubt you know accurately the computed distance of that planet from the sun, and also that of our own planet. Could you tell me now, how would you calculate the distance in inches, say from London Bridge to the nearest portion of Jupiter's disc, at twelve o'clock on the first of April? . . . I am not asking the distance, you know," said Mr Jobbles, smiling sweeter than ever; "I am only asking how you would compute it."[64]

Here is a factoid worthy of Aurora's English education, now elevated to a determinant of whether or not a career civil servant is worthy of a new job and a raise. Ironically, the clerk found most deserving by the new system is Alaric Tudor, whose morally suspect obsession with numbers, especially those computed in pounds, leads him from financial speculation to fraudulent trust guardianship.[65]

After Alaric's misdeeds have been punished by a public trial, six months in Millbank prison, and emigration to Australia, Trollope suitably rewards the novel's remaining clerks, Henry Norman and Charley Tudor, with ascension to the landed gentry and a transfer to Weights and Measures, respectively, as well as marriage to the younger Woodward sisters. Charley's fortuitous reassignment then becomes the subject of a brief exchange in Parliament, with Mr Nogo objecting to the apparently preferential treatment that Charley has received. In Charley's defense, Mr Whip Virgil notes that his "'name was now respectably known in the lighter walks of literature,'" and that

> "he would, if permitted, read the opinion expressed as to his style of language by a literary publication of the day; and then the House would see whether or no the produce of the Civil Service field had not been properly winnowed; whether the wheat had not been garnered, and the chaff neglected." And then the right honourable gentleman read some half-dozen lines, highly eulogistic of Charley's first solitary flight.[66]

In other words, Charley's promotion is justified not by competitive examination but rather by literary exertion and is proven not by a commissioner but rather by a reviewer. Trollope thereby concludes his repudiation of fact with an endorsement of writing as a profession.

Recognizing Status in Charles Dickens's *Hard Times*

Conceived as a weekly serial by Charles Dickens at the behest of his publishers, Bradbury & Evans – who were concerned about the flagging sales of *Household Words* – *Hard Times* appeared in both serial and volume form one year after *Villette* and two and three years, respectively, in advance of *Aurora Leigh* and *The Three Clerks*.[67] Given the recent history of the Preston strike, discussed in the previous chapter, reviewers overwhelmingly expected "a story of overwork, small wages, poor food, and scanty clothing; and we took it up, rather expecting to meet with a tale of the Mary Barton school, and with some curiosity to see how even so experienced an author as Mr Dickens would meet Mrs Gaskell on her own ground."[68] Judged with such preconceptions in mind, the novel met with an equivocal response at best: *Blackwood's Edinburgh Magazine*, for instance, censured it as a "lamentable *non sequitur*"[69]; the writer for *The Critic*, full of praise for Dickens in general, found that "*Hard Times* has fewer beauties and more defects than any thing he has yet produced"[70]; John Forster's *Examiner* more positively declared "*Hard Times* reads admirably in a volume"[71]; and John Ruskin judged *Hard Times* "in several respects, the greatest" work written by Dickens, even as he acknowledged that it partakes of "the colour of caricature," "brilliant exaggeration," and "a circle of stage fire."[72]

Later academic critics have largely followed early reviewers' bias towards "condition-of-England" readings, beginning with F. R. Leavis, who in *The Great Tradition* focused subsequent decades of critical attention on a novelistic "intention [so] peculiarly insistent . . . that the representative significance of everything in the fable—character, episode, and so on—is immediately apparent as we read."[73] Read in these terms, however, the novel presents, as Welsh admits, a noticeable "lack of a coherent program for the improvement of either education or industrial relations."[74] This absence leaves critics interested in these topics either, like Robert Caserio, to concede Dickens's "reactionary political ideas" while investing them with greater complexity at the level of form or, along with Patrick

Brantlinger, to contest the dominance of such ideas by observing that the novel more ambivalently shows how "the factory owners, their allies, and also their opponents, all use political economy and 'tabular statements' to excuse their moral and legal failures."[75]

Regardless of specific approach, critics have generally come to agree that *Hard Times* manifests a number of interpretive problems. The first emerges out of expectations that the novel is primarily concerned with the condition of England question, to which it provides a response that many find insufficient. Even settling upon industrialization as the subject of the work presupposes that its structure permits a clear identification of the primary plot and its dominant character; however, as Welsh observes, "*Hard Times* is also a multi-plot novel, and it is not easy to locate the affective center or to name with confidence the protagonist."[76] This difficulty is magnified by the apparently unfinished or schematic quality of many of the characters, who seem to be caricatures rather than realistic individuals.[77] Although praised by the otherwise critical reviewer in *Blackwood's* as "beautifully sketched," Stephen Blackpool has been found by subsequent critics as particularly wanting in depth.[78] All of these problems converge in critical responses to the circus, in that Sleary and company as embodiments of the universal panacea, Fancy, while perhaps amusing, hardly offer a credible alternative to the factory system and the hard-fact school.

Although complicit in expectantly limiting *Hard Times* to "a story, certainly sad—perhaps tragical—but true, of the unfortunate relationship between masters and men which produced the strike of Preston," the *Blackwood's* reviewer, in broader comments about Dickens, does suggest an alternative and largely unexplored perspective from which to interpret the novel.[79] Dickens, the reviewer writes, is "perhaps more distinctly than any other author of the time, a *class* writer, the historian and representative of one circle in the many ranks of our social scale. Despite their descents into the lowest class, and their occasional flights into the less familiar ground of fashion, it is the air and the breath of middle-class respectability which fills the books of Mr Dickens."[80] While he uses the word "class," the reviewer's emphasis on characterological traits – not just "respectability," but later " intelligent, sensible, warm-hearted" – and his definitional vagueness about this "circle of society" that "in itself is a realm of infinite gradation" with "perhaps a different meaning in the lips of every individual who says the words," suggests that what differentiates "the wide middle ground" from "the rich and the poor" is not reducible to economics but instead comprehends a whole set of social behaviors and collective practices.[81] What he means, in other words, is not just "class" but also "status."

Applying this observation to *Hard Times* itself provides a compelling response to the interpretive problems outlined above. If the novel is primarily interested in the fine distinctions of middle-class status, then it need not be found wanting for failing to resolve the condition of England question. This shift in theme from industrialization to status also renders *Hard Times*, unambiguously, Thomas Gradgrind, senior's story. Retired from the "wholesale hardware trade" and "now looking about for a suitable opportunity of making an arithmetic figure in Parliament," Gradgrind possesses both the commercial background and the authoritative aspirations of an amorphous middle eager to assert its public status.[82] Moreover, if the characters in the novel, including the unfortunate Stephen Blackpool, are intended to represent individual facets of a highly differentiated status system, then concerns about their verisimilitude seem misdirected; as in Hogarth's classic *Industry and Idleness* (1747) or Thackeray's more recent *The Book of Snobs* (1848), caricature might be more appropriate to Dickens's method.[83] Finally, refocusing attention on the novel in this way sheds an entirely new light on the itinerant Sleary and his horse riders: they do not offer a way of life or locus of value diametrically opposed to Coketown, but instead provide the necessary approbation of Gradgrind's successful practice of his middle-class status.

At the beginning of the novel, Gradgrind asserts, quite famously, that his status rests in "'facts. Facts alone are wanted in life. Plant nothing else, and root out everything else'" (7). By the end of *Hard Times*, Dickens has done him one better, unearthing birth, wealth, force, and finally fact itself, by identifying each possible warrant for public domination with one or more representative characters, whose respective loss of status before the end of the narrative then undermines his or her associated warrant. Their systematic repudiation leaves, in Mrs Gradgrind's dying words, "'something—not an Ology at all—that [Gradgrind] has missed, or forgotten'" (149). This figure "of wonderful no-meaning," I argue, is middle-class status, which is provocatively constructed by Dickens on the basis of a series of categorical negations unaccompanied by substitutions announced via patterns of consumption, and which therefore can be confirmed only through its recognition from those in a position to be dominated (150).

"Those are the antecedents, and the culmination"[84]

As already discussed in Chapter 1, consanguinity and longevity were perennial weak points in the aspirations for status made by middle-class Victorians; *Hard Times* reminds readers of a number of period-appropriate strategies for eliding this problem of birth. Most succinctly, Dickens's narrator dismisses the manufacturing of noble pedigrees, such as those conjured up by Baptist Hatton in Benjamin Disraeli's *Sybil* (1845) or resold in the secondary soul markets of North's *The City of the Jugglers*, as a "mean claim (there is no meaner)" (194). Emulation also merits just enough pejorative attention to appear in the behavior of the nameless "many of the Gradgrind school" who "liked fine gentlemen; they pretended that they did not, but they did. They became exhausted in imitation of them; and they yaw-yawed in their speech like them; and they served out, with an enervated air, the little, mouldy rations of political economy, on which they regaled their disciples" (95). Public association by members of the middle classes with their gentler counterparts is treated at greater length and by means of specific personalities. When not fatiguing themselves by impersonation, members of the Gradgrind party "went about recruiting; and where could they enlist recruits more hopefully, than among the fine gentlemen who, having found out everything to be worth nothing, were equally ready for anything" (95). Thus arrives in Coketown that younger son of "a good family and better appearance," that "handsome dog who can make you a devilish fine speech," that "thorough gentleman, made to the model of the time; weary of everything, and putting no more faith in anything than Lucifer," Mr James Harthouse (96, 97, 91–2). And the nouveau-riche Josiah Bounderby cements his sense of himself as a "Conqueror" by keeping at a cost of "a hundred a year" his own "captive Princess," Mrs Sparsit, whose claims to gentility arise from her consanguineous connection to the Scadgerses and her union by marriage to the Powlers (37). Both Harthouse and Sparsit, then, signify in their persons birth in service to middle-class status.

For his part, Harthouse also represents a significant threat to his middle-class patrons, not through any active malice but rather through an amoral and at times uncomfortably familiar "smoothness so perfectly diabolical" (172). A lifetime of cultivated boredom has led him to a "conviction that indifference was the genuine highbreeding (the only conviction he had)" (170). This conviction allows Harthouse both to understand perfectly the impetus to rob banks – "'fellows who go in for Banks must take the consequences,'" he tells the Bounderbys, "'If there were no consequences, we should all go in for Banks'" (139) – and to repudiate the wonder of friendship as readily as any utilitarian, since "it was as much against the precepts of his school to wonder, as it was against the doctrines of the Gradgrind College" (133). Dissuaded by statute and unfettered by friendship, Harthouse, without "any earnest wickedness of purpose in him," begins to go in not for a bank, but for a banker's wife, engaging in a slow seduction of Louisa that she escapes just short of consummation (135). "Publicly and privately, it were much better for the age in which he lived," the narrator judges, "that he and the legion of whom he was one were designedly bad, than indifferent and purposeless. It is the drifting icebergs setting with any current anywhere, that wreck the ships" (135). This mixing of biblical and maritime metaphors seems especially designed for Dickens's middle-class readers, who were both the motive force behind the nineteenth-century's evangelical revival and the commercial investors most likely to be interested in ships meeting with accidents at sea.

Harthouse himself is wrecked on the "ingenuousness," "fearlessness," "truthfulness," and "entire forgetfulness of herself" of Sissy Jupe (171). Managing to touch "the cavity where his heart should have been—in that nest of addled eggs, where the birds of heaven would have lived if they had not been whistled away," she accesses his capacity for shame by appealing to his pride in the status of birth (172). She begins their interview by wondering aloud "'what your honour as a gentleman binds you to do,'" raising a blush that makes evident the "blood" guaranteeing Harthouse's social position (172). Through a series of rhetorical maneuvers recently mapped with admirable precision by Victor Sage, Sissy uses Harthouse's care for his own reputation against him, ultimately forcing him to acknowledge himself "'James Harthouse a Great Pyramid of failure'" (174).[85] He agrees to leave Coketown, never to return. That he is so defeated by Sissy, who is "'[o]nly a poor girl—only a stroller,'" dramatically undercuts the value of gentle birth in the novel, thereby partially unhinging status from its most venerable source of legitimacy (174).[86]

Consumed by the same pride in "ancient stock" that betrays Harthouse in his final confrontation with Sissy, Mrs Sparsit reveals a slightly different, but no more appealing side of status supported by birth (36). Unable to afford the smooth indifference permitted by his financial independence, she cultivates instead a "self-laudatory . . . ladylike deportment" that permits her to maintain a sense of superiority to "the rude business aspect" of her domestic service at the bank (87). She directs her barely disguised passive-aggressive resentment upon Louisa – whom she persists in calling "Miss Gradgrind" even after the latter's marriage to Bounderby – participating vicariously in her emotional entrapment by Harthouse through jealous surveillance:

> Mrs Sparsit saw James Harthouse come and go; she heard of him here and there; she saw the changes of the face he had studied; she, too, remarked to a nicety how and when it clouded, how and when it cleared; she kept her black eyes wide open, with no touch of pity, with no touch of compunction, all absorbed in interest. In the interest of seeing her, ever drawing, with no hand to stay her, nearer and nearer to the bottom of this new Giants' Staircase. (153)

The key term in this passage, used twice in quick succession, is "interest," with its palimpsestic combination of active attention, shared participation, material investment, selfish advantage, and financial indemnity, whether for a legal injury or an outstanding debt. For all of her assumed superiority to her business surroundings, Mrs Sparsit has thoroughly absorbed the vocabulary that was prescribed for personal success and broader economic health by the self-appointed entrepreneurial heirs of Adam Smith.

Smith would likely find Mrs Sparsit's self-interest in the developing affair neither rational nor enlightened, but even he would be hard-pressed to fault her industry. In fact, her zealous pursuit of her own "gratified malice" towards Louisa leads to Mrs Sparsit's own loss of status, and through her, to the further diminution of gentle birth as a warrant for domination (158). Shadowing Louisa through the storm, both meteorological and emotional, of book two, chapter eleven, she sacrifices her ladylike deportment until reduced by woods and weather to the state of "an old park fence in a mouldy lane" (160). Having lost Louisa in the rain, she finds Bounderby in London, discloses the alleged infidelity, and attempts to salvage her dignity with an aristocratic faint. Instead, in the chapter that immediately follows Harthouse's humbling acquiescence to Sissy Jupe, Mrs Sparsit is grammatically reduced from subject to object through a series of transitive verbs, being shaken off upon the floor, unceremoniously "recovered" by means of violently "potent restoratives," "hustled" onto a train, "carried" back to Coketown, "crammed" into a coach, and born off to Stone Lodge (175). Reprising the language of interest with which he had described her several chapters earlier, Dickens writes, "Regarded as a classical ruin, Mrs Sparsit was an interesting spectacle on her arrival at her journey's end; but considered in any other light, the amount of damage she had by this time sustained was excessive, and impaired her claims to attention" (175). That her story will be discredited by Louisa's presence in her father's house is an almost unnecessary confirmation of Mrs Sparsit's, and by extension birth's, loss of legitimacy when presented before the novel's locus of aspiring middle-class status.

It is on the strength of a letter of introduction from Gradgrind that Harthouse gains entry into Josiah Bounderby's home and business. Already resident at both is Sparsit, who presides in "State humility" over the tea she serves at the former and jealously broods as "Bank Dragon . . . over the treasures of the mine" at the latter (40, 87). As Leavis was among the first to note, Bounderby's affiliations with these two aristocratic embellishments to his environs extend beyond a common setting to include a shared attitude; together, Leavis writes, they "form a trio that suggests the whole system of British snobbery" (247). Whereas Harthouse and Sparsit recursively remind others of the relative privilege due to them from their pedigrees, Bounderby elevates himself by proclaiming the most vociferous rejections in *Hard Times* of any sort of status grounded in gentle birth. His own myth of himself as an entirely self-made man without mother or father, with a childhood spent, first, in the chandler's shop of "the wickedest and the worst old woman that ever lived," his alcoholic grandmother, and, second, on the streets, "where everybody knocked [him] about and starved [him]," is only the most flagrant example of his efforts to exempt himself from the influence of family connections (18).[87]

That, rejecting filial antecedents, Bounderby still believes himself deserving of middle-class status becomes abundantly clear on his birthday. Waiting at Stone Lodge for the return of the family principals, he recites for Mrs Gradgrind a resume of his own meteoric rise from the gutter: "'Vagabond, errand-boy, vagabond, labourer, porter, clerk, chief manager, small partner, Josiah Bounderby of Coketown. Those are the antecedents, and the culmination'" (18). In the supposed absence of the advantages of birth, Bounderby's legitimacy rests primarily in the power of his wealth, a fact implied in the narrator's opening description of him as "a rich man: Banker, merchant, and what not," and confirmed by Mr Childers's admission to him soon after that "'if you mean that you can make more money out of your time than I can of mine, I should judge from your appearance, that you are about right'" (16, 28). At this early stage in the novel, at least, Bounderby's wealth-secured status is sufficient to impress even Gradgrind, who looks upon him "as if Mr Bounderby had been Mrs Grundy" (16).[88]

Bounderby certainly invites the comparison, dispensing self-aggrandizing and censorious opinions to all within earshot, whether they ask for them or not. Not everyone is convinced, of course – Louisa remains nonplussed by his "[c]heerless and comfortless, boastfully and doggedly rich" manner even after marriage, and the circus performers nearly "'pith [him] out o' winder" (97, 33) – but enough people endorse his authority that the narrator is brought to confide that it was "one of Bounderby's most exasperating attributes . . . that he not only sang his own praises but stimulated other men to sing them. There was a moral infection of clap-trap in him" (37). In fact, Bounderby's is not an idiosyncratic but rather a representative failing of those the novel represents as legitimizing their status through wealth. Among the "fictions of Coketown" is one articulated by any "capitalist there, who had made sixty thousand pounds out of sixpence," and who "always professed to wonder why the sixty thousand nearest Hands didn't each make sixty thousand pounds out of sixpence, and more or less reproached them every one for not accomplishing the little feat" (60). Bankruptcy does "sometimes happen in the best regulated families in Coketown," but even the failures of men like Nickits, "who, in his determination to make a shorter cut than usual to an enormous fortune, overspeculated himself by about two hundred thousand pounds," enrich Coketown's banker, who finds himself, "'like a maggot [got] into a nut,'" now in possession of that ultimate status symbol of wealth, a country estate (126–7).

Bounderby's only pecuniary loss in the novel is the one hundred and fifty pounds stolen from the bank; his loss of status before the end, however, is considerably greater, and occurs in two stages. First, his repudiation of the power of birth, in the form of the story he has told and has induced others to tell about his childhood depravations, is exposed as a lie before "the busiest of the neighbours to the number of some five-and-twenty" by his doting mother, Mrs Pegler (191). Filled with "impatient mortification" throughout the scene, Bounderby is at the end reduced to

> a blustering sheepishness . . . at once extremely crestfallen and superlatively absurd. Detected as the Bully of humility, who had built his windy reputation upon lies . . . he cut a most ridiculous figure. With the people filing off at the door he held, who he knew would carry what had passed to the whole town, to be given to the four winds, he could not have looked a Bully more shorn and forlorn, if he had had his ears cropped. (192, 194)

Crucially, Gradgrind stands among the five-and-twenty, and it is his interrogation of Mrs Pegler that publicizes the truth behind Bounderby's lies. Throughout the scene, as Bounderby swells "larger and larger . . . redder and redder," Gradgrind is "shocked by the possibility which dawned upon him" and ultimately feels himself "innocently placed in a very distressing predicament"; implicitly, the possibility he realizes is that his earlier innocent endorsement of Bounderby's wealth-legitimated claim to serve as Coketown's Mrs Grundy has been founded upon false deserts (192–3). Second, Bounderby's attempt to salvage his legacy by establishing another "windy reputation," built this time not upon the past but upon the future, also fails spectacularly. Seeking to justify his status post facto, Bounderby makes "a vain-glorious will" intended to memorialize himself through the perpetual maintenance of "five-and-twenty Humbugs, past five-and-fifty years of age" on his country estate, everything and everyone taking on the name of Bounderby "with a vast amount of Bounderby balderdash and bluster" (217). This scheme comes to naught, as he dies five years later, his "precious will" embarking on a "long career of quibble, plunder, false pretenses, vile example, little service and much law" (218). Soon to be consumed in Chancery, a process represented to such memorable effect in Dickens's just-completed *Bleak House*, Bounderby's wealth alone is thus represented by *Hard Times* as another insufficient warrant for establishing lasting middle-class legitimacy.

Shorn, forlorn, and victim of a fatal fit before the end of the novel, Bounderby is for most of the story appropriately caricatured as a "Bully," one who uses force to dominate others. Whether verbally stunning Mrs Gradgrind through "three sonorous repetitions of . . . pride in having at any time of his life achieved such a great social distinction as to be a nuisance," blasphemously swearing "by the Lord Harry" while badgering Stephen Blackpool about his fellow weavers' union, or discharging his "coarsely blurted . . . loud outbreaks . . . like a Rocket, at his father-in-law's head" during their confrontation over Louisa's alleged infidelity, Bounderby consistently relies upon bellicose forms of speech (18, 111, 176–9). When especially agitated – as he is in the last of the aforementioned examples – he escalates to physical violence, "screwing," "smiting," "knocking," and otherwise assaulting individuals and objects (175–6). As Blackpool recognizes during his unfortunate interview, this predisposition to force also guides Bounderby's and by extension the other Coketown employers' business practices. "'Look how you considers of us, and writes of us, and talks of us, and goes up wi' yor deputations to Secretaries o' State 'bout us,'" he enumerates, "'and how yo are awlus right, and how we are awlus wrong, and never had'n no reason in us sin ever we were born. Look how this ha' growen an' growen, Sir, bigger an' bigger, broader an' broader, harder an' harder, fro year to year, fro generation unto generation'" (113). Proving Blackpool's point about the deteriorating relations between "masters" and "hands" at the end of this chapter, Bounderby fires him for speaking the truth when commanded to do so.

Bounderby's fondness for the "strong hand" and his and the other "united masters" impulse towards collective action align them in surprising ways with what is surely the most significant long-term threat to middle-class aspirations to public authority in the Victorian period, the growing numerical and productive power of those closer to the bottom of the social scale (114, 88). The Preston strike to which critics so often allude in connection with *Hard Times* – and which did receive explicit attention in *Household Words* during the novel's serialization – was a single point on this increasingly visible line of domination legitimized by force. The most visible representative of this third, and for Dickens false, form of status is Slackbridge.

"An ill-made, high-shouldered man, with lowering brows, and his features crushed into an habitually sour expression," the union delegate exhibits little that is personally appealing (105).[89] However, it is the ugliness of his words that is most at issue in the novel, which painstakingly records Slackbridge's repeated descents from biblical diction to threats of violence. Thus, in his opening speech to Coketown's factory workers, he marries an allusion to "the God-created glorious rights of Humanity, and upon the holy and eternal privileges of Brotherhood" with a call to "crumble into dust" the factory owners (104-05). Similarly, in his public denunciation of Blackpool for refusing to join the union, Slackbridge, with "violent scorn" escalates in his name-calling from Esau to Judas to Castlereagh, thus progressing from one biblical figure who sold his family birthright to another whose betrayal enabled the crucifixion of Jesus to the historical politician associated with the violent repression of the Irish Rebellion of 1798 and the massacre at Peterloo in 1819. During Blackpool's subsequent address, he also expostulates with increasing violence, first shaking "his head as if he would shake it off," then "laugh[ing], fold[ing] his arms, and frown[ing] sarcastically," and finally jumping to his feet "gnashing and tearing" (107). At the end of the meeting, the physical, even militant, threat posed by his bombastic rhetoric is subtly highlighted when "Slackbridge acted as fugleman" to the crowd (109). Although some of those present at this and the later assembly of workers resist his excesses, "these were pygmies against an army; the general assemblage subscribed to the gospel according to Slackbridge, and gave three cheers for him, as he sat demonstrably panting at them" (183).

No dramatic comeuppance is needed to discredit Slackbridge as an individual; however, containing the democratic force that he represents cannot be accomplished solely on the grounds of his mouth-breathing. It is for this reason that the novel includes the pathetic character of Blackpool, whose quiescence in the face of repeated provocations and final lingering death promises that the numerical majority will be no threat to *Hard Times*'s middle-class readers. Thus, upbraided by Bounderby for inquiring about a divorce, he polishes the banker's "brazen full-stop" on his way out (61); trapped in his house by his alcoholic spouse, he promises Rachael, "'I nevermore will see or think o' anything that angers me, but thou, so much better than me, shalt be by th' side on't'" (70–1); about to be ostracized by his lifelong neighbors and coworkers, "not a grain of anger with them was in his heart" (108); and, finally, on the brink of death from his fall down the Old Hell Shaft, he counsels, "'But in our judgments, like as in our doins, we mun bear and forbear'" (201). As melodramatic, saccharine, even irritating as Blackpool's attitude and fate are for many readers and critics, they make perfect sense as elements within Dickens's dilution of force as a legitimate warrant for status.

With birth, wealth, and force discredited, all that remains is fact, "the one thing needful" according to the title of the opening chapter in the schoolroom and the focus of attention for the vast majority of the novel.[90] Every bit as topical as the Preston strike, the "tabular statements" and "blue books" alluded to with such frequency throughout *Hard Times* represent what Oz Frankel identifies as the nineteenth-century's new "*print* statism," itself a symptom of Poovey's broader epistemological unit of "the modern fact."[91] Carolyn Berman convincingly locates Dickens's novel specifically within the epistemological and rhetorical contexts established by mid-century Blue Books, with their combination of numerical tables and charts purporting to represent without distortion the modern facts of nineteenth-century life alongside pathos-inducing interviews and individual anecdotes.[92] Exposing the insufficiencies of fact, as contained in government-sponsored reports and as deployed by utilitarian reformers, occupies Dickens in his industrial, educational, and domestic subplots, and thus an entire crowd of characters contends to represent this final warrant for middle-class status. A much smaller number of characters links all three subplots together, with two in particular demonstrating to Gradgrind the full extent of the problem with entrusting public authority to those whose sole claim to legitimacy rests upon being "replete with facts" and "trained to mathematical exactness" (16). Both educated by having "imperial gallons of facts poured into them until they were full to the brim" and then apprenticed in different capacities within Bounderby's temple of wealth – where both witness Harthouse's performance of the indolent superiority of birth and later participate in the robbery investigation that authorizes Blackpool's second condemnation by the delegate of force – Bitzer and Tom Gradgrind, junior, together represent fact in its least edifying form in *Hard Times* (8).

The model pupil in M'Choakumchild's model schoolroom, Bitzer shows the consequences of the perfect realization of fact. His thorough schooling ensures that Bitzer remains as unphased as a child by Gradgrind's imperative to define a horse as he is later unimpressed by Harthouse's command of appearances: he wonders aloud to Mrs Sparsit whether fashionable dress is "'worth the money'" and finds Harthouse's likely gambling "'ridiculous . . . because the chances are against the players'" (94). He is also proof against the allure of wealth for its own sake, viewing his Christmas gratuity as merely an opportunity to "'put by a little'" (90). Even the prospect of the force derived from numerical preponderance only inspires Bitzer with factual schemes for advancing individual self-interest: "'As to their combining together; there are many of them, I have no doubt, that by watching and informing upon one another could earn a trifle now and then, whether in money or good will, and improve their livelihood. Then, why don't they improve it, ma'am! It's the first consideration of a rational creature, and it's what they pretend to want'" (90). Bitzer has so perfectly learned this foundational lesson of the school of fact that he has relieved himself of the need to care for his own mother by having her confined to Coketown's workhouse under the provisions of the 1834 Poor Law Amendment Act.[93]

Tom, by contrast, provides an example of the consequences of a perverse indoctrination into fact. Like Bitzer exercising himself "diligently in his calculations relative to number one," Tom is already two-thirds of the way along the professional trajectory enumerated earlier by Bounderby – he is clerk at the bank – by the time Harthouse arrives on the scene (71). Unlike Bitzer, Tom quickly falls under the spell of aggressive indifference cast by his new friend, to whom he later confesses that he games and loses prodigiously. Since moving out of his father's house, Tom has been, the narrator reveals, a slave to "groveling sensualities" brought on by his strict education in fact; these same propensities also lead him to pimp his sister to Bounderby, to brag about his accomplishment in the first evening of his acquaintance with Harthouse – who uses this confirmation of Louisa's one emotional vulnerability to lead her gradually down Sparsit's "mighty Staircase, with a dark pit of shame and ruin at the bottom" – and, ultimately, to rob the bank, framing Blackpool for the crime (101, 150). He is, the narrator judges, "a monster . . . a hypocrite . . . incapable at last of governing himself" (101).

Bitzer's perfect and Tom's perverse realizations of fact collide in book three, chapter eight, "Philosophical." Alerted by Sissy at the side of the Old Hell Shaft, Tom has fled to Sleary's circus, where he is absurdly separated from his former middle-class status. Sleary first hides Tom in plain sight, as "one o' them black thervanth" in a Jack the Giant killer routine (207). Denied even the role of the thieving English boy, Tom descends a bit further down the status scale, to similitude with a "monkey" and at last to a "deplorable object," once he justifies his actions to his father by an appeal to the apparently overdetermining force of statistics: "'So many people are employed in situations of trust; so many people out of so many, will be dishonest. I have heard you talk, a hundred times, of its being a law. How can *I* help laws?'" (209). Bathed afterwards by Sleary in beer, Tom is at last redressed as a "Jothkin," a country bumkin with no middle-class status whatsoever for his final flight from Liverpool abroad. At this moment, Bitzer appears to arrest Tom, "his colourless face more colourless than ever, as if he ran himself into a white heat" that provides a pointed contrast to Tom's recent status as a "comic blackamoor" (210, 209). Just as Tom had cited the facts of his education to rationalize his dishonesty, Bitzer now recites the "catechism" of "self-interest" that he learned at Gradgrind's school, which lesson thoroughly absorbed makes him inaccessible to any definition of his heart that exceeds "the facts related by Harvey relating to the circulation of the blood" (211). That Bitzer's goal of watching and informing upon Tom in exchange for a trifle to improve his own livelihood is frustrated in part by a horse whose reality exceeds any narrowly factual definitions only further proves the insufficiencies of his education. In this climactic scene, therefore, Gradgrind is presented with the extreme ends of a continuum predicated upon fact. In Tom's case, fact has led to vagabondage, whereas for Bitzer fact has resulted in a pale imitation of humanity. In both cases, fact has proven a poor warrant for middle-class status.

"Mere fables . . ."[94]

All of which leaves Gradgrind at the end of *Hard Times* in the somewhat incongruous position of having witnessed the systematic diminution of some of the most significant forms of legitimacy supporting the exercise of middle-class domination. That he nevertheless retains his own right to an especially empowered version of public authority is clear from his continued possession, into a point of "futurity" distant enough to age him into "a white-haired decrepit man," of his seat as Coketown's MP (218). Given the ritualized brutality of contested elections, during which Gradgrind's position as the father of a bank robber would surely be raised, his lingering status among his own constituents would have to be considerable to allow him to overcome his own familial baggage.[95] We as readers are never in a position to see what the voters of Coketown value in their representative, but we are witness to two extended scenes in which Gradgrind's legitimacy is confirmed through public recognition. During both of the chapters in which he interacts at length with the members of Sleary's Horse-riding, Gradgrind is evaluated and ultimately approved by its itinerant members once he explicitly distances himself from the more conventional warrants of middle-class status.

In book one, chapter six, "Sleary's Horsemanship," Gradgrind and Bounderby walk to the Pegasus's Arms public house with the express purpose of expelling Sissy from the model school. Placed immediately in conversation with Childers and Kidderminster, Bounderby repeatedly asserts his status on the basis of his wealth, "rattling his money and laughing" (30). Far from impressed, Childers quickly alters his address from "'gentlemen,'" inclusive of both, to "'Sir,'" directed exclusively thereafter at Gradgrind (28). Insulting and then "feigning unconsciousness of Mr Bounderby's existence," Childers seeks "to conciliate" Gradgrind, whom readers know, courtesy of the narrative's focalization, he sees as a "gentleman" (31). Once the entire company of performers arrives and Sissy returns, Bounderby even more egregiously insults them by his command of "plain Fact" (33). Rejecting both the advice and the example of his friend, Gradgrind offers Sissy a place in his home and at his school, prompting Sleary to forgive him even past efforts "'that keepth a prethiouth thight of money out of the houthe'" and to address him consistently as "'Thquire'" (35).

Much later, in the final confrontation with Bitzer, Sleary witnesses Gradgrind's repudiation of fact as he pleads ineffectually for Tom's freedom; in response, the circus master arranges an elaborate escape act, complete with horse, dog, and pony show. Offered "a handsome remuneration in money," Sleary suggests instead a more personal set of gifts – in election parlance, treats – for the members of his company, who perform in this instance the role of Gradgrind's loyal constituents (213). After lunch, Sleary recognizes Gradgrind's status more personally by taking him into his confidence about the reappearance of the now-dead Jupe's dog, Merrylegs, and about the insufficiency of "'Thelf-interetht'" to explain either canine or human conduct (215). They part with a handshake, one of the most basic forms of acknowledgment and a staple of the election canvass.

The need of a character like Gradgrind for the endorsement of a social outsider like Sleary helps to explain why the *Blackwood's* reviewer quoted earlier remains so imprecise in his definition of the social circle represented in Dickens's fiction. As depicted in *Hard Times*, at least, middle-class status cannot be known by those claim it, but only acknowledged after the fact by others who do not aspire to it themselves. Extending this fictional logic to the fiction in which it appears, we can see that what was at stake in the serialization of the novel, then, was not merely the sales figures for *Household Words*, but rather Dickens's own legitimacy as a unique weekly purveyor of information, opinion, and public authority. That his readers voted, as it were, with their expanded purchase of the magazine, implies both that they were willing to confirm the Inimitable's status and that the epistemologically unstable nature of middle-class status may best serve those accustomed to deal, not in "the howling ocean of tabular statements" but in "mere fables about men and women" (42).[96]

Notes

1. Both Blackwood and Eliot's more liberal friend, Frederick Harrison, who had advised her about the legal details of the Transome inheritance, commented upon the diverse readership obtained by *Felix Holt, the Radical*, with Blackwood assuring Eliot that the novel's "politics are excellent and will attract all parties" and Harrison writing that "each party and school are determined to see their own side in it . . . all quite convinced that it has been conceived from their own point of view" (Blackwood to Eliot, 26 April 1866; Harrison to Eliot, 19 July 1866; both reprinted in vol. 4 of *The George Eliot Letters*, 247, 285). Whether the novel's politics should be conflated with the rather less nuanced conservatism of the "Address" has been questioned by

both Hilda Hollis, "Felix Holt: Independent Spokesman or Eliot's Mouthpiece?," who judges that without the *Blackwood's* piece, "the absolute identification of an author and her character would be seen as naïve" (158); and Helen Kingstone, "The Two Felixes," who agrees that "Eliot's stance on reform in *Felix Holt*, so often equated with Matthew Arnold's, has been oversimplified due to a questionable elision of the author with her eponymous hero, and of two distinct embodiments of 'Felix Holt' in two different publications" (42).
2. Eliot finally agreed to write the "Address" in a letter to John Blackwood dated 9 November 1867 – "Felix Holt is immensely tempted by your suggestions, but George Eliot is severely admonished by his domestic critic not to scatter his energies" – and recorded in her journal that she had begun the piece on 22 November and sent it off on 4 December, and replied to Blackwood's final payment for and approval of the revised text in a letter dated 30 December: "I am much obliged to you for your handsome cheque, and still more gratified that the 'Address' has been a satisfaction to you" (both letters appear in vol. 4 of *The George Eliot Letters*, 397, 412; Eliot's journal entries may be found on p. 131 of *The Journals of George Eliot*).
3. [George Eliot], "Address to Working Men, by Felix Holt," 6. As Scott Thompson explains, the "popular analogy" comparing "society to a living organism" was "employed by Spencer and others—most notably, Comte—as a way of conceptualizing the interdependence of society"; reversing course somewhat from Spencer, however, who "views 'individual desires' as a positive driving force behind the success of the living social body, Eliot considers what happens to the 'delicate dependence' of the organism when the body becomes diseased; if one part of the body goes wrong, the entire organism feels the effects" (142).
4. [Eliot], "Address," 1, 5.
5. Ibid. 7. That, even in possession of these desiderata, "the aristocratic and mercantile classes" presumably reading *Blackwood's* have allowed the social body to become infected by their own sharp practices, remains implied but never stated (1).
6. Ibid. 8.
7. Ibid. 11.
8. "Numerical representation," Poovey writes, "is particularly central to" *A History of the Modern Fact*,

> because, once they were purged of the last vestiges of supernaturalism, numbers came to epitomize the peculiarity written into the modern fact. On the one hand, as signs of (what looks like or passes as) counting, numbers seem to be simple descriptors of phenomenological particulars, and because the mathematical manipulation of numbers is governed by a set of invariable rules, numbers seem to resist the biases that many people associate with conjecture or theory. On the other hand, however, because numbers also constitute the units of a system of knowledge production that is biased toward deduction – that is,

mathematics – numbers inevitably carry within them the traces of a certain kind of systematic knowledge: to assign numbers to observed particulars is to make them amenable to the kind of knowledge system that privileges quantity over quality and equivalence over difference. (4)

9. According to Lawrence Goldman, the "real bond" of the early leaders of the statistic movement at Cambridge "came from an intellectual contempt for the method of Ricardian economics as it was developed in the 1820s and 1830s and a related desire to base economic and social analysis on inductive procedures" (594).
10. Theodore M. Porter, *The Rise of Statistical Thinking 1820–1900*, 27. Flint similarly observes that statistical figures "both derived their authority from, and helped to underpin, the theories of political economy, which allowed impersonal market forces, rather than considerations of human compassion, to determine the direction of commercial development" (3).
11. "Crime rates, birth rates, suicide rates," writes Stephen Stigler in his *History of Statistics*, presented "such an appearance of stability in large numbers over time that even the existence of free will seemed to be called into question" (172).
12. Porter 11, original emphasis; Joseph W. Childers, "Industrial Culture and the Victorian Novel," 77.
13. This list is necessarily selective, since, as Alexander Welsh notes in passing, by "1854 as many as sixteen new departments of government were empowered to inspect and report on local government and private institutions" (*George Eliot and Blackmail*, 66).
14. Welsh, *George Eliot and Blackmail*, 41. The most elementary indication of this triumph of the Modern Fact was that "numerical information (eventually) became the British government's preferred mode of knowledge" (Poovey, *History*, 5).
15. Betensky, 26.
16. [John Robertson], "Exclusion of Opinions," 45.
17. Ibid. 69. Poovey discusses Robertson's article at greater length on pp. 315–6 of *History*.
18. Betensky, 27. Additionally, it "can be argued that most inductive sciences advance rapidly through observation of something 'wrong' in the field of view" (Welsh, *George Eliot and Blackmail*, 35).
19. As social investigation was integrated into Britain's imperial enterprise, sometimes under the guise of ethnology, the same forms of measurement that had been applied to England's poor were increasingly turned onto colonized subjects. Middle-class resistance to sociological measurement stemmed, with greater frequency as the century progressed, from a desire to maintain racial distinctions that were integral to the administration of the Empire.
20. Pamela K. Gilbert, *Mapping the Victorian Social Body*, xii, xvii.
21. On the exchange between Quételet and Keverberg, alternatively spelled Koverberg, see Stephen M. Stigler, *The History of Statistics*, 163–9.

The mathematics necessary to resolve the complexities of statistical sampling would not be developed until the 1880s, through the combined efforts of Francis Galton, Francis Ysidro Edgeworth, and Karl Pearson. On this late-century revolution in statistical methods, see Stigler, 265–362; and Porter, 255–314.

22. As Flint remarks, "Figures rendered hardship more tangible. Moreover, they both derived their authority from, and helped to underpin, the theories of political economy, which allowed impersonal market forces, rather than considerations of human compassion, to determine the direction of commercial development" (3).

23. Quételet's 1835 invention of the figure of the "average man," initially a methodological innovation designed to embody the mean values of those physical characteristics collected from individual army recruits, regional laborers, or other discrete constituencies, became over time a point of ideological opposition by those who demurred at Quételet's readiness to perform "moral measurements" as well. On resistance to the "average man," see Stigler, 171.

24. "Paradoxically, again, one of the complaints directed against political economy in the nineteenth century was not that it was insufficiently systematic, or even that its system had no grounds, but that once the science of wealth abandoned its providential foundation it had no basis for authority beyond the self-interest of its practitioners (or those the political economist served)" (Poovey, *History*, 236).

25. Gary F. Langer, *The Coming of Age of Political Economy, 1815–1825*, 85.

26. Porter, 8, 149. On the deterministic implications of social statistics, see also Stigler, 172.

27. Welsh, *George Eliot and Blackmail*, 75. Observing that from "the individual perspective, quantification itself is often a threat, and at some point the progress of the one and not the many ought to be defended," Welsh identifies

> three conditions of society that affected individuals directly and indirectly intensified the need for privacy or secrecy, and these conditions are interrelated: a self-regulating economy; social mobility and choice of occupation; and representative government. Each depends on the rise of knowledge and communication and partakes of that liberated condition that in turn enforces a new sense of accountability; each contributed to a weakening of the sense of community. (*George Eliot and Blackmail*, 58–9, 72)

Flint also documents reactions against government Blue Books and statistical knowledge more broadly, especially in the 1850s (3–4).

28. Among the earlier critics of political economy and utilitarianism, including a majority of imaginative writers, Langer lists Coleridge, Cobbett, Southey, and Peacock, as well as the stable of writers at *Blackwood's*, Wordsworth, Byron, "Alexander Baring, the parliamentary leader of

the commercial interest, and the so-called Birmingham School, led by Thomas Attwood" (84; see also 14–15).
29. As Brantlinger writes, succinctly, "There is no lack of evidence of utilitarian hostility to imaginative literature" (*Spirit*, 24).
30. In his sweeping account of *The Social Novel in England*, Cazamian describes a collision in the 1830s through 1850s between idealism, "a general awakening of practiced and moral activity" (3) with a renewed value in "sensation and emotion" (4), and what he calls individualism, an approach to the social informed by utilitarian thought and political economy, which was "as cold-blooded as it was abstract" (6). Aligning idealism with the social novel and individualism with the nascent social sciences, he summarizes their mutual antipathy as "human sensitivity opposing social rationalism" (6).
31. Porter, 57.
32. It is worth noting that Charlotte Brontë's repudiation of conventional warrants for social status extends beyond simply fact. In chapter 27, Lucy describes Ginevra Fanshawe's "incapacity to conceive how any person not bolstered up by birth or wealth, not supported by some consciousness of name or connection, could maintain an attitude of reasonable integrity." That she characterizes Ginevra's position as one of "obstinate credulity" makes clear Lucy's feelings about birth and wealth; and although she concedes that the "World . . . held a different estimate," she nevertheless asserts, "I am not quite wrong in mine" (*Villette*, 385).
33. Brontë, *Villette*, 72–3. Lucy's reception at Boue-marine contrasts with her recent treatment at the London hotel once frequented by her two uncles. Once fully rested, Lucy establishes this admittedly slim familial connection with the hotel waiter, who adopts a "ready and obliging courtesy" despite her obviously meagre economic resources (58).
34. Ibid. 156–7.
35. Ibid. 312.
36. Ibid. 313. This passage provides a point of entry for Karen Chase Levenson's broader consideration of mid-Victorian novelists' reimagining of happiness as "plot and not, or just, conclusion" ("'Happiness is not a potato,'" 168).
37. Brontë, *Villette*, 313.
38. Ibid. 342.
39. Ibid. 85. The foreignness of Madame Beck's constant surveillance is raised repeatedly: after witnessing the first search of her possessions, Lucy pronounces Labassecour "a foreign land" (85); Madame Beck confides to Lucy "that ruinous consequences would ensue if any other method were tried with continental children" (89); much later, she also exempts Lucy from further observation because of "quelquechose de bien remarquable dans la caractère Anglais" [something very remarkable in English character] (366).

40. Ibid. 90, 90, 290.
41. Ibid. 89, 146.
42. Ibid. 145, 369.
43. Ibid. 219.
44. Ibid. 617.
45. This hyphenated label was applied by EBB to the manuscript that would become *Aurora Leigh* in a letter to Robert Browning dated February 27, 1845. It appears in *The Letters of Robert Browning and Elizabeth Barrett Browning 1845–1846*, I.32, and is reproduced in the Norton Critical Edition of *Aurora Leigh*, 330.
46. Elizabeth Barrett Browning, *Aurora Leigh*, I.413–4.
47. Ibid. I.400–6. Aurora's education in England by her aunt, which she compares to "water torture" (I.468), contrasts with her earlier instruction in Italy by her father, who "taught me what he had learned the best / Before he died and left me, – grief and love" as well "out of books / He taught me all the ignorance of men" (I.185–6, I.189–90). Aurora eventually rediscovers her father's collection of "Books, books, books!" while living with her aunt and so enlarges her education on her own (I.832).
48. Ibid. I.856–8.
49. Ibid. I.860–2.
50. Ibid. I.702–9.
51. Ibid. I.525–7.
52. Ibid. II.309, II.199.
53. Ibid. II.217–20.
54. Ibid. V.481–5.
55. As enumerated by Lady Waldemar, Romney's other intellectual principals are "Proudhon, Considerant, and Louis Blanc, . . . (with a place for Sue)," all of whom she says she "'quotes from . . . prettily enough / Perhaps, to make them sound half rational / To a saner man than'" Romney when she pursues him for a husband (III.583–96).
56. Ibid. II.479–85 and VIII.430–6.
57. Ibid. VII.540–1, IX.865–9.
58. Introducing the reader to the Civil Service department of Weights and Measures, Trollope facetiously refers to the "noise of battle booming" around the "paramount . . . question of the decimal coinage," a subject of special concern to the secretary and his subordinates:

> Then what statistical work of the present age has shown half the erudition contained in that essay lately published by the secretary on 'The Market Price of Coined Metals'? What other living man could have compiled that chronological table which is appended to it, showing the comparative value of the metallic currency for the last three hundred years? Compile it indeed! What other secretary or assistant-secretary belonging to any public office of the present day, could even read it and live? (*The Three Clerks*, 2)

59. In his introduction to *The Three Clerks*, N. John Hall refers to the competitive examination system as Trollope's "*bête noire*" (ix). That he remained sore on the subject for years is evident from the opening chapter of *The Bertrams* (1859), "Vae Victis" – translated by that later novel's editor, David Skilton, as "Woe to the vanquished" – which bemoans, "Competitive examinations will produce something that shall [only] look to be strong; that shall be swift, if it be only for a start of twenty yards" (1, 3).
60. Anthony Trollope, *The Three Clerks*, 3, 116, 305.
61. Charley Tudor, the third clerk, is also tested, but under the lax pre-examination methods of Mr Oldschoole in Internal Navigation, who bids him complete a fair copy of a newspaper article, declare his willingness to serve the Queen, and confess his only-partial mastery of arithmetic (11–12). Charley's lackluster performance is sufficient to get him the job and, perhaps, to justify the impetus for, if not the fact-driven form of, Hardlines's reforms. Mr Oldschoole is himself eventually examined by "those Magi of the Civil Service office," as to "the exact use of the Internal Navigation Office" (515); when his answers are found unsatisfactory, his entire office is shuttered and its clerks pensioned, reassigned, or turned out altogether.
62. Ibid. 57. Extending the alimentary metaphor, Mrs Woodward, sympathetic mother to the three clerks' future wives, predicts that with the advent of the examination system, the world "'will soon be like a fish-pond, very full of fish, but with very little food for them. Everyone is scrambling for the others' prey, and they will end at last by eating one another'" (112).
63. Ibid. 120.
64. Ibid. 120.
65. Alaric's moneyed misadventures, along with those of Undy Scott, Mr M'Buffer, and others, are more than sufficient to qualify *The Three Clerks* for inclusion among the financial fictions discussed in Chapter 2. At one point, Trollope overtly signals his awareness of recent banking scandals in a reference to "the roguery of the Sadleirs and Camerons, of the Robsons and Redpaths of the present day" (342).
66. Ibid. 525.
67. According to John Forster's *Life of Charles Dickens*, this fictional gambit paid off: "He more than doubled the circulation of this journal" (2.66).
68. "Hard Times for these Times," 489.
69. "Charles Dickens," 453.
70. "Hard Times," 513.
71. "Hard Times. For these Times," 568.
72. Ruskin, John. "Unto This Last," 159.
73. F. R. Leavis, *The Great Tradition*, 227. Beginning in the 1970s, the text also became the object of numerous alternative methods and

conclusions. Those focused on connecting *Hard Times* to other historical topics include John Baird, who reconstructs the "memorial" to the failed divorce bill of 1854 "woven deeply into the texture of the narrative" ("'Divorce and Matrimonial Causes,'" 401); Paul Schacht, "Dickens and the Uses of Nature," and Joseph Butwin, "*Hard Times*: The News and the Novel," who in their respective studies reconnect the novel's weekly installments to surrounding articles in *Household Words*; and K. J. Fielding and Anne Smith, who, in "*Hard Times* and the Factory Controversy," seek to adjudicate among Dickens's and Harriet Martineau's mutual recriminations over the novel, ultimately finding that Dickens was more sinned against than sinning in the exchange. Approaching the novel from a somewhat less historicist direction are John Kucich, who reads the text in light of a persistent "dialectic of excess and restraint . . . resolved outside of any single character" that animates much of Dickens's fiction (*Excess and Restraint in the Novels of Charles Dickens*, 180); Katherine Kearns, who reexamines the novel's patterns of figurative language in order to argue that Louisa Gradgrind serves as "a potent sign within the text of *Hard Times*, a figure that embodies Dickens's resistance to realism's co-opting of language to its causes" ("A Tropology of Realism in *Hard Times*," 876); Francesca Orestano who reveals a stylistic predilection for entropy-inducing lists in "Charles Dickens and the Vertigo of the List"; and Nils Clausson, who, in "Dickens's Genera Mixta," locates the novel at the generic intersection point of the comedy of humors and Menippean satire. Martha Nussbaum even cites *Hard Times* in *Poetic Justice* as a foundational example of social justice grounded in sympathetic identification with distant others; although Nussbaum's own critique is, itself, questioned by Paulette Kidder in "Martha Nussbaum on Dickens's *Hard Times*" for its omission of Dickens's frequent religious references.

74. Welsh, *Dickens Redressed*, 151.
75. Robert Caserio, "The Name of the Horse," 11; Brantlinger, "Dickens and the Factories," 282. Among the most sophisticated factory-focused readings of the novel is Patricia Johnson's "*Hard Times* and the Structure of Industrialism," which reexamines the novel's bivalent deployment of "the physical structure of the factory itself as both the metaphor for the destructive forces at work on its characters' lives and as the metaphor for its own aesthetic unity as a novel," ultimately arguing that Dickens problematizes the industrial city by metonymically associating its inhabitants with both "the fuel and eventually the waste products, of the factory system" (129, 132).
76. Welsh, *Dickens Redressed*, 150.
77. Despite her personal vitriol, Harriet Martineau is typical in *The Factory Controversy* when she judges, "Master and man are as unlike life in England, at present, as Ogre and Tom Thumb: and the result of the

choice of subject is simply, that the charm of an ideal creation is foregone, while nothing is gained in its stead" (36). A rare dissent to this general opinion appears in *The New Quarterly Review and Digest*: "In 'Hard Times' the characters are strongly drawn, but they are true flesh and blood: it is easy to fancy that all and each of them live and move in the world around us, and that they are not mere puppets called forth by an arbitrary will to play a part according to the dictates of the machinist" ("Hard Times for these Times," 489). A much better predictor of subsequent opinion comes from *The Critic*:

> He has carried his bad habit of caricature to an excess unknown before, even to himself. There is scarcely a natural character in the whole book. Sissy, Louisa, and her brother, are tolerably free from exaggeration; but all the rest are more fitted for *Punch* than for a sober narrative professing to paint life as it is to-day. ("Hard Times," 513)

I am grateful to Deborah Logan for leading me to the original full text of Martineau's response.
78. "Charles Dickens," 454. Stephen J. Spector, "Monsters of Metonymy," speaks for many critics when he asserts that

> Dickens bestows hardly a single spark of his vitalizing genius upon Stephen Blackpool and Rachael, *Hard Times*'s thwarted working-class lovers. Like Victor Frankenstein's creation, a monstrous assemblage with limbs and features ironically chosen for their beauty, Stephen and Rachael are automatons compounded of such Victorian middle-class virtues as industry, honesty, self-denial, chastity, and deference. Where Frankenstein's unattractive child entertains, Dickens' beau ideal of the industrial worker bores. (365)

79. "Charles Dickens," 454.
80. Ibid. 451.
81. Ibid. 452.
82. Charles Dickens, *Hard Times*, 13. Hereafter cited parenthetically in the text.
83. An alternative defense of Dickens's methods of characterization appears in Thomas Kelly's "Character in Dickens' Late Novels." For observations with particular relevance to *Hard Times*, see 390–1, 393, 395–6.
84. Dickens, *Hard Times*, 18.
85. Victor Sage, "Girl Number Twenty Revisited," esp. 330–5. That Harthouse, at the moment he is outmaneuvered by Sissy, identifies himself with "the Great Pyramid" and, immediately afterward, writes to his brother that he is "going in for camels," points to Egypt as an alternative venue for his diabolical smoothness (174). Although better connected to France than to England at midcentury, Egypt under Abbas I (1848–54) and Said Pasha (1854–63) was subject to British influence over the building of the Suez Canal and railway projects; additionally,

ancient Egypt and its surviving artifacts served as the primary objects of analysis for British Egyptologists led by British Museum field specialist Samuel Birch.
86. The aristocratic Harthouse's defeat by the virtuous Sissy offers a fictional example of what Pam Morris, in *Dickens's Class Consciousness*, describes as a shift away from eighteenth-century faith in "elitism of birth" and towards a nineteenth-century belief in "an elitism of individual worth" (6). In an observation particularly relevant to my reading of middle-class status as predicated in part upon the rejection of gentle birth, Morris writes, "However, unlike self-evident ties of blood, ties of affiliation need to be defined in opposition to what they are not; an affiliated group can experience its identity only by reference to those who are different and not of the group. Class affiliation, therefore, depends upon the power to exclude and marginalize, as well as to interpellate" (6).
87. Even Bounderby's manner of dress, which explicitly rejects fashionable norms, makes perspicuous his repudiation of gentle birth: "So, Mr Bounderby threw on his hat—he always threw it on, as expressing a man who had been far too busily employed in making himself, to acquire any fashion of wearing his hat—and with his hands in his pockets, sauntered out into the hall. 'I never wear gloves,' it was his custom to say. 'I didn't climb up the ladder in *them*. Shouldn't be so high up, if I had'" (21).
88. Bounderby's capacity to impress others with his legitimacy extends beyond Gradgrind to unnamed "third parties" and "[s]trangers, modest enough elsewhere," who "started up at dinners in Coketown, and boasted, in quite a rampant way, of Bounderby. They made him out to be the Royal arms, the Union-Jack, Magna Carta, John Bull, Habeas Corpus, the Bill of Rights, An Englishman's house is his castle, Church and State, and God save the Queen, all put together" (37). He is thus associated in the public mind with the very symbols used by propagandists of all political persuasions to justify national chauvinism and international expansionism.
89. As Pam Morris observes, "Despite public approval for the 'respectable poor', it was in fact upon vociferous reiterations of the uncouth behaviour and moral degeneracy of the 'vulgar poor' that the middle class depended to construct their sense of class identity and worth" (8).
90. This allusion to the biblical narrative of Mary and Martha from the Gospel of Luke is surely deployed to outrage the novel's original readers at the sacrilegious pretensions of its fictional utilitarians. Ironically, it also invests Dickens's own efforts to describe the negative assertion of middle-class status with an aura of sacredness that can only be justified through negation.
91. The first two phrases come from *Hard Times* (42, 75). In *States of Inquiry*, Frankel explains how these forms of "official reportage"

were designed primarily to bring various disenfranchised constituencies within the sphere of political discourse, and hence governmental control:

> Exchange of knowledge and texts thus operated through multifarious paths, implicating governments and legislatures, the disenfranchised populations—now the object of national attention—and diverse communities of readers who recognized the state in its published documents. Conversely, through fact-finding enterprises, the state conjured up its subjects, publics, and spheres. It also fashioned itself a target of observation and scrutiny. I term this field of communication between the state and its constituencies *print* statism (following Benedict Anderson's notion of *print* capitalism). (2, italics original)

92. In addition to offering a pithy one-paragraph history of the Blue Book, Berman argues that "*Hard Times* reveals a convergence between government reports, novels, and the periodicals that digested them. All three rivals in the print marketplace sought to represent, to educate, and to speak *to* and *for* the public. *Hard Times* caricatures a representative government trying to apprehend its subjects. By implication, it also probes a flourishing print culture trying to apprehend its audience" ("'Awful Unknown Quantities,'" 563).
93. It is in response to decisions like this that Nussbaum writes, "At the limit, the character Bitzer shows us the extreme unreliability of the feeling of satisfaction when not linked to any more probing ethical evaluation, for whatever makes that empty vessel of self-interest feel pleased fills the reader with anxiety and even horror" (*Poetic Justice*, 50).
94. Dickens, *Hard Times*, 42
95. Dickens's familiarity with the parliamentary election process is apparent from the Eatanswill episode in *Pickwick Papers*. For more on this and other Victorian novels' representations of election ritual, see Pionke, *The Ritual Culture of Victorian Professionals*, 123–58.
96. A number of critics – among them Razak Dahmane, "'A Mere Question of Figures'"; Nussbaum, *Poetic Justice*; and Starr, "Manufacturing Novels" – focus productively on the ways in which *Hard Times* reflects on novel reading and writing.

Chapter 5

Legitimizing the Subjection of Middle-Class Women in Mid-Victorian Fiction

Dickens concludes his own "mere fable" of *Hard Times* by enumerating the futures of his principal "men and women." Some appear to get what they deserve – Mrs Sparsit reduced to the disagreeable companion of her impecunious blood relative, Lady Scadgers; Tom penitent and reconciled by letter with Louisa but struck down by fever during his attempted return to England; and Sissy rewarded for her unstatistical steadfastness to her own father and the Gradgrind family with "happy children" of her own (219) – but not everyone. Bitzer, for instance, receives no long-term comeuppance for his lack of compassion, whether for Tom or his own mother, and instead is made "a show of" by Bounderby "as the rising young man, so devoted to his master's great merits" (217). More egregiously, Rachel, despite her manifold virtues, remains "a woman working, ever working, but content to do it," while bestowing her unique "compassion on a degraded, drunken wretch of her own sex, who was sometimes seen in the town secretly begging of her, and crying to her" (218).

With only one exception, the format for these visions of futurity consists of a single paragraph whose glimpse of things to come is confirmed in its final sentence. Louisa, however, looks forward to a divided fate. First, the narrative denies her Sissy's more conventional happy ending with an abrupt reversal of its rhetorical epiphora:

> Herself again a wife—a mother—lovingly watchful of her children, ever careful that they should have a childhood of the mind no less than a childhood of the body, as knowing it to be even a more beautiful thing, and a possession, any hoarded scrap of which, is a blessing and happiness to the wisest? Did Louisa see this? Such a thing was never to be. (219)

After this emphatically non-parallel negation of one possibility, the novel offers Louisa a slightly more affirmative consolation in the form of service as a kind of universal maiden aunt, "all children loving her" and she seeking "to beautify" with "imaginative graces and delights" the "lives of machinery and reality" enjoined upon "her humbler fellow-creatures" (219).

The question of why some characters experience retributive narrative justice and others do not, and of why Bitzer in particular maintains a smooth upward trajectory at the bank while Rachel and Louisa remain comparatively trapped by circumstances not of their own making is a troubling one. That one young man of a perversely factual nature gets ahead whereas two women, who otherwise have comparatively less in common at the level of age, class, or demonstrated character, remain left behind suggests gender as the irreducible determinant of their respective destinies. Adjudicating his characters' futures in 1854, Dickens certainly would have found the overdetermining force of "The Woman Question" difficult to ignore. The demographic revelation of the 1851 census that there were roughly 360,000 more females than males in England, and just over 510,00 more females than males in Great Britain, made it a "modern fact" that these so-called "surplus women" could not be expected to find their social fulfillment in marriage.[1] Whether marriage itself offered a guarantee of connubial happiness was also under public scrutiny. As John Baird has meticulously reconstructed, 1854 witnessed a first and second reading of a Divorce and Matrimonial Causes Bill, which, although ultimately withdrawn, nevertheless "is woven deeply into the texture" of *Hard Times*.[2] Stephen Blackpool's inability to win a legal divorce from his wife features prominently: even after his death, it is the implacable force of his matrimonial bond that continues to connect Rachel to his "degraded, drunken wretch" of a widow. Somewhat more subtle but no less unbreakable are the vows taken by Bounderby and Louisa: he cannot seek legal divorce from her once she has permanently returned to her father's house, because she has not actually committed adultery with Harthouse; and she cannot even attempt to become "herself again a wife—a mother" until his death five years after the conclusion of the narrative, at which point she would have to compete in a marriage market oversaturated with younger, less baggage-encumbered, but still "surplus" women.

Although Dickens's own authorial baggage with respect to his female characters and Victorian women more broadly has been well documented, for the purposes of this chapter, what interests me more than the Inimitable's unique forms of misogyny is the way in which especially Louisa's fate may be inflected by more than just individual predilection.³ All the negative assertions of value considered thus far might be described as applying to fictionalized members of the middle class without particular regard to gender. Of course – since birth was usually determined by patrilineal inheritance; wealth disproportionately accumulated by the same, as well as through a maturity spent working and maintaining control over one's wages; force most often discharged, and in the case of social disturbances repulsed, in the public sphere; and even facts amassed, analyzed, and deployed for gain overwhelmingly in professional or political circles – no particular regard might be required to nevertheless produce a bias favoring the construction of male, as opposed to female, middle-class status. Moreover, as now three generations of feminist history, social and cultural analysis, and literary criticism have shown, such systemic favoritism on the basis of gender was anything but accidental.⁴ Neither matriarchal angel nor independent social agent at the end of *Hard Times*, Louisa, I wish to suggest, serves as not an inimitable but rather a typical example of the effects of a final, explicitly gendered repudiation required of female characters throughout Victorian fiction. In order to demonstrate their fitness for middle-class status, Louisa and her sisters must disavow the exercise of masculine authority.⁵

The expectation of such social self-abnegation was quite literally written into the very statute that in 1832 set out to define the pecuniary limits of the middle class itself. The £10 franchise that the First Reform Act used to elevate roughly 300,000 citizens of England and Wales into parliamentary voters applied exclusively to "male persons."⁶ This gendered definition of personhood enshrined into law a distinction that had previously been a matter of custom, neatly closing a loophole that "in the seventeenth and eighteenth centuries" had allowed "a few women, by virtue of the strange franchise arrangements . . . to exercise the right to vote."⁷ Two years later, the New Poor Law not only inspired a bevy of orphan narratives, its bastardy clause simultaneously insulated middle-class men from the effects of philandering with their female servants, thereby protecting the newly enfranchised from financial encumbrances upon their £10 households, and reinforced women's primarily domestic duties by making even the mothers of illegitimate children solely responsible for their offspring's welfare.⁸

That the mothers of legitimate children, regardless of social class, could not expect their maternal responsibilities to be accompanied by anything resembling custodial rights became scandalously visible following the separation of prominent society hostess and author Caroline Norton, née Sheridan, from her husband, abusive barrister George Chapple Norton.[9] George hid their three sons from her in Scotland and Yorkshire, confiscated all of her earnings as an author, and in 1836 unsuccessfully sued then-Prime Minister, Lord Melbourne, for "criminal conversation" (adultery). Her reputation destroyed, Caroline Norton nevertheless publicized the details surrounding their separation and her continued lack of access to her own children and campaigned successfully in favor of the Custody of Infants Act 1839.[10] Legally empowering in that it allowed a mother to petition the courts for sole custody of children under age seven and the right of access to older children, the act was also socially limiting, in that it confirmed that children of tender years were the primary responsibility of their mothers, whose authority was confined to nurturing within the domestic sphere.[11]

A similarly normalizing impulse to restrictively define women's proper sphere as in the home underlies many of the industrial reforms of the 1840s. Thus, Lord Ashley persuaded MPs of the need for the Mines and Collieries Act 1842, which prohibited the underground employment of women and girls, in part by appealing to their sense of gendered propriety: among the miners, Ashley noted "girls . . . of all ages, from seven to twenty-one. They commonly work quite naked down to the waist, and are dressed—as far as they are dressed at all—in a loose pair of trousers . . . nothing can be more graphic and touching than the evidence of many of these poor girls"; he went on to quote the testimony of pregnant women, who worked until the day they gave birth and returned to the mines after recovering "never longer than ten or twelve days"; and concluded by citing the "moral effects of the system," which leaves women "wholly unfit for the duties of their sex . . . wholly disqualified from even learning how to discharge the duties of wife and mother."[12] Comparable rhetoric was also deployed during the debates over the 1844 and 1847 Factories Acts, both of which limited the number of daily hours, to twelve and ten, respectively, that could be worked by child-laborers and women operatives.[13] Of course, middle-class women were discouraged from working at all and, until the founding of Queen's College, London (1848) and Bedford College for Women (1849), did not have schools to which they could go to be academically accredited for any occupation. Those forced to seek wages by exigent financial circumstances were generally governesses, lady companions, and teachers of young children of both sexes and older girls, with literary piece work – often completed anonymously or pseudonymously – as authors, translators, or reviewers also available if only rarely equitably remunerated.

The hegemony of home-bound domesticity within mid-century Britain's social horizon of expectations for middle-class women perceptibly fractured after the results of the 1851 Census became known and debated. Additionally, the evidence and arguments provided by the lives of a few remarkably pioneering women added further anecdotal fuel to the rhetorical fire of "The Woman Question." Perhaps most famously, Florence Nightingale's well-publicized work as a nurse and medical administrator during the Crimean War (1854–6), when she was christened "the Lady with the Lamp" for her late-night rounds among the beds at Scutari, showed that middle-class women's supposedly natural domestic inclinations could be channeled into a form of paid vocational service. Nightingale was quick to elevate nursing into a profession in its own right, publishing *Notes on Hospitals* and *Notes on Nursing* in 1859 and using £40,000 donated to the Nightingale Fund to establish the Nightingale Training School for nurses at St. Thomas's Hospital, London, in 1860.[14] Also active in the 1850s and 1860s was Barbara Leigh Smith, whose friendship with Elizabeth Rayner Parkes formed the nucleus of the Langham Place group, publisher of the *English Woman's Journal* (1858–64), a monthly periodical marketed explicitly to middle-class women featuring regular articles on contemporary social issues, book reviews, a correspondence column, and brief summaries of public affairs. Smith had already authored *A Brief Summary, in Plain Language, of the Most Important Laws Concerning Women* (1854) and, in 1855, formed a committee to petition the House of Commons for a reform of the laws governing married women's property. Although unsuccessful in introducing a Married Women's Property Bill in 1857, Smith, now Bodichon, did campaign that same year in favor of the Matrimonial Causes Act, which established a less expensive and time-consuming process for divorce, albeit one still weighted in favor of husbands.[15] In 1859, Bodichon was also among the founders of the Society for Promoting the Employment of Women, whose advocacy in favor of training for women, to be for example printers and bookkeepers, complemented the efforts of the Society of Female Artists (1855–69) to offer women the chance to exhibit and sell their paintings and works of plastic art.

Subsequent decades saw incremental improvements in occupational and educational opportunities for women, along with substantial setbacks that demonstrated the depth of resistance to full political or social equality. The 1860s, for instance, although crowned by the founding of Girton College at Cambridge and women ratepayers' enfranchisement in municipal elections in 1869, also witnessed the passage of the Contagious Diseases Acts 1864, 1866, 1869 – according to which women presumed to be prostitutes in garrison towns could be forced to undergo a physical examination for venereal diseases – and the defeat of then-MP John Stuart Mill's suggestion to remove the "male" modifier of "persons" from the bill that would go on become the Second Reform Act 1867. In 1870, the first Married Women's Property Act allowed women to retain control of their wages and investments after marriage, to inherit sums less than £200, and to control inherited family property independently of their husbands. Such relative financial autonomy indirectly incentivized married women to pursue paid employment, as they, unlike Norton in the 1830s, would retain the right to any wages, copyrights, and investments.[16] Also in 1870, the Education Act granted women the right to serve on and to vote for candidates of local school boards. And, later in the decade, the founding of both Lady Margaret Hall and Somerville College (1878) provided women with a presence at Oxford. As at Cambridge's Girton, however, female students remained barred from taking university degrees and accessing university resources (most notably, the Bodleian Library). Moreover, these developments did not translate to women's enfranchisement by the Third Reform Act 1884, nor did they provide women with right of entry into the learned professions of law, medicine, and the clergy.

The Overdetermination of Female Agency

As even this brief survey of the more perspicuous developments and deferrals of Reform-Era middle-class women's history suggests, Victorian purveyors of fictionality, regardless of gender, would have addressed a reading public whose standards of plausibility with respect to female agency were vastly overdetermined.[17] Hence the consistency with which nineteenth-century novels, including works now celebrated for their feminism – among those previously discussed, Charlotte Brontë's *Jane Eyre*, *Shirley*, and *Villette*; Elizabeth Gaskell's *North and South*; Wilkie Collins's *The Woman in White* and *No Name*, and George Eliot's *Felix Holt* – feature middle-class women characters whose fictional legitimacy is secured, at least in part, through a repudiation of their claims to masculine authority. By initially focusing specifically on authors and texts generally read by twentieth- and twenty-first-century critics as progressive on the subject of gender, I hope to establish the ubiquity of this distinctly gendered negative assertion of value regardless of competing social commitments. At the same time, I shall identify strategic alternatives to a direct confrontation over male prerogative that nevertheless trouble the gendered status quo and advance the claims to middle-class status of female characters. The chapter concludes with a lengthier reading of Charlotte Yonge's *The Clever Woman of the Family* (1865), which may initially appear to share little ideological ground with its more liberal contemporaries. And yet, setting aside the text's deliberate humbling of its titular "clever woman" – an inevitable, perhaps even constitutive element in the construction of her and other women characters' middle-class status – one can discern Yonge self-consciously replicating her contemporaries' strategies for exposing, eroding, and redirecting normative and exclusively domestic answers to the pressing Woman Question.

Appearing in the late 1840s and early 1850s, and thus bracketing the dramatic demographic facts of the 1851 Census, Brontë's novels all feature strong female protagonists who must discipline themselves to the gendered limits imposed upon them by nineteenth-century society even as they reveal the unjust and often precarious bases of Victorian patriarchy. Thus, before completing Jane's impressive rise from penniless orphanhood to moneyed upper-middle-class status with a final slip under the coverture of domesticity – shorthanded by her declaration, "Reader, I married him"[18] – *Jane Eyre* strategically enlists its readers' own standards of plausibility concerning women even as it seeks to undermine their normative expectations about gender.[19] For instance, capitalizing upon what her readers would have known of middle-class women's limited employment opportunities in the 1840s, Brontë has Jane serve as both teacher at Lowood and governess at Thornfield before allowing her to comment on just how unfulfilling, even socially dangerous, such limitations may be. Reflecting on her comparatively easy circumstances at Thornfield, Jane thinks,

> Millions are condemned to a stiller doom than mine, and millions are in silent revolt against their lot. Nobody knows how many rebellions besides political rebellions ferment in the masses of life which people earth. Women are supposed to be very calm generally: but women feel just as men feel; they need exercise for their faculties, and a field for their efforts, as much as their brothers do; they suffer from too rigid a restraint, too absolute a stagnation, precisely as men would suffer; and it is narrow-minded in their more privileged fellow-creatures to say that

> they ought to confine themselves to making puddings and knitting stockings, to playing on the piano and embroidering bags. It is thoughtless to condemn them, or laugh at them, if they seek to do more or learn more than custom has pronounced necessary for their sex.[20]

The novel also depicts its male and female protagonist according to the period's standards of masterful mature masculinity and comparatively slighter and younger femininity, then deliberately maims Rochester in body and manner so that Jane can serve as a suitable helpmeet, thereby revealing the absurd extremes required to achieve the allegedly domestic bliss of a companionate marriage.[21]

Shirley similarly domesticates the at times unseemly expressions of independence by Caroline Helstone and Shirley Keeldar through a double marriage to the Moore brothers.[22] Moreover, the novel humbles both of its heroines through illness, which in Caroline's case requires prolonged nursing by her rediscovered mother, Mrs Prior, and in Shirley's case a troubled confession to Louis Moore that she may be infected with rabies. Finally, Shirley, with her "man's name" and "man's position" inspiring her "with a touch of manhood" must also be made to acknowledge her place without the inner circle of men who plan the defense of Hollow's Mill.[23] Before arriving at these narratively plausible solutions, however, the novel allows Caroline and Shirley to chaff articulately against the emotional, occupational, and broadly social constraints preventing women from achieving full independence and happiness. Among the barriers, they both agree, is marriage itself, with Caroline cannily anticipating one of the troubling revelations in the 1851 Census: "'I wonder we don't all make up our minds to remain single.'"[24] The novel also presents women with credible alternatives to marriage, in the form of powerful sororal bonds such as those between Caroline and Shirley, as well as maternal relations such as those connecting Caroline to Mrs Prior.[25] In both cases, it appears that women might be sufficient unto themselves.[26]

Some four years later, this possibility of self-sufficiency is realized by Lucy Snowe in *Villette*, who ends her narrative the successful, single directrice of a pensionnat in the Faubourg Clotilde. Before arriving at this position of relative autonomy – which she attains under the aegis of M. Paul Emmanuel's planning and initial financing and marketing, as well as the benevolent proprietorship of M. Miret – Lucy samples the mid-century employment opportunities available to her, serving as lady-companion to Miss Marchmont, governess of Mme. Beck's children, and teacher of girls and young women at the latter's school. Although Lucy rarely voices the same overt critiques of the social limitations placed upon women articulated by Jane, Caroline, and Shirley, as narrator she does include episodes that more subtly represent the same sentiments. For instance, while still a child she observes the even younger "little Polly" learning to sew and "occasionally starting when the perverse weapon swerving from her control – inflicted a deeper stab than usual; but still silent, diligent, absorbed, womanly."[27] Once an adult, Lucy demonstrates that she has thoroughly internalized the mechanisms of female self-restraint, repeatedly curbing her own feelings and imagination so effectively that she needs no external surveillance to constrain her within gendered boundaries: beset by an aching longing "for something to fetch me out of my present existence" after a thunderstorm, she gives herself a figurative "knock on the head"; discovering within herself a "keen relish for dramatic expression," Lucy binds her new-found feelings "with the lock of a resolution which neither Time nor Temptation has since picked"; and recognizing the inappropriateness of her unreciprocated feelings for Dr John, "I closed the eyes of my dead [feeling], covered its face, and composed its limbs with great calm."[28] Perhaps the best indication of Lucy's capacity to renounce all claims to inappropriately masculine agency is her final choice of a friend-cum-lover: when alive, the mercurial M. Paul Emmanuel manifests all the signs of what we now recognize as verbal and emotional abuse; after his implied death, he as effectively overdetermines the now white-haired, narrating Lucy's fate as Frank had done for Miss Marchmont.[29]

Never working for wages and attaining only a temporary financial independence by her novel's end, Gaskell's Margaret Hale very rarely challenges male authority directly. Her most overt transgression of gendered propriety occurs during the riot, when she admonishes Thornton to "'go down this instant, if you are not a coward. Go down and face them like a man,'" and then, when violence appears imminent, lifts "the great iron bar of the door" to the family's domestic apartments "with an imperious force" and rushes out to confront "that angry sea of men, her eyes smiting them with flaming arrows of reproach."[30] Margaret's error is at this moment primarily one of unfeminine intent – "personally disinterested," in Catherine Gallagher's estimation, "she acts out an abstract sense of justice"[31] – one for which she is checked immediately by a "sharp pebble . . . grazing forehead and cheek, and drawing a blinding sheet of light before her eyes."[32] Afterward, she must endure, first, hearing her defense of Thornton attributed to his sister by Bessy Higgins, and, second, witnessing her potentially unfeminine assertion of self misinterpreted by the Thornton household as a symptom of normatively-expected romantic attraction.[33] That their incipient union on the final pages of *North and South* transforms Margaret's proffered loan of £18,057 into Thornton's capital outright – obviating his need to "pay much better interest" than the "two and half percent" currently accrued at the bank – only reinforces the novel's earlier repudiation of phallic authority for women.[34] Even as it reaffirms middle-class women's fundamentally circumscribed roles, however, the novel also amplifies their importance, investing the Higgins daughters, living and dead, and Margaret with the power to forestall Nicholas's alcoholism, and returning repeatedly to the profound effects of mothers upon sons.[35] Also, without damaging Thornton physically, Gaskell nevertheless echoes Brontë's treatment of Rochester by humbling her male protagonist with bankruptcy in order to make him a suitable marriage partner.

Appropriate to their place in the history of sensation fiction, Collins's *The Woman in White* and *No Name* render monstrous the extremes of femininity and masculinity seemingly inevitably created by the social prohibition against fully autonomous women. In the former, Collins focuses on the potential for personal and financial exploitation that inheres in the period's unbalanced gender norms. All of the novel's female characters remain unambiguously bound in their feminized places, which in half-sister Laura and Anne's overlapping case results in mental instability, social interchangeability, and involuntary incarceration; Laura is additionally defrauded of £20,000 outright and a life-interest in £10,000 more (worth roughly £300 annually). Even Marian, undoubtedly the strongest, most independent, and appealing woman in the novel, succumbs to the force of circumstances before she can disrupt the male plot against her sister. Stripping off her silk dress and the "cumbersome parts of my underclothing," and clothing herself in "a petticoat of dark flannel" and "black travelling cloak" in order to engage in some clandestine evening sleuthing, Marian claims that "no man could have passed through the narrowest spaces more easily than I."[36] However, her gender-bending espionage exposes her to the evening's "cruel rain," and she contracts a fever, suffers a violation of her diary, and is sadly reduced in the much of the late narrative to a "worn and wasted" version of her former self.[37] She ends the novel a maiden aunt, deprived even of her own more modest property of somewhat less than £700.[38] Much of Collins's narrative energy in *The Woman in*

White is devoted to representing the extreme forms of male mastery that propagate within the Victorians' hothouse of female dependency, from the choleric and abusive faut-baronet Sir Percival Glyde; to the passive-aggressive invalidism of Frederick Fairlie; to the unctuous master criminal and double agent Count Fosco; to the initially weak then colonially remastered Walter Hartright, whose actions during his private investigation of the Glyde-Fosco conspiracy veer frequently outside the limits of the law.[39] Collins's point seems to be, in a riff on the novel's preamble, that, under the present one-sided division of phallic authority, women had best prepare to endure whatever outrages overmastering men can conceive.[40]

In his subsequent novel, *No Name*, Collins then features a young woman, Magdalen Vanstone, who refuses to acquiesce in her own victimization by a legal system designed to reinforce the social power of men. Juxtaposed with her older sister, Norah, who is a model of resignation, Magdalen repeatedly and egregiously transgresses the normative middle-class prescriptions against too-assertive women in an effort to regain their lost inheritance and status. As detailed in Chapter 1, she fails spectacularly, in the process descending the social ladder from disinherited upper-middle-class woman to, briefly, governess-in-training, actress, fraudster, suspected poisoner, housemaid, and, finally, helpless, penniless, near-homeless invalid. What I wish to stress here is the assiduity with which the narrative recuperates Magdalen through repudiations of masculine authority. Initially, her body itself rebels against her unfeminine frenzy of self-assertion, first while at St. Crux, where she begins to develop hand tremors and finds herself "feeling old and weak and worn, in the heyday of her youth," and later and more catastrophically at Aaron's Buildings, where she sickens until "too weak and helpless to support herself—a woman apparently in the last stage of illness."[41] The first six weeks of her convalescence are described as an "oblivion," which presumably means that even her most basic bodily functions must be attended to by others.[42] Informed of her total dependence upon Kirke, she does not rebel against his care, but rather expresses herself "'very, very grateful for all your goodness to me.'"[43] Once mostly recovered, Magdalen receives a letter from Norah detailing how "the recovery of the lost fortune was her sister's triumph, not hers," and she "victoriously trample[s] down all little jealousies and all mean regrets," saying "in her heart of hearts, 'Norah has deserved it!'"[44] Finally, she destroys the Secret Trust, her "only claim to the fortune" of her father.[45] It may not have been the death that Mrs Oliphant thought that she deserved, but this cycle of renunciation does place Magdalen back within the bounds of middle-class femininity as defined by earlier fictions.

As in the novels discussed above, in *No Name* Collins also implicitly critiques the very gendered order he appears to affirm through Madgalen's rehabilitation. The sororal bond between Magdalen and Norah both motivates the former's transgressive plotting and enables her to accept as a gift the fortune that she was unable to win as a prize of her stratagems.[46] The men Magdalen must associate with throughout her misadventures never quite attain the monstrous proportions of Glyde or Fosco, but the unforgiving speculator Matthew Vanstone, the vain and weak-hearted Noel Vanstone, and the fraudulent and domineering Wragge are hardly models of ideal masculinity. And the final love-match between Kirke and Magdalen is beset from the improbability of its beginning and Kirke's own lingering doubts about the gap in their ages, which, at forty-one and twenty, are not so dissimilar to those of many prudent Victorian middle-class unions.

In a text as dedicated to revealing the overdetermining forces at work in the lives of individuals and society as Eliot's *Felix Holt*, it is unsurprising to find women consistently interpellated within circumstances defined by men. As Esther tells Felix during their walk in the country, "'A woman can hardly ever choose . . . she is dependent on what happens to her. She must take meaner things because, because only meaner things are within her reach.'"[47] Despite her unexpected inheritance, the vast majority of which she refuses, Esther, herself, ultimately chooses between the two forms of marital dependence represented by Felix and Harold. Mrs Transome is similarly circumscribed by "a hard, unalterable past" embodied by Jermyn and the "bitterness of . . . helpless bondage" to the overbearingly indulgent Harold.[48] And, within her own sphere, Mrs Holt must submit to the overmastering scrupulousness of Felix concerning the sale of her late husband's patent medicines.[49] However, the novel's determinism does not discriminate on the basis of gender, since *Felix Holt*'s male characters, too, remain bound within the elaborate social web of Treby's past and present. Felix, for instance, is punished with a gunshot to the shoulder and conviction for manslaughter at the Loamford Assizes for presuming to assert his authority over the election-day riot. Harold returns to Treby as heir to a fortune, only to discover that he has been dispossessed by the legal maneuvers of unscrupulous ancestors who, it turns out, are not even his blood relations, and so must accept his own bastardy, renounce his courtship of Esther and leave Transome Court long enough for there be "silence about the past."[50] And the villainous Jermyn pays for his at-times criminally overreaching assertiveness by going "to reside at a great distance: some said 'abroad,' that large home of ruined reputations."[51]

In dramatically limiting the agency of both male and female characters – although, perhaps, not to equal degrees – Eliot subtly pushes back against the normative assumptions that had preserved the "male" modifier of persons in the Second Reform Act. Echoing the prominence of the maternal in Gaskell's prior contribution to the industrial novel, Eliot also recursively returns to the centrality of mothers in the lives of Esther, Harold, and Felix. Finally, she elevates women's effect upon the process of social improvement by allowing that, when "a woman feels purely and nobly, that ardour of hers which breaks through formulas too rigorously urged on men by daily practical needs, makes one of her most precious influences: she is the added impulse that shatters the stiffening crust of cautious experience."[52] Traditionally-defined masculine authority may be off limits for women, and often also for men, in *Felix Holt*, but women nevertheless have an important, hitherto underappreciated role in Eliot's meticulously woven social fabric.

Beyond Anti-Feminism in *The Clever Woman of the Family*

Chronologically situated between *No Name* and *Felix Holt*, Yonge's *The Clever Woman of the Family* only reservedly partakes of the sensationally affecting excesses and realistically overdetermining constraints of its near contemporaries.[53] Instead, the novel marshals its strongest feelings and most meticulous details for the gendered social and spiritual salvation of its eponymous "clever woman," Rachel Curtis. Critical discussion of Yonge's work generally and of *Clever Woman* specifically has focused overwhelmingly on whether it merits feminist recovery, remains cripplingly anti-feminist, or requires a more intersectional approach – via Tractarian aesthetics, postcolonial theory, or disability studies, for instance – to best appreciate its merits.[54] The problem to be overcome for most critics is Yonge's consistent, unapologetic, High Church conservatism, which manifests most perspicuously in what Tamara Wagner has aptly labeled the "salutary humiliation" of its protagonist.[55]

The ideological divide between Yonge and many of her enduringly more popular contemporaries yawns widest in narrative asides, such as that "a woman's tone of thought is commonly moulded by the masculine intellect, which, under one form or another, becomes the master of her soul."[56] Reflective, perhaps, of Yonge's own devotional relationship with John Keble and written without irony, rhetorical qualification, or the interposition of a dramatic speaker, this narrative assertion of men's spiritual mastery would be glaringly incongruent if transplanted into any of the novels discussed above.[57] And yet they, like *The Clever Woman of the Family*, accede to the social imperative that their female protagonists must repudiate masculine authority in order to authorize their claims to middle-class status. Moreover, despite its doctrinally inflected conservatism, Yonge's novel mounts a robust and multifaceted critique of Britain's patriarchal culture in the 1860s that deploys elements also present in these alternative fictions. Indissolubly linking Rachel's own final social position to her marriage and her renunciation of cleverness, the text nevertheless also reserves a significant and laudatory place for disinterestedly intelligent women. In sum, when read in the intersectional context of its generic peers, Yonge's *The Clever Woman of the Family* reveals both the legitimating power and the long-term precariousness of middle-class status grounded in the subjection of women.

"'What nonsense I talked in those days'"[58]

The reader first meets Rachel on her twenty-fifth birthday, which, she tells her elder sister Grace, is "'the very day I had fixed for hauling down the flag of youth'" (35). Orphaned at fifteen by the death of her father, with "the palm of cleverness conceded to her ever since she could recollect" by the members of her domestic circle, including her somewhat fragile mother, Rachel is the joint heiress, with Grace, to the family estate in the fictional seaside town of Avonmouth (41). Having "considerably surpassed in acquirements and reflection all the persons with whom she came into frequent contact," Rachel has nurtured herself by reading "periodical literature, instead of by conversation or commerce with living minds," and is, as a result, "isolated as a sort of pedant" (41–2). Newly arrived at her legal majority, Rachel is determined that she "'will no longer be withheld from some path of usefulness! I will judge for myself, and when my mission has declared itself, I will not be withheld from it by any scruple that does not approve itself to my reason and conscience'" (38).[59] She mutters this declaration while correcting the copy books of "half-grown lads," arrogating to herself the gendered qualifications of reason and conscience and hinting at the ways in which this determination to be socially useful will overstep normative expectations for upper-middle-class women (37). In fact, Rachel has already cast both herself and her sister as outside the pale of the period's matrimonial prescriptions for women, since, as "'the maiden sisters of Avonmouth,'" they are "'husband and wife to one another, as maiden pairs always are'" (36). Rachel is, furthermore, at loggerheads with the neighborhood curate, Mr Touchett; unwilling to consult her mother's man of business, Mr Cox; maintaining a "deadly feud" with the neighboring doctor, Mr Frampton; and accustomed to discount the "old-world prejudices" of her father's friend, the magistrate Mr Grey (347, 344). In sum, as a clever woman, Rachel claims a freedom to act that supersedes the authority of every professional man of her acquaintance.

The novel follows Rachel down several paths of potential usefulness, consistently stymying her each time she seeks to assert masculine authority for herself. First, and least problematic initially, is her self-appointed "domestic mission" to take "care of Fanny, poor dear helpless Fanny" – her cousin, also twenty-five, recently widowed, and about to return from Australia with seven young children, the youngest an infant daughter – and to assume responsibility for "training her and forming her boys as a most sacred office" (38). Her "heart throbbing with Britomart's devotion to her Amoret," Rachel meets Fanny and her family at the train station and is swiftly stunned into silence by the energy of six young boys (45). She recovers sufficiently by the next day to rebuff Touchett's every offer of clerical advice and assistance, but finds herself repeatedly checked by invocations of "the Major," without consulting whom Fanny refuses to make any significant decisions; "Three Majors in one speech," Rachel bristles before the second day of the Temple family's return is concluded (55). Determined to eradicate Fanny's "foolish clinging habits of reliance" upon this male "counter influence" (60), Rachel then attempts to educate, supervise, and discipline the two oldest boys, but only succeeds in alienating them and their mother, who angrily bids her, "'Go away! If anything is to be done to my boys, I'll do it myself," ending her brief flash to temper with "'Oh, I wish the Major would come!'" (75). The cousins are quickly reconciled, but Rachel resigns all plans of teaching her nephews, and once the Major, now a Colonel, does, in fact, arrive, Fanny grants him pride of place at her table: "Lady Temple and her guests sat down to dinner. Rachel meant to have sat at the bottom and carved, as belonging to the house; but Fanny motioned the Colonel to the place" (111–2). Rachel is, thus, outmaneuvered by the habitual discipline of a regimental family and its reliance upon a man of rank to manage important household duties.

Even while in the first blush of her Spenserian ecstasy, Rachel embarks on a second useful mission, one which might most charitably be understood as a campaign of public improvement through the dissemination of enlightened information. She begins orally with Fanny, whose serendipitous employment of "a young woman whose health had quite given way over her lace pillow" allows Rachel to wax eloquently "over the crying evils of the system . . . holding Fanny fast to listen by a sort of fascination, in her overpowering earnestness" (50). A woman with strong and well-informed opinions about a trade employing girls and women to make products destined for their more fortunate female counterparts does not unduly transgress against normative gendered expectations. However, Rachel's opining quickly expands to include the desirability of "female medical men – I mean medical women," a critique of daily morning church services and the feeble efforts of Mr Touchett's "penny-whistle choir," and a lecture to Alick Keith on the true meaning of heroism, citing a well-publicized incident from the recent Indian Mutiny (1857–8) as an example (56, 58, 148). She also graduates from a desire to improve her nearest interlocutors in conversation to an imperative to influence a broader segment of society through publication.[60] In her first prospective article, she decries the perils of "curatolatry," Yonge's own invented term for the "sickly mixture of flirtation and hero worship, with a religious daub as a salve to the conscience" directed by young women at clergymen like Touchett (104). The final product, "Curatocult," is succeeded by "Human Reeds," a thinly disguised admonition directed at women such as Fanny for allowing herself to be influenced by men such as Colonel Colin Keith, and "Military Society," a more direct verbal assault on her nemesis and his ilk. Rachel's overreaching assertion of rhetorical authority is met with the polite refusal of her polemical manuscripts, the revelation that Alick Keith won the Victoria Cross for the very act with which she sought to educate him, and the unexpectedly pleasurable realization that Colin Keith possesses "strength, and acuteness of powers superior to her own" (174).[61] That she goes on to confuse Colin Keith's intellectual attentions for more romantic intentions only further cements her back within the normalizing confines of Victorian domesticity.[62]

Rachel's third, largest, and most public-facing scheme of usefulness allows her to act upon her powerful convictions about the lacemaking trade. Ironically re-presenting some of the central efforts of the Langham Place group, she co-founds a residential "asylum . . . in which young girls might be placed to learn handicrafts that might secure their livelihood, in especial, perhaps, wood engraving and printing," with the ultimate goal "to render the whole self-supporting . . . by the publication of a little illustrated periodical" (229).[63] Local girls and young women could thus be removed from the tyranny of their pillows and bobbins, thereby improving their lot and presumably raising the wages of those left behind by a reduction in the pool of available labor, and Rachel herself could be supplied with a venue ready to publish her articles without a "dull [presumably male] editor to hamper, reject or curtail" (229).[64] Her partner in this parody of the Victoria Press is an artistically inclined supposed clergyman, though "unhappily not in orders," Rd. R. H. C. L. Mauleverer, a stranger to Avonmouth introduced while assisting her rescue of an injured dog from rising sea water (228).[65] "Never since she had grown up to be a thinking woman," the narrator explains, "had Rachel been so happy as with this outlet to her activity and powers of managing, 'the good times coming at last'" (231). She quickly begins canvassing for funds among her immediate neighbors and, when their "few five-pound notes" and "scanty supply of guineas and half-guineas" are insufficient to her needs, sells the horse on which many of her improving discussions with Colin Keith occurred, and then solicits everyone on the subscriber list of the Christian Knowledge Society in the name of the Female Union for Englishwoman's Employment, or F. U. E. E. (232).[66] Depositing all of the funds received in her own name at the Avoncester Bank, Rachel soon has enough "to justify beginning on a small scale" by renting a house just outside St. Norbert, "the very large and fashionable watering-place in the next indentation of the coast," to be presided over by a matron of Mauleverer's choosing (237, 230). The three children selected for the initial experiment, including the precocious Lovedy Kelland, are thereby largely placed beyond the supervision of either Rachel or a local clergyman, since the suburb of North Hill turns out to be "part of a great moorland parish" and, therefore, "almost pastorless" (239).[67] Nevertheless, as the solicitor and keeper of the F. U. E. E.'s funds, as well as its most vocal public proponent, Rachel assumes primary responsibility for the project's well-being, a position of authority that would ordinarily be assumed by a man.

The "good times" do not last at the F. U. E. E., which Rachel soon finds "a heavy drain on her private purse," although she is "happy" to exercise the "rigid economy" required to meet the "constant small expenses entailed by the first setting on foot [of] such an establishment" (267). In her zeal to supply the fledgling charity with sufficient funds, Rachel even seeks to monetize the Curtis family's land trust, Burnaby's Bargain, to provide additional income and supplies Mauleverer with all of the family's paperwork related to it.[68] Other characters begin to evince concern once they learn that the charity's children are not to be allowed to go home to their families for Christmas, and Colin Keith takes it upon himself to visit North Hill. He comes away suspicious, telling Rachel that the matron, Mrs Rawlins, reminds him "'strongly of a face I saw in India . . . a very handsome sepoy havildar whom we took at Lucknow; a capital soldier before the mutiny, and then an ineffable ruffian'" (319).[69] Soon after, both mothers lament their respective child's absence to Rachel, who begins to feel "as if there were a general conspiracy to drive her distracted" (321). In fact, Fanny Temple, Colin Keith, Alick Keith, and Ermine Williams do meet without her to discuss how best to undermine her blind confidence in her agent, Mauleverer.[70] Ultimately, they provide her with empirical proof, in the form of a plagiarized woodcut, for which Rachel has already advanced twenty pounds, that he may be neither the artist nor the pastoral steward that he has represented himself to be. Returning home "in a kind of dreamy bewilderment," Rachel is then met with testimony from the Curtis's former servants, the Rossiturs, who have set up their own shop and have been supplying the F. U. E. E., that they have not been paid for two months; adding to this discrepancy between her account books and Mauleverer's payments is the salacious detail that Mrs Rawlins has been seen at the "the-a-ter . . . dressed out in pink feathers" (331, 332). Simultaneously, Fanny makes an unscheduled visit to the asylum, discovers evidence of child abuse, removes both of the Avonmouth girls, and proceeds straight to the Curtis home, where, in a final embarrassment, Conrade Temple yells from the carriage in front of the assembled household and guests, "'Oh, Aunt Rachel, your F. U. thing is as bad as the Sepoys. But we have saved the two girls that they were whipping to death, and have got them in the carriage'" (340). Every member of her domestic and social circle, then, witnesses the consequences of Rachel's overreaching as announced by the youngest eldest son of the novel.[71]

Among the guests who hear Conrade's announcement is Mr Grey, and before long Rachel finds herself being deposed and her cleverwoman's assumption of masculine authority about to be tried more publicly. When she attempts to arrest the incipient proceedings, he tells her, in no uncertain terms, that the case is more serious than that of "'a silly girl who has been taken in by a sharper'" and that she has, "'for want of proper superintendence, or the merest rational precaution'" – recall her opening claim to act upon reason and conscience – made herself "'accountable for all this'" to a degree that her protestations now verge on "'obstruction to the course of justice'" (346). Briefly, her feminine cleverness has approached criminality.[72] It soon ascends to lethality bordering on perdition, as Rachel insists on nursing Lovedy Kelland – who is lethargic, emaciated, shockingly abused, and "unwilling to attempt to swallow" – with the aid of her own "homeopathic book" (349, 347). When Alick Keith diagnoses Lovedy with diphtheria, Rachel quickly resigns her place to a more traditional medical man, Dr Macvicar, but is unable to assist when called upon to perform the more feminine task of praying with the dying child, because the same reading that has made her a "sort of a pedant" has also led her into religious doubt.[73] Rachel herself recovers from her own bout with diphtheria just in time to serve as witness at Mauleverer's trial, conducted in "full view of faces which were far more familiar than she could have wished" (384). Under cross-examination, she is forced to admit that she had neither sought nor received any positive assurance from Mauleverer that the bills for the F. U. E. E. had been paid, and "being the Clever Woman of the family, only rendered her the more sensible both of the utter futility of her answer, and of the effect it must be producing" (386). The case against him is dismissed on the weakness of Rachel's testimony, which to "her excited, morbid apprehension, magnified by past self-sufficiency, it was as though all eyes were looking in triumph at that object of general scorn and aversion, a woman who had stepped out of her place" (387). Although found not guilty of embezzling F. U. E. E. funds, Mauleverer is quickly indicted for an earlier, similar fraud perpetrated on the Williams family when he was known as Maddox; in this second trial, thanks to the assiduity of Colin Keith, he is found guilty and sentenced to fourteen years of penal servitude. Prior to this more satisfying exercise of justice, Rachel learns, to her consternation, that she had been suspected of having had romantic feelings for Maulever, that if Dr Macvicar had not arrived before Lovedy's death she might have "been looking forward to a worse business than this at the next assizes," and that she had never even been in possession of true title deeds for Burnaby's Bargain (409). Proposed to by Alick, she makes a "full surrender of herself," becoming, in her own words, "a commonplace woman . . . just like other women, for I know I could not live without him" (420, 430). Her pejorative cleverness cured by "a meek submission, very touching in its passiveness and weary peacefulness," Rachel regains her faith under the tutelage of Alick's uncle, the reverend Mr Clare, and by the end of the novel normatively ascends to motherhood (431).[74]

"'Chafing against constraint and conventionality'"[75]

Although the thoroughness with which Yonge subjugates her female protagonist's impulses to assume the agency of a man may exceed that of Brontë, Gaskell, Collins, or Eliot, the difference is one of degree rather than kind. Moreover, while devoting so much of her narrative to the repudiation of Rachel's claims to phallic authority, Yonge also replicates and even amplifies the patriarchally disruptive strategies of her progressive peers. Thus, Rachel waxes fulsomely and articulately about the restrictions placed upon women's ability to act in the public sphere:

> "Here is the world around one mass of misery and evil! Not a paper do I take up but I see something about wretchedness and crime, and here I sit with health, strength, and knowledge, and able to do nothing, nothing – at the risk of breaking my mother's heart! . . . I know that every alley and lane of town or country reeks with vice and corruption, and that there is one cry for workers with brains and with purses! And here am I, able and willing, only longing to task myself to the uttermost, yet tethered down to the merest mockery of usefulness by conventionalities." (37–8)

She also quite perceptively links these conventionalities to the over-determining expectation of marriage, despite the statistical evidence proving the impossibility of this end for large numbers of women.[76]

Such occupations as were historically available to middle-class women are represented thoroughly in the novel. Rachel's mother and sister conscientiously perform the "quiet Lady Bountiful duties" expected of them, and the individual poor of Avonmouth benefit from their efforts, even as Rachel hints that this sort of lady's aid may be "too small and easy to satisfy a soul burning at the report of the great cry going up to heaven from a world of sin and woe" (42). Somewhat more promising is the provision of education to the young, a duty which Rachel herself discharges through her Sunday school classes and her aborted attempt to tutor Fanny's sons. She is succeeded in the latter task by Alison Williams, the younger sister of Ermine, who has been forced by "present reduced circumstances" to find work as a governess (95). "'Is it not a flagrant abuse,'" Rachel judges, "'that whether she have a vocation or not, every woman of a certain rank, who wishes to gain her own livelihood, must needs become a governess? A nursery maid must have a vocation, but an educated or half-educated woman has no choice; and educator she must become, to her own detriment, and that of her victims'" (56).[77] Although Alison proves herself highly capable – not just at maintaining discipline among Fanny's boys but also, thanks to her "firmness," at saving Conrade from the same diphtheria that kills Lovedy and afflicts Rachel (376) – her particular case does not invalidate Rachel's more general critique. Indeed, the abuse suffered by the girls at the F. U. E. E. is coincident upon installing a woman with no natural facility for educating children in charge of the asylum.[78] Alison's sister Ermine earns her share of their household's wages as a professional writer, under the pseudonym "the Invalid"; reviewer, a task she describes as "pleasant and improving, not to say profitable" (122); and, when the male editor of the *Traveller's Review* magazine is on holiday, shadow subeditor, in which capacity she recruits Colin Keith to copy the text of letters of rejection because her hand "betrays womanhood" (166). As the founding editor of and a significant contributor to *The Monthly Packet* (1851–94), Yonge knew this branch of women's employment well, and so her hints about the need for Ermine to write under a pseudonym and disguise her handwriting should carry particular weight when measuring the precise limits to female agency still enforced in the literary world.[79] Even professional nursing makes a brief appearance in the novel, in the person of the "nice little Sister, rather young . . . but who turned out thoroughly efficient, nearly as good as doctor" whom Colin Keith engages to take care of Mrs Rawlins, a. k. a. Maria Hatherton, after her arrest when her daughter also shows symptoms of diphtheria (363).[80]

This same Sister exemplifies a form of sororal bonding particular to Yonge's High Church milieu. Anglican Sisterhoods had begun to be established under the auspices of the Oxford Movement in the 1840s, providing devout Anglican women with an acceptably Protestant form of convent life, the women living in an independent all-female commune and providing charitable service to the nearby public.[81] *The Clever Woman of the Family* also features other, less denominationally specific forms of social bonds for women outside of heteronormative marriage.[82] Well into their twenties and thirties, respectively, the pairings of Grace and Rachel Curtis and Ermine and Alison Williams have sustained their consanguineous sisters without having to rely upon fathers, brothers, or husbands. After Rachel marries Alick, the highly eligible Grace appears simply to strengthen her ties to her widowed mother rather than to seek male companionship; in like manner, once Ermine and Colin Keith wed, Alison is taken in as permanent companion by Fanny Temple. Provocatively, Ermine describes her sister's new relationship with Fanny in matrimonial terms, telling Colin, "'when you go to Avoncester, I think you may as well get a license for the wedding of Alison Williams and Fanny Temple at the same time. There has been quite a courtship on the lady's part'" (528).[83]

Grace and Alison's second round of domestic partners also begins to highlight the centrally important role assigned to mothers in Yonge's novel. For all of her fretful anxiety, Mrs Curtis succeeds in protecting Rachel from the most scandalous gossip surrounding her relationship to Mauleverer, and she similarly warns Fanny against the ways that her conduct as a young new widow might be misconstrued by her Avonmouth society neighbors.[84] As a mother herself, Fanny provides for her seven children, presumes to visit the F. U. E. E. without an appointment, adroitly divides her forces once inside to allow for a full investigation, bears away the abused children, and is proclaimed by Rachel the "heroine" of the story (376). Rachel demonstrates her improvement as a character through her own willingness to serve as temporary foster mother to her infant nephew, Alexander, after the death of his biological mother, and once she and Alick have their own daughter, Una, Rachel worries with him about how to contain the "perilous" cleverness of their offspring (547). Young Alexander becomes the long-term foster child of Colin and Ermine, who has already shown her maternal gifts by raising her brother's daughter, Rose, for the three years prior to the main story. Even more so than the maternal figures of *Shirley* and *North and South*, these three younger mothers of *The Clever Woman of the Family* especially promise to exercise formative influence over the lives of their numerous and still developing offspring.

Rachel and Ermine's husbands, the Keith cousins Alick and Colin, are, along with Alick's uncle, the Rev. George Clare, the novel's most idealized male authority figures. All also exhibit physical disabilities, highlighting the degree to which Yonge has invested in her contemporaries' strategy of representing masculinity as always already compromised. Both veterans of the recent pacification of India, Alick and Colin carry with them tangible evidence of their service. Like Rochester, Alick is missing a hand; he is also subject, when under stress, to recurrent attacks of malarial fever sufficiently severe to be described as "failure of the physical powers" (475).[85] Colin suffers from what the narrative repeatedly refers to as a "weak chest," a general vulnerability to cool or inclement weather consequent upon still carrying a musket ball embedded in his torso.

The effects of this remnant of India are perceptible in his appearance, which Ermine pronounces "worn and altered" when she first sees him again after their long separation and "much thinner" when he returns from a brief visit to Scotland (120, 244).[86] Mr Clare, whose combination of gentle saintliness and profound erudition are sufficient to bring Rachel back to the High Church Anglican fold, is blind. This does not prevent him from navigating his garden without assistance or even chaperoning Rachel on a shopping trip to London, but it does place limits on his capacity of independent action: he must have a live-in curate or a full-time familial assistant to fulfill all his pastoral duties and keep up his house.[87]

The patriarch of the Keith clan, Lord Keith, also suffers and finally dies from physical vulnerability, even as he exhibits characterological infirmities that are more typical of the novel's class of less excellent men. First described as giving "the impression of a far greater age than fifty-eight; there was the stoop of rheumatism, and a worn, thin look on the face," Lord Keith succeeds in getting "himself rigged out in London . . . so that he looks ten years younger" when he returns to court Fanny and, ultimately, to marry Alick's sister Bessie (179, 245). Unfortunately, he is quickly back to being supposedly "laid up with sciatica" before, finally, dying from a combination of "a blow from the end of a scaffold-pole" and a lack of immediate medical attention (440, 450). Looking old or young, in good health or bad, however, he is "a hard, self-seeking man, who has been harsh and grasping towards his family," and who definitively reforms his behavior with respect to Colin and Ermine's marriage only when faced with death and in need of a guardian for his infant son and heir (295). Edward Williams, the brother of Ermine and Alison and the first victim of Maddox's fraud, is differently but no less seriously flawed as a character. Predisposed to live "with his head in the clouds," Edward is left "too broken-hearted" by the death of his wife "to care for vindicating himself" or nurturing his still-living daughter (124). After Colin retrieves him from Russia in time for Maddox's trial, Edward seems to Ermine "not so much changed as exaggerated . . . most loving when roused, but infinitely more inclined to fall off into a muse" (491); unfiltered by filial sympathy, Grace's impression is that he looks "a wreck of a man, stunned and crushed," although he does exert himself during the trial and, after, is capable of thanking Colin if not of rebuilding his paternal relationship to Rose (494). Not surprisingly, perhaps, the novel's villain, Maddox, displays the most extreme faults of male character: addicted to gambling, he seduces and eventually abandons Maria Hatherton, embezzles from Edward, emotionally traumatizes Rose, relatively impoverishes Ermine and Alison, commits forgery, and seems "to take a kind of pleasure in explaining the whole web, almost" (500). However, Maddox also begins life "a respectable ironmonger's son," receives no parental support to transfer from a commercial to a more artistic middle-class fraction, and does nothing positively criminal until Edward's lackadaisical supervision combines with his own inclination to gambling – which we now recognized as a form of disabling addiction – to provide him with more temptation than he can resist. He is responsible for his actions but also recognizably middle-class in his aspirations and not entirely unsympathetic in his weakness to over-determining circumstances.[88]

"Really large-minded and generous"[89]

Given how it treats its antagonist, it is little wonder that *The Clever Woman of the Family* expends considerably more narrative energy in rehabilitating readers' opinions of its protagonist and, by extension, of the right sort of strong-minded woman. Even in the midst of her schemes of usefulness, Rachel's intentions remain overwhelmingly disinterested, her frustrations eminently justified, and her ideas generously accessible to contrary evidence and adverse judgments. When Ermine's identity as the Invalid is revealed to her, for instance, she responds with "a genuine simplicity that almost looked like humour," accepts that there "'may be something'" to the idea that she allows her own preconceived notions to blind her to exceptional particulars, and praises her sister as generally more perceptive than herself (313). Alick admires her "'real truth and unselfishness'" and thinks "'her wildest blunders better than parrot commonplace'" (416, 484). Even Colin Keith, who first judges her a "'detestable, pragmatic, domineering girl,'" is converted, finding Rachel "'showing to great advantage'" at Bishopsworthy (166, 525). Moreover, although the F. U. E. E. fails spectacularly, it serves as the catalyst for lasting philanthropy, in the form of a "tidy industrial school" in Avonmouth paid for in part by the proceeds of Burnaby's Bargain (433).

Rachel's virtues come to light with particular clarity during the crisis of Bessie's accident, premature childbirth, and death. Consistently popular, apparently clever, and successful in pleasing everyone except Alick, Bessie not only outshines Rachel for much of the novel but also periodically makes her the object of her own "demon of teasing" (274). On her deathbed, Bessie admits, "'I never thought I should have loved you so well, when I quizzed you. I did use you ill then,'" and she dies "supported in Rachel's arms" (473, 474). After her death, Rachel helps to sort through Bessie's possessions and private papers, perceiving in them sad proof of Bessie's "'vanity of vanities, all is vanity,'" an "accumulation of expensive trinkets . . . evidently for her own gratification" (508). She and Colin also find outstanding bills confirming that Bessie "'must have greatly exceeded her means, and have used much cleverness and ingenuity in keeping the tradesmen quiet,'" and suggesting that she may have neglected and thereby contributed to the incipient death of Lord Keith (510). Bessie's is a species of cleverness entirely unfamiliar to Rachel, who ends the novel unselfishly "'awake to larger interests, and doing common things better for being the Clever Woman of the family'" (545).

This late appraisal is made by Ermine, who had, much earlier, recognized Rachel's worth and similarity to her own younger self.[90] However, what Rachel, and through her the reader, comes to understand, is that Ermine best exemplifies Yonge's standard of clever womanhood. "'The most superior person I ever knew,'" Rachel pronounces her indignantly to Mrs Menteith, Ermine combines intellect with empathy, principled action with careful observation, publicity with anonymity, and influential agency with the renunciation of masculine authority. Without her subtle intervention, neither of Maddox's frauds would have been exposed, but she did not, herself, seek to act as the prosecutor. Even the ultimate paterfamilias of the novel, Lord Keith, ultimately bends to her and relies upon her to preserve his patrilineal inheritance by fostering young Alexander. In an unambiguous acknowledgment of intelligent and self-abnegating women as *a*, and perhaps *the*, necessary and sufficient condition of men's middle-class status at mid-century and after, the novel's final words are spoken by one such woman, Rachel, about another, both now married: "'commend me to such a Clever Woman of the family as Ermine Keith'" (547).

Notes

1. The actual figures cited by Edward Cheshire in "The Results of the Census of Great Britain in 1851, with a Description of the Machinery and Processes employed to obtain the Returns," a paper read before the BAAS and subsequently published in the *Journal of the Statistical Society of London* one month prior to the serialized start of *Hard*

Times, were 358,420 and 512,361 more females than males in England and Great Britain, respectively, yielding a relative proportion of 100 males to every 105 females. Cheshire noted that the latter number was "as many as would have filled the Crystal Palace 5 times over" and should be judged a "remarkable fact when it was considered that births during the last 13 years had given the reversed proportion of 105 *boys* to 100 *girls*" (46). Parsed by age and marital status, these numbers became even more startling in light of "revelations that two-thirds of women aged 20–4 and one third of women aged 24–35 were unmarried" (Dreher, 4).
2. Baird, 401.
3. The essays reprinted in Lillian Nayder's edited collection, *Dickens, Sexuality, and Gender*, provide an excellent one-volume introduction to the range of approaches to and interpretations of Dickens's vexed representations of women from the mid-1980s through the first decade of the twenty-first century. The discovery in February 2019 of a trove of letters revealing that Dickens had attempted to have his wife Catherine confined to a lunatic asylum in order to more easily carry on his affair with actress Ellen Ternan made international news and has added an unavoidably unsavory dimension to subsequent critical understandings of his female characters.
4. Among the now-classic works of feminist history, cultural and social theory, and literary criticism with special relevance for Victorian studies are Amanda Anderson's *Tainted Souls and Painted Faces*, Nancy Armstrong's *Desire and Domestic Fiction*, Leonore Davidoff and Catherine Hall's *Family Fortunes*, Sandra Gilbert and Susan Gubar's *Madwoman in the Attic*, Elizabeth Langland's *Nobody's Angels*, Mary Poovey's *Uneven Developments*, and Elaine Showalter's *A Literature of the Their Own*.
5. In Lacanian terms, they must deny their claim to the symbolic phallus. Lacan's most definitive discussion of the symbolic phallus appears in "La signification du phallus" (1966), translated as "The Signification of the Phallus" in Alan Sheridan's *Écrits: A Selection*, 281–91.
6. According to Vanden Bossche, the First Reform Act "raised the number of eligible voters in England and Wales from 366,00 to 653,000, an increase from 11 percent to 18 percent of the adult male population . . . This modest increase meant that, even after passage of the Act, four out of five adult males—*and, of course, all women*—did not have the right to vote" (1, emphasis added). "The History of the Parliamentary Franchise," prepared by Neil Johnston, Senior Library Clerk specializing in elections at the House of Commons Library, provides a similarly-sized differential between the pre- and post-Reform electorate – at 516,000 and 809,000, respectively, for all of Great Britain and Ireland – but estimates that "the Great Reform Act of 1832 probably increased the total electorate by over 50%" (4).

7. Derek Heater, *Citizenship in Britain*, 107. The UK Parliament website confirms that "[b]efore 1832 there were occasional, although rare, instances of women voting" ("The Reform Act 1832"). Johnston similarly defines "Ancient voting rights in England" as "[r]estricted to males by custom rather than statute" and "not specifically prohibit[ing] women's suffrage" (6, 7; see also 19). Even as they were prevented from voting in parliamentary elections, unmarried women continued to be enfranchised in parish vestry elections by the Vestries Act 1818 (37).
8. The New Poor Law also briefly empowered female ratepayers to vote in the election of poor law guardians, but this right was rescinded by the Municipal Corporations Act 1835, which redefined "the local electorate . . . by inserting the words 'male persons'" (Johnston, 38).
9. On Norton's life and writing, see Diane Atkinson's *The Criminal Conversation of Mrs Norton*, Alan Chedzoy's *A Scandalous Woman*, Randall Craig's *The Narratives of Caroline Norton*, and Gail Savage's "Caroline Norton (1808–1877)."
10. Writing a letter to the editor of the *British and Foreign Review* that was printed in the *Examiner* on 26 August 1838, during the ongoing debate over the Custody of Infants Bill, Norton responded to the former periodical's recent *ad hominem* attack by repudiating any desire for gender equality: "I believe the beauty and devotion of a woman's character mainly to depend on the consciousness of her inferiority to man, and that the greatest suffering a right-minded and pure-hearted woman can feel, is to be *unable* to respect and look up to her husband" (531).
11. The Custody of Infants Act became the statutory basis for the "tender years doctrine," according to which custody disputes involving young children were summarily decided in favor of mothers well into the 1960s in Britain and the United States.
12. *The Annual Register, 1842*, 165, 166, 167–8.
13. During the 1844 debate, Lord Ashley, again, "dwelt particularly on the extensive prevalence, in many factories, of employing women for continuous lengths of time so great, as to preclude, especially in the case of mothers, the possibility of their attending to their natural duties" and "adverted still more earnestly to the fearful effect produced upon the morals through the promiscuous way in which males and females are intermingled in their working hours" (*The Annual Register, 1844*, 109). The sponsor of the 1847 bill, Oldham MP John Fielden, similarly stated, "The house and children of a labouring man can only be kept clean and healthy by the assiduous labour of a well-trained, industrious wife" (*The Annual Register, 1847*, 111).
14. That Nightingale became the pioneering example of female nursing rather than her Crimean War contemporary, British-Jamaican volunteer Mary "Mother" Seacole (1805–81), speaks to the relative privilege afforded to white, socially well-connected women as compared with women of color even during this early period of limited opportunities

for all women. Seacole's autobiography, often credited as the first published by a black woman in Britain, *Wonderful Adventure of Mrs Seacole in Many Lands*, was first published in 1857 and includes details of her initial medical training in Jamaica and her self-funded work on behalf of British soldiers in Crimea.

15. On the shortcomings of the 1857 Matrimonial Causes Act, as well as the importance of Caroline Norton's well-publicized marriage to its passage, see Poovey's "Covered but not Bound," reprinted as chapter three of *Uneven Developments*.

16. On the relationship between the Married Women's Property Act 1870 and the legal doctrine of couverture, see Rachel Ablow, "'One Flesh,' One Person, and the 1870 Married Women's Property Act."

17. The socially and culturally overdetermined limits of plausibility in the Victorian period may well have meant, for instance, that the creation of a young woman protagonist whose intentions and actions fully realize the expectations of twenty-first-century feminist narrative would have been inconceivable to most nineteenth-century authors; such a character would almost certainly have been met with hostile incredulity by a commercially prohibitive percentage of period readers. Which is to say that the feminism of nineteenth-century fictions must be sought in subtler forms than fully "woke" heroes and heroines.

18. Brontë, *Jane Eyre*, 473.

19. Marrying Rochester may allow Jane to solemnize the supernatural bond of their love, but it also ensures that control of Jane's inheritance will pass from her to him, given that the laws of couverture remained in effect for a further 23 years after the novel was published, and perhaps more than 60 years after the main events were set. Even before the narrative's romantic climax, of course, Jane had already begun the process of renouncing the social independence created by her uncle's legacy by disbursing the money among her cousins.

20. Brontë, *Jane Eyre*, 114–15.

21. In adapting the form of the bildungsroman in *Jane Eyre*, Brontë also makes a generic statement about the suitability of women's characters for narratives of development.

22. Commenting on the "chiasmal marriages—that of bold Robert to shy Caroline and that of domestic Louis to adventurous Shirley," Plotz notes that "both women's roles will be essentially passive and observant, both men emotionally stolid, but vicariously attached to a larger world of mills and markets" (158).

23. Brontë, *Shirley*, 200. The restraints that Shirley herself places upon Caroline during and after the attack on the mill, physically preventing her from joining her eventual husband, Robert Moore, because "'Men never want women near them in time of real danger'" (341), lead Rosemarie Bodenheimer to dismiss altogether "any pretenses about the nature of [Brontë's] feminism" (295).

24. Brontë, *Shirley*, 217.
25. Although there are critiques of society's unfairly normative expectations for women and demonstrations of sororal and maternal coupling throughout the novel, volume two, chapter one, "Shirley and Caroline," offers readers a concentrated synecdoche of all three strategic feminist alternatives in one place.
26. Like *Jane Eyre*, *Shirley* also makes a statement about gender on the basis of a formal choice about genre, in this case placing two women at the heart of an historical novel set during the Napoleonic wars and the Luddite disturbances. The novel also includes a biting dismissal of Milton's depiction of Eve, thereby implicitly claiming a superior verisimilitude for itself and the novel more generally over poetry when it comes to the depiction of women (320).
27. Brontë, *Villette*, 18–19. The backstory of Miss Marchmont, whose afflicted spinsterhood emerges out of the dragging death of her young lover Frank, offers another instance of *Villette*'s nod to women's overdetermined position (see esp. 50). Lucy's second employer, Mme. Beck, "ought to have swayed a nation . . . In her own single person, she could have comprised the duties of a first minister and a superintendent of police," but, as she is a woman, "her powers" are confined to the "too limited sphere" of her school (91). Even the flighty Ginevra Fanshawe, who, Lydia-Bennett-like, scandalously elopes with Count de Hamal near the story's end, is described by herself and later excused by Lucy as a product of her limited financial circumstances and upbringing (see 67–8, 280).
28. Ibid. 134–5, 174, 366.
29. M. Paul's choleric outbursts and subsequent emotionally manipulative reconciliations are too numerous to cite, although it is worth noting that his controlling impulses do manifest once as a physical blow. In order to secure a final interview with Lucy, who is anxious to excuse him, he strikes Mme Beck when she will not leave the classroom of her own pensionnat:

> She was opening her lips to retort; I saw over all M. Paul's face a quick rising light and fire; I can hardly tell how he managed the movement; it did not seem violent; it kept the form of courtesy; he gave his hand; it scarce touched her I thought; she ran, she whirled from the room; she was gone, and the door shut, in one second." (601)

30. Gaskell, *North and South*, 177–8.
31. Gallagher, *Industrial Reformation*, 172. In Gaskell's own words, Margaret is concerned that "Mr Thornton might be smitten down,—he who she had urged and goaded to come to this perilous place" (179).
32. Gaskell, *North and South*, 179.
33. Bodenheimer reads "Margaret's insistence that her act [during the strike] is a representative piece of women's work" as a "defensive

meaning" actuated by shame at "having left the protected women's place for one of unwomanly publicity" (299).
34. Gaskell, *North and South*, 435.
35. As one example among many, note Thornton's request to his mother that she help him "'as you helped me when I was a child . . . when my father died'" now that he has come to bankruptcy and his "great comfort to have had this conversation" (425). Such instances are sufficiently frequent to serve as a structural element for Gallagher, who writes, "Much of the plot of *North and South* turns on the relationships Mrs Hale and Mrs Thornton have with their sons, and several of the characters' comments highlight the social importance of mothers. Indeed, on one occasion the familial metaphor is used to express a belief in social maternalism" (*Industrial Reformation*, 168–9).
36. Collins, *The Woman in White*, 342.
37. Ibid. 357, 431.
38. Marian first appears in the novel as an erotic silhouette topped by a head pronounced "ugly" because of its incongruously male appearance: "the dark brown on her upper lip was almost a moustache. She had a large, firm, masculine mouth" (58); Walter is "almost repelled by the masculine form and masculine look of the features in which the perfectly shaped figure ended" (59). Marian soon confirms this appearance in her manner, advising Walter to conquer his disappointment at Laura's engagement in explicitly gendered terms: "'Crush it!' she said . . . 'Don't shrink under it like a woman. Tear it out; trample it under foot like a man!'" (96).
39. Ironically, the most authentic among the novel's monstrous men is Fairlie, who is the only one not to live under a false name or false pretenses. Referring to Walter and his fellow protagonists, Tamara Wagner writes, "The antiheroes of Collins's novels eschew Victorian fashions of a muscular masculinity, anticipating the rise of the new fin de siècle antihero but also harking back to the sentimental heroes of the late eighteenth-century novel of sentiment or sensibility" ("'Overpowering Vitality,'" 471).
40. The novel's preamble actually begins, "This is the story of what a Woman's patience can endure, and what a Man's resolution can achieve" (33).
41. Collins, *No Name*, 655, 697.
42. Ibid. 707. As Wragge tells Magdalen once she has begun to recover, "'Somebody was wanted to take care of you, while you were not able to take care of yourself'" (714).
43. Ibid. 716.
44. Ibid. 726.
45. Ibid. 735.
46. As ably summarized by Helena Michie, the "moral of the story, depending as it does on the symmetry of the two sisters' relation to

marriage, family, and inheritance, is that feminine passivity will reap the very rewards that female aggression seeks and fails to achieve" (409). Additionally, Debra Morris argues that, as in *North and South*, in *No Name* and other Collins novels, "maternal figures are important. They provide a way to assess his sympathy toward women and their effacement in a society that places so much meaning on inheritance and name, the cultural domain assigned to the father. . . . Throughout her adventures Magdalen plays out various maternal narratives before embracing the traditional one, and these narratives fail specifically *because* they allow her to express herself as a sexual subject." (271, 273).

47. Eliot, *Felix Holt*, 223.
48. Ibid. 293, 294.
49. The limitations placed on Esther, Mrs Transome, and Mrs Holt are, for Lesjak, symptomatic of "restrictions on pleasure" built into the Victorian novel: "The unredeemed pleasures in all these texts—the impulses of which are often expressed through these novels' heroines—testify both to the oppressive strictures which govern women's lives, specifically, and to a longing, more generally, for social spaces inclusive of larger domains of experience" (*Working Fictions*, 13).
50. Eliot, *Felix Holt*, 398.
51. Ibid. 397.
52. Ibid. 373.
53. The most sensational scenes in the novel seek to motivate readers' horror at the abuse, both physical and emotional, of children: thus, Lovedy, "with a fugitive action of terror," unpins "the thin coarse shawl on her neck . . . revealing the terrible stripes and weals of recent beating" (337); and Rose, after a paroxysm of weeping for an untruth "wrested from her by terror," recounts to Colin Keith a memory of "dreadful letters in light over the door" and lions "growling in papa's dressing room" manufactured the night her father's seal was likely stolen to traumatize her into remaining silent about an ongoing affair between her father's agent and her nurse (306–7). Even in these terror-infused scenes, however, Yonge does not go to the extremes that one might expect from some of her peers in the sensational sixties, including Collins, but also Braddon and Reade. Such reserve, Susan Colón argues in "Realism and Reserve," is even more at work in her meticulous depictions of domestic space, whose accumulated "minutia of ordinary life" do not hint at the overdetermining force of past decisions or present social expectations, as they might in Eliot, but rather provide evidence for Yonge's commitment to Tractarian aesthetics:

In the proliferation of quotidian detail, specific incidents do not necessarily declare their typological significance. Whereas poetry is precalculated to draw attention to its ontological status as indirect discourse with a meaning beyond its surface, realism requires readers to sift through common life in search of typological significance. Consequently, realism can train the reader to look for potential reserved truths in the midst of entirely unsacramental activity and details. (228)

Yonge's fictional reliance upon Tractarian aesthetics also receives extensive treatment in Gavin Budge's *Charlotte M. Yonge*, which "argues that Tractarian ideas enabled Yonge to formulate a feminist position which, as expressed in her fiction, questioned or subverted many aspects of Victorian gender ideology" from the perspective of what Budge labels "conservative feminist critique" (13, 25).

54. Labeling the text "an explicitly anti-feminist novel," Janice Fiamengo acknowledges that "*The Clever Woman of the Family* (1865) is a difficult text for the feminist critic, at least for those of us who believe that the oppressed don't enjoy their oppression" ("Forms of Suffering in Charlotte Yonge's *The Clever Woman of the Family*," 80). More interested in feminist recovery, Laura Fasick stipulates that "Yonge's fiction, despite its social conservatism, insists upon the autonomy and dignity of women as independent moral beings" ("The Ambivalence of Influence," 145). And, in her "Introduction – Novelist with a Reserved Mission" to the August 2010 special issue of *Women's Writing* dedicated to Yonge, Wagner summarizes that recent "interest in Yonge revolves precisely around the need to do away with any easy typecasting of nineteenth-century domestic women novelists. Instead, she has become a central figure in a reconsideration of simplistic dichotomies of feminist versus antifeminist writers" (214). The issue's subsequent essays include Colón's excavation of Yonge's realism as Tractarian reserve; Susan Walton, "Charlotte Yonge: Marketing the Missionary Story," and Teresa Huffman Traver, "'The Ship that Bears through the Waves,'" both of which approach Yonge's thematics of imperialism, and Elizabeth Hale's exploration of Yonge's representations of physical disability in "Disability and the Individual Talent."

55. Wagner's subsequent parenthetical observes that "salutary humiliation" is "a common, almost obligatory plot-element in Yonge's fiction" ("'Everything was a system with Rachel,'" 43). June Sturrock similarly describes *The Clever Woman of the Family* as a "narrative of salutary punishment" ("*Emma* in the 1860s," 328).

56. Charlotte Yonge, *The Clever Woman of the Family*, 506. Hereafter cited parenthetically in the text. For a sympathetic reading of the "conservative feminist" potential of this passage, see Budge, pp. 297–8.

57. According to Barbara Dennis, *Charlotte Yonge*, Keble arrived as vicar of Otterbourne, Hampshire, Yonge's home, in January 1836, when Yonge was only twelve, and throughout her "impressionable youth and in the early years of her fame as a novelist all the famous names from the developments in the church were visitors to Keble" and, through him, to Yonge as well (3).

58. This judgment on her own younger self is pronounced by Rachel after marriage (537).
59. According to Sturrock, Rachel's determination is in this instance typical of many of the female characters created by Yonge, who "never presents a woman as frustrated because she is not married; she is far more likely to express the frustrations of being without appropriate work, as she does in *The Clever Woman of the Family*" ("Something to Do," 36).
60. As Rachel confides to Ermine Williams, "'If I can make myself useful with my pen, it will compensate for the being debarred from so many more obvious outlets'" (105). Rachel is not at this point aware of Ermine's own rather more successful work as an author, of which more in the following subsection.
61. Rachel's realization of her mistake with Alick Keith makes her feel "more disconcerted than ever had been her lot before" and, despite his self-deprecation, she ends the evening having "never felt so beaten down and ashamed of herself" (281, 288).
62. Despite the "sudden humiliation" that accompanies finally learning of Colin Keith's longtime attachment to Ermine Williams, Rachel does have the honesty and disinterestedness to "honour them both . . . out of the innermost depths of her candid heart" when discussing the matter with her mother later that same day (272, 277).
63. Signaling her awareness of Bodichon and Parkes's efforts, Yonge has Rachel plan to submit "Curatocult" once it has been rejected by the *Traveller's Review*, to the *Englishwoman's Hobbyhorse* – where it is also declined – and describes Rachel as reading the report of the Social Science Congress while waiting for Bessie Keith's train to arrive (159, 192). As noted in the Broadview edition, both passages are thinly-veiled references to the *English Woman's Journal*, which included such reports among its articles.
64. Although focused primarily on Yonge's *The Stokesley Secret* (1861), Leslee Thorne-Murphey's broader observation that Yonge is invested in "revealing the mixed motives that masquerade as philanthropy, in an attempt to come to a more thorough and beneficial understanding of worthy charity work" applies with equal facility to Rachel's combination of altruism and self-interest with respect to the F. U. E. E. ("The Charity Pig," 281).
65. Middle-class readers with even a passing knowledge of French were surely meant to be on their guard against this nominalized portmanteau of "*mauvais lever*," literally "bad riser," more colloquially "social climber" or "bounder."
66. It is at the mischievous suggestion of Bessie Keith that Rachel almost makes her appeal on behalf of the Female Union for Lace-makers Employment, or F. U. L. E., the Scots spelling of "fool," and only a last-minute intervention by Alick Keith prevents her from doing so. In this

incident of unfortunate acronyms, Yonge was surely thinking of the Langham Place group again and their equally unappealing Society for Promoting the Employment of Women, or S. P. E. W.

67. From Yonge's High Church perspective, this absence of clerical supervision, which Rachel values just short of decrying pastoral "meddling," is the clearest signal she can give of the troubles to come (239). In fact, Dennis refers to *The Clever Woman of the Family* as Yonge's "most forceful indictment of a secular foundation" (69).

68. Once she surrenders the paperwork, "Rachel was in higher spirits than ever. To oblige the estate to pay £140 a year to the F. U. E. E. was beyond measure delightful, and though it would be in fact only taking out of the family pocket, yet that was a pocket she could not otherwise get at" (270).

69. Yonge's repeated references to "the mutiny" indicate the degree to which even her resolutely domestic novel relies upon its readers' lingering outrage over this most recent and dangerous symptom of colonial unrest to establish the relative merits of its male and female characters.

70. As Fanny tells the others, "'if those people are deceiving Rachel, who knows what they may be doing to the poor children'" (326).

71. In "Feminist Social Reform and the Problems with Patriarchy in Charlotte Yonge's *Clever Woman of the Family*," Audrey Fessler reads the downfall of the F. U. E. E. somewhat differently. Rather than attribute the charity's "catastrophic collapse" to Rachel's non-normative overreaching, Fessler identifies the cause as the "socially mandated reliance on male aid. Ironically, the very society that requires Rachel to rely on male guidance to accomplish her indisputably worthy goals cannot furnish a single man who will publicly and honestly help her to reach those goals" (52).

72. The criminalizing of Rachel's cleverness is of a piece with what Budge describes as "Yonge's often challenging portrayals of a middle class sliding into deliquescence for want of self-discipline" and an overweening faith in "the effects of rationalism" (105).

73. Rachel recalls this incident during her own subsequent illness: "'Tell me of my Saviour,' the dying child had said; and the drawn face had lightened at the words to which Rachel's oracles declared that people attached crude or arbitrary meanings; and now she hardly knew what they conveyed to her, and longed, as for something far away, for the reality of those simple teachings" (372). Herein, for Yonge, lies the true problem with female cleverness – it leads to a loss of religious faith.

74. Critics invested in Yonge's feminist recuperation must simply accept the limitations of Rachel's story: Fiamengo describes her narrative trajectory as "re-education through humiliation" until "marriage and motherhood decisively cure her insubordination" (80); and Emily Morris writes, in "Imperfect and Alternative Marriages in Charlotte Yonge's *Heartsease* and *The Clever Woman of the Family*," that, certainly,

"Rachel is reformed, after being severely punished for her desire to be something other than a wife" (40).

75. This phrase is also a description of Rachel, made in this case by Ermine Williams, who is defending her to Colin Keith (168).
76. "'Is it for any better reason than because no mother can bear to believe her daughter no longer on the lists for matrimony? Our dear mother does not tell herself that this is the reason, but she is unconsciously actuated by it'" (38).
77. Reflecting on Yonge's career as a professional writer, her "life-long involvement in schools," and her "encouragement of women's colleges" in her later life, Budge asserts that Yonge "probably did as much as any other single figure in the nineteenth century to promote women's education" (38).
78. Mrs Rawlins turns out to be Maria Hatherton, Maddox's accomplice in his fraud of the Williams family and the mother of his illegitimate child. While working at the Williams home as nurse to their daughter, Rose, she has already exhibited her potential for abuse, euphemistically rendered as "tyranny in the nursery" (310).
79. On Yonge's extensive work at *The Monthly Packet*, see Kristine Moruzi's "Never Read Anything that Can at All Unsettle Your Religious Faith." On the strength of her periodical experience, one suspects, and despite Yonge's own at times considerable sales as a novelist – she was able to outfit a mission ship to Melanesia using the proceeds from *The Heir of Redclyffe* (1853) – there are also a number of hints that literary labor does not pay particularly well. For example, it is only with the aid of Alison's final wages from her work as a governess at Cliff Cottages that the sisters can consider taking a domestic holiday or buying either "a respectable Sunday mantle" or a cheap edition of *Ivanhoe* (85).
80. Sadly, "all the care and kindness of the good Sisters at St. Norbert's" are insufficient to save Alice Hatherton, whose mother remains "in a dull, silent, tearless misery, quietly doing all that was required of her, but never speaking nor giving the ladies any opening to try to make an impression upon her" (373).
81. Livia Arndal Woods offers a succinct history of the Anglican Sisterhood movement on pp. 152–4 of "'What are they to do with their lives?'"; regarding *The Clever Woman of the Family* specifically, Woods writes that "comparing these two women," Rachel and the unnamed Sister, might lead the reader to intuit that if "Rachel had only spent her time fostering her feminine skills . . . she might have helped to stave off a child's death – she might have been useful." (156). Simmons, in the Introduction to the Broadview edition of Yonge's novel, somewhat differently draws attention to how, "when the Sisterhood in St. Norbert's provides a refuge for one of the characters," Yonge may be hinting "that for women of less means than Grace, communities of women with an emphasis on nursing offer a way of doing good" (15).

82. As Fasick observes, "Yonge at least envisions various possibilities for women within domesticity, including contented spinsterhood and life-long companionate relationships with other women" that, when "pitted against Victorian heterosexual ideology with its concomitant sense of the 'redundancy' of unmarried women," offers "some sense of empowerment" (146).
83. Fanny and Alison's final companionate relationship is, perhaps, the most striking example in *The Clever Woman of the Family* of what Emily Morris refers to as a Yonge's broader novelistic predilection for "alternative unions that take place in spite of, and with more ease and joy than, traditional patriarchal marriages" (35).
84. Mrs Curtis, "rather glad to have a witness to the surprise" the news causes Rachel, finally tells her daughter about the gossip from which she has been screening her in the presence of the elderly Miss Wellwood (403). Her advice to Fanny is made much earlier, both in the novel and in the process of gossip-mongering, and without any witnesses: "'Understand me, my dear, I am not at all afraid of your – your doing anything foolish, only to get talked of is so dreadful in your situation, that you can't be too careful'" (152).
85. Alick must also have extensive physical scarring, since he is described as "almost shattered to pieces" by "a general smash of all the locomotive machinery" on one side of his body (120, 284).
86. Colin also keeps two convalescent house guests, "a rheumatic sergeant" and "an exemplary consumptive tailor," prior to his marriage to Ermine (304).
87. Clemence Schultze reflects, "It is striking how feminized are the chief male characters in this book, their masculinity partaking of aspects related to home and nurture. All have suffered injury and/or illness, and have been the objects of care; they become considerate and perceptive carers for the women" ("Absent Fathers and Faithful Wives," 83).
88. Located somewhere between the compromised characterological positions of Edward and Maddox is Charley Carleton, "a regular case of a bad shilling" whose inopportune attentions to Bessie precipitate her fatal "tumbling over a [croquet] hoop," but who, after his forgiveness by Alick, accepts "a situation in a new field of labour, in a spirit of manful duty that he had never evinced before" (452, 465, 504).
89. A final, unspoken appraisal of Rachel's character by Colin, who has now been thoroughly converted to Ermine's point of view (512).
90. Ermine's comparison between Rachel and herself begins somewhat condescendingly – "'she is just what I should been without papa and Edward to keep me down, and without the civilizing atmosphere at the park" – before conceding the advantage to her younger counterpart – "'I was not her equal in energy and beneficence'" – and admitting "'I feel for her longing to be up and doing'" (168).

Afterword

As the wife of the eldest surviving member of the Keith clan, with the young heir literally "scrambling to his place" in her lap "as one who felt it his own nest and throne," Ermine holds the lineal and financial future of this traditionally military family in her hands (543). That she can be trusted with her charge seems amply demonstrated by her conduct throughout the prior years of her family's disgrace, her fortune's dissipation, her body's disability, and her immediate society's confinement to the "circumscribed view" afforded by her sitting room and small garden (79). Within the domestic limits of Mackarel Lane, Ermine practices with near ascetic discipline the negative assertions of value discussed in the individual chapters of this book; crucially, though, her individual deserts, by themselves, are not enough to change her or her sister's circumstances. Ermine needs disinterested recognition before she can assume the social place she has already earned by her exquisitely appropriate behavior. With this necessity in mind, one might read *The Clever Woman of the Family* as narrating the characterological developments required for Rachel to be able to perceive, articulate, and thereby secure Ermine's middle-class status. Not only, then, does Yonge's novel reveal the precarious reliance of mid-century men such as Alick and Colin Keith on women's renunciation of masculine authority, it also makes perspicuous the epistemologically fraught nature of a broader middle-class status that could only be warranted by the timely approbation of strategic absences.

In making the representation of McKeon's "sociohistorical condition of status inconsistency" also a problematic inherent to the novelistic re-presentation of a hierarchically unstable society, Yonge demonstrates a fundamental aesthetic congruity with her fellow Reform-era novelists that transcends their at times substantial ideological differences. Thus, one might describe the essential narrative trajectory of *No Name* as positioning Magdalen to be able to affirm the long apparent virtues of Norah even as she shreds the newly rediscovered Trust. In *Felix Holt*, the discursive, physical, and legal trials of Felix similarly teach him to perceive the social worth of Esther Lyon. North's *The City of the Jugglers* arguably seeks to make such individual acts of recognition valid more generally, to show society as a whole how to appreciate the value of genius in the abstract. Finally, Dickens's *Hard Times* provides in Sleary and his fellow itinerants an external vantage already able to appraise social worth once the vagaries of the plot put them in the position to do so. In every case, the final act of recognition appears as both socially requisite and phenomenologically unlikely, except insofar as each writer has subtly molded readers' standards of plausibility through artful fiction.

The novelistic imperative to legitimate middle-class status in this way – through the representationally unstable repudiation of more conventional warrants that would then be recognized as deserving by characters and readers subtly groomed into doing so – waned in the 1880s. A dramatic rise in novel readers brought on by universal state-sponsored primary education and dramatic reductions in printing costs drove the primary target for narrative fiction downmarket, with a corresponding retreat into more abstract and "highbrow" forms by the smaller number of "serious" novelists influenced by the art-for-art's-sake movement. The comparatively more unified mid-century literary culture of middle-class readers supporting predominantly middle-class writers responding to their unique status anxieties had fractured into a recognizably modern portfolio of distinct market segments. With this change in readership came a shift in form, as the more capacious three-decker was replaced by the comparatively tighter one-volume novel, which could rarely afford the loose bagginess required to tease out the complexities of status grounded in absence.

Moreover, by the time the Third Reform Act 1884 added roughly six million working-class voters to the electorate, proportionately reducing the relatively static number of those identified as middle class to a small fraction of the whole, that more affluent, privileged, and increasingly socially-dominant minority had enjoyed a full century of discursive and a half-century of statutory existence. Their moment of existential crisis had passed, and with it the need to define themselves through the repudiation of values ordinarily associated with the upper and lower extremes of the social spectrum. By the 1880s, one could claim a middle-class lineage stretching back four generations and acknowledge the wealth earned by oneself and one's male antecedents through employment in the learned professions or the burgeoning managerial class. Force in its more vulgar forms might still be condemned, but the rise of competitive athletics in public schools, at university, and increasingly in hours of leisure – the Amateur Athletic Association of England was founded in 1880 – allowed for its acceptable social sublimation, while Britain's rising tide of overseas military engagements during the so-called "Scramble for Africa" associated martial prowess with imperial stature. Even statistics grew less objectionable in the 1880s, as mathematicians developed the formulas necessary to produce accurate results from rigorous sampling. Finally, although they continued to be excluded from the electorate, middle-class women occupied a slowly increasing share of the labor market, with the New Woman novels of the 1880s and 1890s offering a productive point of entry into the more fluid norms of gender emerging in the final decades of the nineteenth century. Which is not to say that theories of status primarily focused on places and periods other than Victorian England could not benefit from paying greater attention to the ways in which systems of domination may rely on absence as much as they do presence, but rather that the specific forms of absence explored here may not transfer seamlessly beyond the Age of Reform.

Nor do I mean to imply that, within the chronological and national bounds of this study, such negatively guaranteed forms of middle-class status were confined to the novel. The fact that Yonge focalizes the need of those who occupy the social middle for disinterested recognition through the dramatic return to middle-class status of Ermine Keith, née Williams, calls attention to what I would propose as an alternative and specifically Victorian manifestation of "novelization" and "novelistic usage," namely literary nonfiction prose. Ermine writes under the pseudonym "the Invalid" for the *Traveller's Review*, to which she supplies everything from articles on Maria Edgeworth's *Practical Education* (1798) to lyrical descriptions "of the heather behind the parsonage" (121); she also agrees to contribute, although not under her standard nom-de-plume, to Rachel's fledgling periodical prior to the collapse of the F. U. E. E. Often appearing first in the serious quarterlies patterned after the *Edinburgh Review* or the *Westminster Review*, monthly miscellanies such as *Blackwood's Edinburgh Magazine* or *Fraser's Magazine for Town and Country*, or weekly magazines led by Dickens's *Household Words* and *All the Year Round*, that together comprise Victorian periodical culture – and, in the case of the latter two categories, alongside serialized novels and novellas, including many of those discussed in earlier chapters – the writings of Victorian "higher journalists," social and cultural critics, polemical historians, and intellectual "sages" such as Matthew Arnold, Thomas Carlyle, John Stuart Mill, John Ruskin, Augusta Webster and a host of greater and lesser luminaries sought to shape public opinion through the performance of disinterested earnestness punctuated by rhetorical virtuosity.

Speaking from the position of the educated middle class to the myriad fractions that comprised the normalizing center of Victorian society, these nonfiction authors recursively return to the epistemological complexities of social categorization, frequently invoking the same negative assertions of value that appear in contemporary fiction. I have already cited John Forster's pejorative, conjoined rejection of Americans' "aristocracy of dollars" and Rufus Griswold's anthologized aristocracy of American poets as an exemplary instance – in this case, of the repudiation of constant scrabbling after wealth – that seeks to constitute a particularly English form of middle-class national and literary identity. Eliot's "Address to Working Men" similarly eschews the exercise of force, as expressed in the newly legislated majority of working-class electors – itself figuratively rendered as mob violence in *Felix Holt* – in order to assert the greater worth of a largely middle-class field of culture, all in a periodical context that blurs the distinction between fictional and nonfictional forms.

With a superabundance of novels from which to choose in the preceding chapters, I have self-consciously avoided the numerous additional novelistic nonfictional examples that lay ready to hand in connection with my five central negative assertions of value. A majority of Carlyle's major works, and many of his more occasional essays, for instance, include vituperative repudiations of birth (*Past and Present* [1843]), wealth (*Hudson's Statue* from *Latter-Day Pamphlets* [1851]), force (*Chartism* [1839]), and fact (*Sartor Resartus* [1833–4]), often palimpsestically layered within a single volume and always written in an anti-mechanical style so distinctive it earned the semi-parodic moniker "Carlylese." Arnold's stylistically smoother reaction to the Hyde Park riots that preceded the Second Reform Act, *Culture and Anarchy* (1867–8), most explicitly rejects force as a basis for social worth, but also skewers over-reverence for birth in its critique of upper-class Barbarians, and takes a swipe at the too-utile reliance upon fact by its dim-witted Philistines. And, throughout the period but especially after mid-century, the mounting urgency of the Woman Question prompted a multitude of approaches to the symbolic phallus, from Ruskin's rather straightforward confinement of women to "Queen's Gardens" in *Sesame and Lilies* (1865) to Mill's botanical figuration of women's overdetermination in *The Subjections of Women* (1869) to Webster's sly troubling of masculine authority in her essays from the *Examiner* collected under the deceptive title of *A Housewife's Opinions* (1878).

Doing interpretive justice to even these few examples remains far beyond the scope of a brief afterword. Instead, it is my hope that *Victorian Fictions of the Middle-Class Status* will prompt a broader range of critical interlocutors to reexamine the myriad absences and status anxieties bequeathed to posterity by the Victorians.

Bibliography

Ablow, Rachel. "'One Flesh,' One Person, and the 1870 Married Women's Property Act." *BRANCH: Britain, Representation and Nineteenth-Century History*. Ed. Dino Franco Felluga. Extension of *Romanticism and Victorianism on the Net*. Accessed 8 May 2020. http://www.branch-collective.org/?ps_articles=rachel-ablow-one-flesh-one-person-and-the-1870-married-womens-property-act

Anderson, Amanda. *Tainted Souls and Painted Faces: The Rhetoric of Fallenness in Victorian Culture*. Ithaca: Cornell UP, 1993.

The Annual Register, or a View of the History and Politics for the Year 1838. London: J. G. & F. Rivington, 1839.

The Annual Register, or a View of the History and Politics of the Year 1842. London: J. G. F. & J. Rivington, 1843.

The Annual Register, or a View of the History and Politics of the Year 1844. London: J. G. F. & J. Rivington, 1845.

The Annual Register, or a View of the History and Politics of the Year 1847. London: F. & J. Rivington, 1848.

The Annual Register, or a View of the History and Politics for the Year 1854. London: F. & J. Rivington, 1855.

Armstrong, Nancy. *Desire and Domestic Fiction: A Political History of the Novel*. Oxford: Oxford University Press, 1987.

Atkinson, Diane. *The Criminal Conversation of Mrs Norton*. New York: Random House, 2012.

Auerbach, Nina. "Incarnations of the Orphan." *ELH* 42, no. 3 (1975): 395–419.

Auerbach, Nina. *Private Theatricals: The Lives of the Victorians*. Cambridge: Harvard UP, 1990.

Baird, John D. "'Divorce and Matrimonial Causes': An Aspect of *Hard Times*." *Victorian Studies* 20, no. 4 (1977): 401–12.

Beaumont, Matthew. "Heathcliff's Great Hunger: The Cannibal Other in *Wuthering Heights*." *Journal of Victorian Culture* 9, no. 2 (2004): 137–63.

Berman, Carolyn Vellenga. "'Awful Unknown Quantities': Addressing the Readers in *Hard Times*." *Victorian Literature and Culture* 37, no. 2 (2009): 561–82.

Berman, Carolyn Vellenga. "Undomesticating the Domestic Novel: Creole Madness in *Jane Eyre*." *Genre* 32, no. 4 (1999): 267–96.

Betensky, Carolyn. *Feeling for the Poor: Bourgeois Compassion, Social Action, and the Victorian Novel*. Charlottesville and London: University of Virginia Press, 2010.

Bisla, Sundeep. "Over-Doing Things with Words in 1862: Pretense and Plain Truth in Wilkie Collins's *No Name*." *Victorian Literature and Culture* 38, no. 1 (2010): 1–19.

Bode, Rita. "Power and Submission in *Felix Holt, the Radical*." *SEL: Studies in English Literature, 1500–1900* 35, no. 4 (1995): 769–88.

Bodenheimer, Rosemarie. "*North and South*: A Permanent State of Change." *Nineteenth-Century Fiction* 34, no. 3 (1979): 281–301.

Bolus-Reichert, Christine. "The Foreshadowed Life in Wilkie Collins's *No Name*." *Studies in the Novel* 41, no. 1 (2009): 22–41.

Bourdieu, Pierre. *Distinction: A Social Critique of the Judgment of Taste*. Translated by Richard Nice. Cambridge: Harvard University Press, 1984.

Brantlinger, Patrick. "Dickens and the Factories." *Nineteenth-Century Fiction* 26, no. 3 (1971): 270–85.

Brantlinger, Patrick. *The Spirit of Reform: British Literature and Politics, 1832–1867*. Cambridge, MA: Harvard University Press, 1977.

Briggs, Asa. "The Language of 'Class' in Early Nineteenth-Century England." In *Essays in Labour History: In Memory of G. D. H. Cole 25 September 1889–14 January 1959*, edited by Asa Briggs and John Seville, 43–73. London: Macmillan, 1960.

Brontë, Charlotte. *Jane Eyre*. Edited by Margaret Smith. Oxford: Oxford University Press, 1993.

Brontë, Charlotte. *Shirley*. Edited by Herbert Rosengarten and Margaret Smith. Oxford: Oxford University Press, 1998.

Brontë, Charlotte. *Villette*. Edited by Margaret Smith and Herbert Rosengarten. Oxford: Oxford University Press, 1990.

Browning, Elizabeth Barrett. *Aurora Leigh: Authoritative Text, Backgrounds and Contexts, Criticism*. Edited by Margaret Reynolds. New York: W.W. Norton, 1996.

Browning, Robert. "Essay on Shelley." In *The Complete Works of Robert Browning: With Variant Readings and Annotations*, edited by Roma A. King, Jr., Allan C. Dooley, Harry Krynicky, and Donald Smalley, 135–52. Vol. 5 of *The Complete Works*. Athens: Ohio University Press; Waco: Baylor University Press, 1981.

Browning, Robert and Elizabeth Barrett. *The Letters of Robert Browning and Elizabeth Barrett Browning 1845–1846*. Edited by Robert B. Browning. 2 vols. London: Smith, Elder, 1899.

Budge, Gavin. *Charlotte M Yonge: Religion, Feminism and Realism in the Victorian Novel*. Oxford: Peter Lang, 2007.

Burn, W. L. *The Age of Equipoise: A Study of the Mid-Victorian Generation*. New York: W. W. Norton, 1964.

Butt, John and Kathleen Tillotson. *Dickens at Work*. London: Methuen, 1957

Butwin, Joseph. "*Hard Times*: The News and the Novel." *Nineteenth-Century Fiction* 32, no. 2 (1977): 166–87.

Butwin, Joseph. "The Pacification of the Crowd: From 'Janet's Repentance' to *Felix Holt*." *Nineteenth-Century Fiction* 35, no. 3 (1980): 349–71.

Calvert, Peter. *The Concept of Class: An Historical Introduction*. New York: St. Martin's, 1982.

Cannadine, David. *Class in Britain*. New Haven: Yale University Press, 1998.

Carroll, Alicia. *Dark Smiles: Race and Desire in George Eliot*. Athens: Ohio University Press, 2003.

Carroll, David. "*Felix Holt*: Society as Protagonist." *Nineteenth-Century Fiction* 17, no. 3 (1962): 237–52.

Caserio, Robert. "The Name of the Horse: 'Hard Times,' Semiotics, and the Supernatural." *Novel: A Forum on Fiction* 20, no. 1 (1986): 5–23.

Cazamian, Louis. *The Social Novel in England 1830–1850: Dickens, Disraeli, Mrs Gaskell, Kingsley*. Translated by Martin Fido. London and Boston: Routledge & Kegan Paul, 1973.

Chancellor, Edward. *Devil Take the Hindmost: A History of Financial Speculation*. New York: Farrar Straus Giroux, 1999.

"Charles Dickens." *Blackwood's Edinburgh Magazine* 77, no. 474 (April 1855): 451–66.

Chase, Malcolm. *Chartism: A New History*. Manchester: Manchester University Press, 2007.

Chedzoy, Alan. *A Scandalous Woman: The Story of Carolyn Norton*. London: Allison and Busby, 1992.

Cheshire, Edward. "The Results of the Census of Great Britain in 1851, with a Description of the Machinery and Processes Employed to Obtain the Returns; also an Appendix of Tables of Reference." *Journal of the Statistical Society of London* 17, no. 1 (March 1854): 45–72.

Childers, Joseph W. "Industrial Culture and the Victorian Novel." In *The Cambridge Companion to the Victorian Novel*, edited by Deirdre David, 77–96. Cambridge: Cambridge University Press, 2000.

"The City of the Jugglers; or, Free-trade in Souls." *Tait's Edinburgh Magazine* 17, no. 199 (July 1850): 453–4.

"The City of the Jugglers; or, Free-trade in Souls." *Westminster and Foreign Quarterly Review* 154, no. 1 (October 1850): 266–7.

Clausson, Nils. "Dickens's Genera Mixta: What Kind of a Novel Is *Hard Times*?" *Texas Studies in Literature and Language* 52, no. 2 (2010): 157–80.

Cody, Lisa Forman. "The Politics of Illegitimacy in an Age of Reform: Women, Reproduction, and Political Economy in England's New Poor Law of 1834." *Journal of Women's History* 11, no. 4 (2000): 131–56.

Collins, Wilkie, *The Woman in White*. Edited by Julian Symons. Harmondsworth: Penguin, 1985.
Collins, Wilkie. *No Name*. Edited by Virginia Blain. Oxford: Oxford University Press, 1993.
Colón, Susan E. "Realism and Reserve: Charlotte Yonge and Tractarian Aesthetics." *Women's Writing* 17, no. 2 (2010): 221–35.
Corbett, Mary Jean. "Orphan Stories and Maternal Legacies in Charlotte Brontë." In *Other Mothers: Beyond the Maternal Ideal*, edited by Ellen Bayuk Rosenman and Claudia C. Klaver, 227–47. Columbus: Ohio State UP, 2008.
Corfield, Penelope J. "Class by Name and Number in Eighteenth-Century Britain." In *Language, History and Class*, edited by Penelope J. Corfield, 101–30. Oxford: Basil Blackwell, 1991.
Craig, Randall. *The Narratives of Caroline Norton*. Cham: Palgrave Macmillan, 2009.
Crossick, Geoffrey. "The Emergence of the Lower Middle Class in Britain: A Discussion." In *The Lower Middle Class in Britain 1870–1914*, edited by Geoffrey Crossick, 11–60. New York: St. Martin's, 1977.
Crossick, Geoffrey. "From Gentleman to the Residuum: Languages of Social Description in Victorian Britain." In *Language, History and Class*, edited by Penelope J. Corfield, 150–78. Oxford: Basil Blackwell, 1991.
Dahmane, Razak. "'A Mere Question of Figures': Measures, Mystery, and Metaphor in *Hard Times*." *Dickens Studies Annual* 23 (1994): 137–62.
David, Deirdre. "Rewriting the Male Plot in Wilkie Collins's *No Name*: Captain Wragge Orders an Omelette and Mrs Wragge Goes into Custody." In *Out of Bounds: Male Writers and Gender(ed) Criticism*, edited by Laura Claridge and Elizabeth Langland, 186–96. Amherst: University of Massachusetts Press, 1990.
Davidoff, Leonore and Catherine Hall. *Family Fortunes: Men and Women of the English Middle Class, 1780–1850*. Chicago: The University of Chicago Press, 1987.
Davis, Jim. "Collins and the Theatre." In *The Cambridge Companion to Wilkie Collins*, edited by Jenny Bourne-Taylor, 168–80. Cambridge: Cambridge UP, 2006.
Dawson, Clara. *Victorian Poetry and the Culture of Evaluation*. Oxford: Oxford University Press, 2020.
Delany, Paul. *Literature, Money, and the Market: From Trollope to Amis*. Houndmills: Palgrave, 2002.
Dennis, Barbara. *Charlotte Yonge (1823–1901): Novelist of the Oxford Movement*. Lewiston: Edwin Mellen Press, 1992.
Dickens, Charles. *Barnaby Rudge*. Edited by Gordon Spence. Harmondsworth: Penguin, 1997.
Dickens, Charles. *Dombey and Son*. Edited by Alan Horsman. Oxford: Oxford University Press, 2001.

Dickens, Charles. *Hard Times*. 2nd ed., Edited by George Ford and Sylvère Monod. New York: W. W. Norton, 1990.

Dickens, Charles. *The Letters of Charles Dickens*. 12 vols. Edited by Madeline House, Graham Storey, and Kathleen Tillotson. Oxford: Clarendon Press, 1965–2002.

Dickens, Charles. *Oliver Twist*. Edited by Fred Kaplan. New York: W. W. Norton, 1993.

Dreher, Nan H. "Redundancy and Emigration: The 'Woman Question' in Mid-Victorian Britain." *Victorian Periodicals Review* 26 no. 1 (1993): 3–7.

Dutton, H. I. and J. E. King. *'Ten Per Cent and No Surrender': The Preston Strike, 1853–54*. Cambridge: Cambridge University Press, 1981.

Earle, Peter. *The Making of the English Middle Class: Business, Society and Family Life in London, 1660–1730*. Berkeley and Los Angeles: University of California Press, 1989.

Eliot, George. *Felix Holt, the Radical*. Edited by Fred C. Thomson. Oxford: Oxford University Press, 1988.

Eliot, George. *The George Eliot Letters*. 9 vols. Edited by Gordon S. Haight. New Haven: Yale University Press, 1954–78.

Eliot, George. *The Journals of George Eliot*. Edited by Margaret Harrison and Judith Johnston. Cambridge: Cambridge University Press, 1998.

[Eliot, George]. "Address to Working Men, by Felix Holt." *Blackwood's Edinburgh Magazine* 103, no. 627 (January 1868): 1–11.

Epstein, James and Dorothy Thompson, eds. *The Chartist Experience: Studies in Working-Class Radicalism and Culture, 1830–1860*. London: Macmillan, 1982.

Fasick, Laura. "The Ambivalence of Influence: The Case of Mary Ward and Charlotte Yonge." *English Literature in Transition, 1880–1920* 37, no. 2 (1994): 141–54.

Fermi, Sarah. "A Question of Colour." *Brontë Studies* 40, no. 4 (2015): 334–42.

Fessler, Audrey. "Feminist Social Reform and the Problems with Patriarchy in Charlotte Yonge's *Clever Woman of the Family*." In *Gender and Victorian Reform*, edited by Anita Rose, 46–57. Newcastle upon Tyne: Cambridge Scholars, 2008.

Fiamengo, Janice. "Forms of Suffering in Charlotte Yonge's *The Clever Woman of the Family*." *Victorian Review* 25, no. 2 (2000): 80–105.

Fielding, K. J. and Anne Smith. "*Hard Times* and the Factory Controversy: Dickens vs. Harriet Martineau." *Nineteenth-Century Fiction* 24, no. 4 (1970): 404–27.

Finn, Margot, Michael Lobban, and Jenny Bourne Taylor, eds. *Legitimacy and Illegitimacy in Nineteenth-Century Law, Literature and History*. London: Palgrave Macmillan, 2010.

Flint, Kate, ed. *The Victorian Novelist: Social Problems and Social Change*. London: Croom Helm, 1987.

Floyd, David. *Street Urchins, Sociopaths, and Degenerates: Orphans of Late Victorian and Edwardian Fiction*. Cardiff: University of Wales Press, 2014.

Forster, John. *The Life of Charles Dickens*. Three volumes in two. Boston: James R. Osgood & Company, 1875.

[Forster, John]. "American Poetry." *The Foreign Quarterly Review* 32, no. 64 (January 1844): 291–324.

Frankel, Oz. *States of Inquiry: Social Investigations and Print Culture in Nineteenth-Century Britain and the United States*. Baltimore: Johns Hopkins University Press, 2006.

Freedgood, Elaine. "Souvenirs of Sadism: Mahogany Furniture, Deforestation, and Slavery in *Jane Eyre*." In *Jane Eyre*, edited by Katie R. Peel, 23–49. Ipswitch: Salem Press, 2013.

Gallagher, Catherine. *The Industrial Reformation of English Fiction: Social Discourse and Narrative Forms 1832–1867*. Chicago: The University of Chicago Press, 1985.

Gallagher, Catherine. "The Rise of Fictionality." In *History, Geography and Culture*, edited by Franco Moretti, 336–63. Vol 1 of *The Novel*. Princeton: Princeton University Press, 2006.

Gash, Norman. *Politics in the Age of Peel: A Study in the Technique of Parliamentary Representation 1830–1850*. London: Longman's, Green and Co., 1953.

Gaskell, Elizabeth. *North and South*. Edited by Angus Easson. Oxford: Oxford University Press, 1982.

Gilbert, Pamela K. *Mapping the Victorian Social Body*. Albany: SUNY Press, 2004.

Gilbert, Sandra and Susan Gubar. *The Madwoman in the Attic: The Woman Writer and the Nineteenth-Century Literary Imagination*. New Haven: Yale University Press, 1979.

Gillman, Susan. "Remembering Slavery, Again." *Caribbean Quarterly* 61, no. 4 (2015): 1–19.

Gilmour, Robin. *The Idea of the Gentleman in the Victorian Novel*. London: George Allen & Unwin, 1981.

Glen, Robert. *Urban Workers in the Industrial Revolution*. London: Croom Helm, 1984.

Goldman, Lawrence. "The Origins of British 'Social Science': Political Economy, Natural Science and Statistics, 1830–1835." *The Historical Journal* 26, no. 3 (1983): 587–616.

Goodlad, Lauren M. E. *Victorian Literature and the Victorian State: Character and Governance in a Liberal Society*. Baltimore: Johns Hopkins University Press, 2003.

Goodway, David. *London Chartism 1838–1848*. Cambridge: Cambridge University Press, 1982.

Grass, Sean. "Piracy, Race and Domestic Peril in *Hard Cash*." In *Pirates and Mutineers of the Nineteenth Century: Swashbucklers and Swindlers*, edited by Grace Moore, 181–95. Surrey: Ashgate Publishing, 2011.

Griswold, Rufus S., ed. *The Poets and Poetry of America*. Philadelphia: Carey and Hart, 1842.
Gunn, Simon. *The Public Culture of the Victorian Middle Class: Ritual and Authority in the English Industrial City 1840–1914*. Manchester and New York: Manchester University Press, 2000.
Gunn, Simon and Rachel Bell. *Middle Classes: Their Rise and Sprawl*. London: Cassell & Co., 2002.
Hack, Daniel. *The Material Interests of the Victorian Novel*. Charlottesville and London: University of Virginia Press, 2005.
Hale, Elizabeth. "Disability and the Individual Talent: Adolescent Girlhood in *The Pillars of the House* and *What Katy Did*." *Women's Writing* 17, no. 2 (2010): 343–60.
Hallam, Arthur Henry. "On Some of the Characteristics of Modern Poetry, and on the Lyric Poems of Alfred Tennyson." *The Englishman's Magazine* 1, no. 5 (August 1831): 616–28.
Hansard's Parliamentary Debates. 3rd Series. London: T. C. Hansard, 1831.
"Hard Times." *The Critic*, September 15, 1854: 513.
"Hard Times. For these Times." *Examiner* September 9, 1854: 568–9.
"Hard Times for these Times." *The New Quarterly Review and Digest of Current Literature, British, American, French, and German* 3, no. 12 (October 1854): 489–93.
Harrison, Brian. "The Sunday Trading Riots of 1855." *The Historical Journal* 8, no. 2 (1965): 219–45.
Harrison, Kimberly. "'Come Buy, Come Buy': Sensation Fiction in the Context of Consumer and Commodity Culture." In *A Companion to Sensation Fiction*, edited by Pamela K. Gilbert, 528–39. Oxford: Wiley-Blackwell, 2011.
Heater, Derek. *Citizenship in Britain: A History*. Edinburgh: Edinburgh University Press, 2006.
Heller, Tamar. *Dead Secrets: Wilkie Collins and the Female Gothic*. New Haven: Yale University Press, 1992.
Heywood, Christopher. "Yorkshire Slavery in *Wuthering Heights*." *The Review of English Studies* 38, no. 150 (1987): 184–98.
Hingston, Kylee-Anne. "'Skins to Jump Into': The Slipperiness of Identity and the Body in Wilkie Collins's *No Name*." *Victorian Literature and Culture* 40, no. 1 (2012): 117–35.
Hobsbawm, Eric. "The Example of the English Middle Class." In *Bourgeois Society in Nineteenth-Century Europe*, edited by Jürgen Kocka and Allen Mitchell, 127–50. Oxford: Berg Publishers, 1993.
Hobsbawm, Eric J. and George F. E. Rudé. *Captain Swing: A Social History of the Great English Agricultural Uprising*. New York: Pantheon Books, 1968.
Hochman, Baruch and Ilja Wachs. *Dickens: The Orphan Condition*. Madison: Fairleigh Dickinson University Press, 1999.

Holcomb, Julie L. *Moral Commerce: Quakers and the Transatlantic Boycott of the Slave Labor Economy*. Ithaca: Cornell University Press, 2016.
Hollis, Hilda. "Felix Holt: Independent Spokesman or Eliot's Mouthpiece?" *ELH* 68, no. 1 (2001): 155–77.
Houston, Gail Turley. *From Dickens to* Dracula: *Gothic, Economics, and Victorian Fiction*. Cambridge: Cambridge University Press, 2003.
Hunt, Aeron. *Personal Business: Character and Commerce in Victorian Literature and Culture*. Charlottesville: University of Virginia Press, 2014.
Huskey, Melinda. "*No Name*: Embodying the Sensation Heroine." *Victorian Newsletter* 82 (Fall 1992): 5–13.
Itzkowitz, David C. "Fair Enterprise or Extravagant Speculation: Investment, Speculation, and Gambling in Victorian England." *Victorian Studies* 45, no. 1 (2002): 121–47.
Jackson, Thomas A. *Charles Dickens: The Progress of a Radical*. London: Lawrence and Wisehart, 1937.
Johnson, Patricia E. "*Hard Times* and the Structure of Industrialism: The Novel as Factory." *Studies in the Novel* 21, no. 2 (1989): 128–137.
Johnston, Neil. "The History of the Parliamentary Franchise." House of Commons Library Research Paper 13/14 1 March 2013. Accessed 5 May 2020. https://commonslibrary.parliament.uk/research-briefings/rp13–14/
Jones, Anna. "A Victim in Search of a Torturer: Reading Masochism in Wilkie Collins's *No Name*." *Novel: A Forum on Fiction* 33, no. 2 (2000): 196–211.
Jones, David. *Chartism and the Chartists*. London: Allan Lane, 1975.
Joyce, Patrick. *Work, Society and Politics: The Culture of the Factory in Later Victorian England*. New Brunswick: Rutgers University Press, 1980.
Kearns, Katherine. "A Tropology of Realism in *Hard Times*." *ELH* 59, no. 4 (1992): 857–81.
Kelly, Thomas. "Character in Dickens' Late Novels." *Modern Language Quarterly* 30, no. 3 (1969): 386–401.
Kent, Christopher. "Probability, Reality and Sensation in the Novels of Wilkie Collins." *Dickens Studies Annual* 20 (1991): 259–80.
Kidd, Alana and David Nicholls, eds. *The Making of the British Middle Class? Studies of Regional and Cultural Diversity Since the Eighteenth Century*. Phoenix Mill: Sutton Publishing, 1998.
Kidder, Paulette. "Martha Nussbaum on Dickens's *Hard Times*." *Philosophy and Literature* 33, no. 2 (2009): 417–26.
Kingsley, Charles. *Alton Locke*. Edited by Ernest Rhys. London: J. M. Dent, 1928.
Kingstone, Helen. "The Two Felixes: Narratorial Irony and the Question of Radicalism in *Felix Holt* and 'Address to Working Men, by Felix Holt.'" *George Eliot Review* 44 (2013): 42–9.

Koo, Seung-Pon. "Esther and the Politics of Multiple Tastes in George Eliot's *Felix Holt, the Radical*." *Feminist Studies in English Literature* 19, no. 1 (2011): 65–90.

Kornbluh, Anna. *Realizing Capital: Financial and Psychic Economies in Victorian Form*. New York: Fordham University Press, 2014.

Kucich, John. *Excess and Restraint in the Novels of Charles Dickens*. Athens: University of Georgia Press, 1981.

Lacan, Jacques. "The Signification of the Phallus." In *Écrits: A Selection*, translated by Alan Sheridan, 281–91. London: Tavistock, 1977.

Lamouria, Lanya. "Financial Revolution: Representing British Financial Crisis after the French Revolution of 1848." *Victorian Literature and Culture* 43, no. 3 (2015): 489–510.

Lamouria, Lanya. "North's *The City of the Jugglers* (1850) and the European Revolutions of 1848." *Victorian Newsletter* 115 (Spring 2009): 16–28.

Langer, Gary F. *The Coming of Age of Political Economy, 1815–1825*. New York: Greenwood Press, 1987.

Langland, Elizabeth. *Nobody's Angels: Middle-Class Women and Domestic Ideology in Victorian Culture*. Ithaca: Cornell University Press, 1995.

Leal, Amy. "Affirmative Naming in *No Name*." *Names: A Journal of Onomastics* 52, no. 1 (2004): 3–19.

Leavis, F. R. *The Great Tradition: George Eliot, Henry James, Joseph Conrad*. 5th printing. New York: New York University Press, 1973.

Lesjak, Carolyn. "A Modern Odyssey: Realism, the Masses, and Nationalism in George Eliot's *Felix Holt*." *NOVEL: A Forum on Fiction* 30, no. 1 (1996): 78–97.

Lesjak, Carolyn. *Working Fictions: A Genealogy of the Victorian Novel*. Durham and London: Duke University Press, 2006.

Levene, Alysa, Thomas Nutt, and Samantha Williams, eds. *Illegitimacy in Britain, 1700–1920*. Houndmills: Palgrave Macmillan, 2005.

Levenson, Karen Chase. "'Happiness is not a potato': The Victorian Cultivation of Happiness." *Nineteenth-Century Contexts* 33, no. 2 (2011): 161–9.

Levine, Caroline. *Forms: Whole: Rhythm, Hierarchy, Network*. Princeton & Oxford: Princeton University Press, 2015.

Lewis, Roy and Angus Maude. *The English Middle Classes*. New York: Alfred A. Knopf, 1950.

Life, Allan and Page Life. "North versus North: William North (1825–1854) in Light of New Documentation." *Victorian Newsletter* 115 (Spring 2009): 55–94.

Life, Page, Patrick Scott, and Allan Life. "A Preliminary Checklist of Writing by and about William North (1825–1854)." *Victorian Newsletter* 115 (Spring 2009): 95–114.

Loesberg, Jonathan. "The Ideology of Narrative Form in Sensation Fiction." *Representations* 13 (Winter 1986): 115–38.

Loftus, Donna. "Capital and Community: Limited Liability and Attempts to Democratize the Market in Mid-Nineteenth-Century England." *Victorian Studies* 45, no. 1 (2002): 93–120.
Lonoff, Sue. *Wilkie Collins and His Victorian Readers: A Study in the Rhetoric of Authorship*. New York: AMS Press, 1982.
MacEachen, Douglas B. "Wilkie Collins and British Law." *Nineteenth-Century Fiction* 5, no. 2 (1950): 121–39.
Markovits, Stefanie. *The Crisis of Action in Nineteenth-Century English Literature*. Columbus: Ohio State University Press, 2006.
Marshall, William H. *Wilkie Collins*. New York: Twayne, 1970.
Martineau, Harriet. *The Factory Controversy; A Warning Against Meddling Legislation*. Manchester: A. Ireland and Co., 1855.
McKeon, Michael. *The Origins of the English Novel 1600–1740*. Baltimore: Johns Hopkins University Press, 1987.
Menke, Richard. "Cultural Capital and the Scene of Rioting: Male Working-Class Authorship in *Alton Locke*." *Victorian Literature and Culture* 28, no. 1 (2000): 87–108.
Meyer, Susan L. "Colonialism and the Figurative Strategy of *Jane Eyre*." *Victorian Studies* 33, no. 2 (1990): 247–68.
Michie, Elsie. "From Simianized Irish to Oriental Despots: Heathcliff, Rochester and Racial Difference." *Novel: A Forum on Fiction* 25, no. 2 (1992): 125–40.
Michie, Helena. "'There Is No Friend Like a Sister': Sisterhood as Sexual Difference." *ELH* 56, no. 2 (Summer 1989): 401–21.
Moretti, Franco. *The Bourgeois: Between History and Literature*. London: Verso, 2013.
Moretti, Franco. *The Way of the World: The Bildungsroman in European Culture*. New Edition. London: Verso, 2000.
Morris, Debra. "Maternal Roles and the Production of Name in *No Name*." *Dickens Studies Annual* 27 (1998): 271–86.
Morris, Emily. "Imperfect and Alternative Marriages in Charlotte Yonge's *Heartsease* and *The Clever Woman of the Family*." In *For Better, for Worse: Marriage in Victorian Novels by Women*, edited by Carolyn Lambert and Marion Shaw, 34–45. London: Routledge, 2018.
Morris, Pam. *Dickens's Class Consciousness: A Marginal View*. Houndmills and London: Macmillan, 1991.
Morris, R. J. *Class, Sect and Party: The Making of the British Middle Class, Leeds 1820–1850*. Manchester: Manchester University Press, 1990.
Moruzi, Kristine. "'Never Read Anything That Can at All Unsettle Your Religious Faith': Reading and Writing in the *Monthly Packet*." *Women's Writing* 17, no. 2 (2010): 288–304.
Murdoch, Lydia. *Imagined Orphans: Poor Families, Child Welfare, and Contested Citizenship in London*. Piscataway, NJ: Rutgers University Press, 2006.

Nayder, Lillian, ed. *Dickens, Sexuality, and Gender*. Farnham, Surrey: Ashgate, 2012. Reprinted by Abingdon, Oxford: Routledge, 2016.
"No Name." *The Athenaeum*, no. 1836 (January 3, 1863): 10–11.
"No Name." *Examiner*, no. 2869 (January 24, 1863): 54–5.
"No Name." *The London Review of Politics, Society, Literature, Art, and Science* 6, no. 132 (January 10, 1863): 46–7.
"*No Name* and *Thalatta*." *Saturday Review of Politics, Literature, Science and Art* 15, no. 377 (January 17, 1863): 84–5.
North, William. *The City of the Jugglers; or, Free Trade in Souls: A Romance of the "Golden" Age*. Edited by Patrick G. Scott. Columbia: University of South Carolina Press, 2008 [facsimile reprint of London: H. J. Gibbs, 1850].
    Digital facsimile reprint available from the University of South Carolina University Libraries. Accessed 9 October 2021. https://digital.tcl.sc.edu/digital/collection/access/id/947/
    Annotated critical edition available from COVE. Accessed 9 October 2021. https://editions.covecollective.org/edition/city-jugglers
Norton, Caroline. "To the Editor of the British and Foreign Review" [printed under the heading "Mrs Norton and the British and Foreign Review"]. *Examiner* 1595 (August 26, 1838): 531.
Nunokawa, Jeff. *The Afterlife of Property: Domestic Security and the Victorian Novel*. Princeton: Princeton University Press, 1994.
Nussbaum, Martha. *Poetic Justice: The Literary Imagination and Public Life*. Boston: Beacon Press, 1995.
Nussbaum, Martha C. "The Stain of Illegitimacy: Gender, Law, and Trollopian Subversion." In *Subversion and Sympathy: Gender, Law, and the British Novel*, edited by Martha C. Nussbaum and Alison L. LaCroix, 150–75. Oxford: Oxford UP, 2013.
[Oliphant, Margaret]. "Sensational Novels." *Blackwood's Edinburgh Magazine* 91, no. 552 (May 1862): 564–84.
Orestano, Francesca. "Charles Dickens and the Vertigo of the List: A Few Proposals." *Dickens Quarterly* 28, no. 3 (2011): 205–14.
Peters, Catherine. *The King of Inventors: A Life of Wilkie Collins*. London: Secker & Warburg, 1991.
Peters, Laura. *Orphan Texts: Victorian Orphans, Culture, and Empire*. Manchester: Manchester University Press, 2000.
Peters, Laura. "Popular Orphan Adventure Narratives." In *A Library of Essays on Charles Dickens: Dickens and Childhood*, edited by Laura Peters, 557–75. Farnham: Ashgate, 2012.
Pionke, Albert D. "'Horn-Handed and Pig-Headed': British Reception of *The Poets and Poetry of America*." *Philosophy and Literature* 41, no. 2 (2017): 319–37.
Pionke, Albert D. *Plots of Opportunity: Representing Conspiracy in Victorian England*. Columbus: Ohio State University Press, 2004.

Pionke, Albert D. "Reframing the Luddites: Materialist and Idealist Models of Self in Charlotte Brontë's *Shirley*." *Victorian Review* 30, no. 2 (2004): 81–102.

Pionke, Albert D. *The Ritual Culture of Victorian Professionals: Competing for Ceremonial Status, 1838–1877*. Surrey, UK: Ashgate Publishing, 2013. Reprinted by Abingdon, Oxford: Routledge, 2016.

Plotz, John. *The Crowd: British Literature and Public Politics*. Berkeley: University of California Press, 2000.

"Police." *Examiner* 1721 (Jan 24, 1841): 59–60.

Poovey, Mary. "Covered but Not Bound: Caroline Norton and the 1857 Matrimonial Causes Act." *Feminist Studies* 14, no. 3 (1988): 467–85.

Poovey, Mary. *The Financial System in Nineteenth-Century Britain*. New York and Oxford: Oxford University Press, 2003.

Poovey, Mary. *A History of the Modern Fact: Problems of Knowledge in the Sciences of Wealth and Society*. Chicago: The University of Chicago Press, 1998.

Poovey, Mary. *Uneven Developments: The Ideological Work of Gender in Mid-Victorian England*. Chicago: The University of Chicago Press, 1988.

Poovey, Mary. "Writing about Finance in Victorian England: Disclosure and Secrecy in the Culture of Investment." *Victorian Studies* 45, no. 1 (2002): 17–41.

Porter, Theodore M. *The Rise of Statistical Thinking 1820–1900*. Princeton: Princeton University Press, 1986.

Pykett, Lyn. "Collins and the Sensation Novel." In *The Cambridge Companion to Wilkie Collins*, edited by Jenny Bourne-Taylor, 50–64. Cambridge: Cambridge UP, 2007.

Randall, Adrian. *Before the Luddites: Custom, Community and Machinery in the English Woolen Industry, 1776–1809*. Cambridge: Cambridge University Press, 1989.

Reade, Charles. *Hard Cash. A Matter-of-Fact Romance*. London: Bradbury, Evans, & Co., 1868.

"The Reform Act 1832." The Reform Acts and Representative Democracy. Living Heritage. *UK Parliament*. Accessed May 5, 2020. https://www.parliament.uk/about/living-heritage/evolutionofparliament/houseofcommons/reformacts/overview/reformact1832/.

Review of *The Imposter; or, Born with a Conscience*. *The Critic* 2, no. 46 (November 15, 1845): 576.

Robb, George. *White-Collar Crime in Modern England: Financial Fraud and Business Morality, 1845–1929*. Cambridge: Cambridge University Press, 1992.

Roberts, J. M. *The Mythology of the Secret Societies*. New York: Scribner, 1972.

[Robertson, John]. "Exclusion of Opinions." *London and Westminster Review* 40, no. 1 (April 1838): 45–72.

Rogers, Philip. "My Word Is *Error*." *Dickens Studies Annual* 34 (2004): 329–50.
Ruskin, John. "Unto This Last." *The Cornhill Magazine* 2, no. 8 (August 1860): 155–66.
Russell, Norman. *The Novelist and Mammon: Literary Responses to the World of Commerce in the Nineteenth Century*. Oxford: Clarendon Press, 1986.
Sage, Victor. "Girl Number Twenty Revisited: *Hard Times*'s Sissy Jupe." *Dickens Quarterly* 29, no. 4 (2012): 325–35.
Salmon, Richard. *The Formation of the Victorian Literary Professional*. Cambridge: Cambridge University Press, 2013.
Saunders, Robert. *Democracy and the Vote in British Politics, 1848–1867: The Making of the Second Reform Act*. London: Routledge, 2011.
Savage, Gail. "Caroline Norton (1808–1877): The Injured Wife, Scandal, and the Politics of Feminist Memory." In *Biographical Misrepresentations of British Women Writers: A Hall of Mirrors and the Long Nineteenth Century*, edited by Brenda Ayres, 169–87. Cham: Palgrave Macmillan, 2017.
Saville, John. *1848: The British State and the Chartist Movement*. Cambridge: Cambridge University Press, 1987.
Schacht, Paul. "Dickens and the Uses of Nature." *Victorian Studies* 34, no. 1 (1990): 77–102.
Schmidgen, Wolfram. "Illegitimacy and Social Observation: The Bastard in the Eighteenth-Century Novel." *ELH* 69, no. 1 (2002): 133–66.
Schultze, Clemence. "Absent Fathers and Faithful Wives: Penelope-Figures in the Novels of Charlotte Yonge." In *Odyssean Identities in Modern Cultures: A Journey Home*, edited by Hunter Gardner and Sheila Murnaghan, 64–85. Columbus: The Ohio State University Press, 2014.
Scott, Patrick. "Introducing a 'Lost' Victorian Novel: The Elusive William North and *The City of the Jugglers* (1850)." *Victorian Newsletter* 115 (Spring 2009): 7–15.
Seacole, Mary. *Wonderful Adventures of Mrs Seacole in Many Lands: With an Introductory Preface by W. H. Russell*, edited by W. J. S. Cambridge: Cambridge University Press, 2013 [reprint of London: James Blackwood, 1858].
Seed, John. "From 'Middling Sort' to Middle Class in Late Eighteenth- and Early Nineteenth-Century England." In *Social Orders and Social Classes in Europe since 1500: Studies in Social Stratification*, edited by M. L. Bush, 114–35. London: Longman, 1992.
Showalter, Elaine. *A Literature of Their Own: British Women Novelists from Brontë to Lessing*. Princeton: Princeton University Press, 1977.
Simpson, Vicky. "Selective Affinities: Non-Normative Families in Wilkie Collins's *No Name*." *Victorian Review* 39, no. 2 (2013): 115–28.

Spector, Stephen J. "Monsters of Metonymy: *Hard Times* and Knowing the Working Class." *ELH* 51, no. 2 (1984): 365–84.
Starr, Elizabeth. "Manufacturing Novels: Charles Dickens on the Hearth in Coketown." *Texas Studies in Literature and Language* 51, no. 3 (2009): 317–40.
Stern, Rebecca. "*The City of the Jugglers* and the Limits of Victorian Fiction." *Victorian Newsletter* 115 (Spring 2009): 46–51.
Stigler, Stephen M. *The History of Statistics: The Measurement of Uncertainty before 1900*. Cambridge: Harvard University Press, 1986.
Sturrock, June. "*Emma* in the 1860s: Austen, Yonge, Oliphant, Eliot." *Women's Writing* 17, no. 2 (2010): 324–42.
Sturrock, June. "Something to Do: Charlotte Yonge, Tractarianism, and The Question of Women's Work." *Victorian Review* 18, no. 2 (1992): 28–48.
Sussman, Herbert. "Industrial." In *A New Companion to Victorian Literature and Culture*, edited by Herbert F. Tucker, 249–63. Oxford: Wiley Blackwell, 2014.
Sussman, Herbert. *Victorian Masculinities: Manhood and Masculine Poetics in Early Victorian Literature and Art*. Cambridge: Cambridge University Press, 1995.
Sutherland, John. *Stanford Companion to Victorian Fiction*. Stanford: Stanford University Press, 1989.
Sutherland, John. "Wilkie Collins and the Origin of the Sensation Novel." *Dickens Studies Annual* 20 (1991): 243–58.
Talairach-Vielmas, Laurence. "Victorian Sensational Shoppers: Representing Transgressive Femininity in Wilkie Collins's *No Name*." *Victorian Review* 31, no. 2 (2005): 56–78.
Taylor, Jenny Bourne. "Nobody's Secret: Illegitimate Inheritance and the Uncertainties of Memory." *Nineteenth-Century Contexts* 21, no. 4 (2000): 565–92.
Taylor, Jenny Bourne. "Representing Illegitimacy in Victorian Culture." In *Victorian Identities: Social & Cultural Formations in Nineteenth-Century Literature*, edited by Ruth Robbins and Julia Wolfreys, 119–42. Hampshire and New York: Macmillan and St. Martin's, 1996.
Teichman, Jenny. *Illegitimacy: A Philosophical Examination*. Oxford: Basil Blackwell, 1982.
Thackeray, William Makepeace. *The History of Samuel Titmarsh and the Great Hoggarty Diamond*. London: Bradbury and Evans, 1849.
Thomis, Malcolm I. *The Luddites: Machine-Breaking in Regency England*. Newton Abbot: David and Charles, 1970.
Thomis, Malcolm I., ed. *Luddism in Nottinghamshire*. Thoroton Society Records Series. Vol. 26. London and Chichester: Phillimore, 1972.
Thompson, James. "After the Fall: Class and Political Language in Britain, 1780–1900." *The Historical Journal* 39, no. 3 (1996): 785–806.

Thompson, Scott C. "Character and Life: Sociological Method in George Eliot's Fiction." In *The Socio-Literary Imaginary in 19th and 20th Century Britain: Victorian and Edwardian Inflections*, edited by Maria K. Bachman and Albert D. Pionke, 136–53. London: Routledge, 2019.

Thomson, Fred C. "The Legal Plot in *Felix Holt*." *SEL: Studies in English Literature, 1500–1900* 7, no. 4 (1967): 691–704.

Thorne-Murphey, Leslee. "The Charity Pig: Altruism and Self-Deceit in Charlotte M. Yonge's *The Stokesley Secret; or, How the Pig Paid the Rent*." *Women's Writing* 17, no. 2 (2010): 268–87.

Traver, Teresa Huffman. "'The Ship that Bears through the Waves.'" *Women's Writing* 17, no. 2 (2010): 255–67.

Trollope, Anthony. *The Bertrams*. Edited and introduction by David Skilton. London: The Trollope Society, 1993.

Trollope, Anthony. *Doctor Thorne*. Edited by Ruth Rendell. London: Penguin, 2004.

Trollope, Anthony. *The Three Clerks*. Edited by David Skilton, introduction by N. John Hall. London: The Trollope Society, 1992.

Trollope, Anthony. *The Way We Live Now*. Peterborough: Broadview Press, 2005.

Valint, Alexandra. "Madeira and *Jane Eyre*'s Colonial Inheritance." *Victorian Literature and Culture* 45, no. 2 (2017): 321–39.

Vanden Bossche, Chris R. *Reform Acts: Chartism, Social Agency, and the Victorian Novel, 1832–1867*. Baltimore: Johns Hopkins University Press, 2014.

Vargo, Gregory. *An Underground History of Early Victorian Fiction: Chartism, Radical Print Culture, and the Social Problem Novel*. Cambridge: Cambridge University Press, 2018.

Vernon, John. *Money and Fiction: Literary Realism in the Nineteenth and Early Twentieth Centuries*. Ithaca: Cornell University Press, 1984.

Wagner, Tamara S. "'Everything Was a System with Rachel': Charlotte Yonge's Modern Mothers and Victorian Childrearing Manuals." *VIJ: Victorians Institute Journal* 43 (2015): 41–66.

Wagner, Tamara S. *Financial Speculation in Victorian Fiction: Plotting Money and the Novel Genre, 1815–1901*. Columbus: The Ohio State University Press, 2010.

Wagner, Tamara S. "Introduction – Novelist with a Reserved Mission: The Different Forms of Charlotte Mary Yonge." *Women's Writing* 17, no 2 (2010): 213–20.

Wagner, Tamara S. "'Overpowering Vitality': Nostalgia and Men of Sensibility in the Fiction of Wilkie Collins." *MLQ* 63, no. 4 (2002): 471–500.

Wahrman, Dror. *Imagining the Middle Class: The Political Representation of Class in Britain, c. 1780–1840*. Cambridge: Cambridge University Press, 1995.

Wallech, Steven. "'Class Versus Rank': The Transformation of Eighteenth-Century English Social Terms and Theories of Production." *Journal of the History of Ideas* 47, no. 3 (1986): 409–31.

Walton, Susan. "Charlotte Yonge: Marketing the Missionary Story." *Women's Writing* 17, no. 2 (2010): 236–54.
Weber, Max. *Basic Concepts in Sociology*. Translated by H. P. Secher. New York: The Citadel Press, 1964.
Weber, Max. *Economy and Society: An Outline of Interpretive Sociology*, 3 volumes, edited by Guenther Roth and Claus Wittich. New York: Bedminster Press, 1968.
Weber, Max. *On Charisma and Institution Building*, edited by S. N. Eisenstadt. Chicago: The University of Chicago Press, 1968.
Weinroth, Michelle. "Engendering Consent: The Voice of Persuasion in *Felix Holt, the Radical*." *Victorians Institute Journal* 33 (2005): 7–44.
Weiss, Barbara. *The Hell of the English: Bankruptcy and the Victorian Novel*. Lewisburg: Bucknell University Press, 1986.
Welsh, Alexander. *Dickens Redressed: The Art of* Bleak House *and* Hard Times. New Haven: Yale University Press, 2000.
Welsh, Alexander. *George Eliot and Blackmail*. Cambridge: Harvard University Press, 1985.
Whitley, Edward and Robert Weidman. "The (After) Life of William North among the New York Bohemians." *Victorian Newsletter* 115 (Spring 2009): 29–45.
Williams, Raymond. *Culture and Society 1780–1950*. New York: Columbia University Press, 1983.
Woodmansee, Martha and Mark Osteen, eds. *The New Economic Criticism: Studies at the Intersection of Literature and Economics*. London and New York: Routledge, 1999.
Woods, Livia Arndal. "'What Are They to Do with Their Lives?': Anglican Sisterhoods and Useful Angels in Three Novels by Charlotte Yonge." *Nineteenth-Century Contexts* 27, no. 2 (2015): 147–63.
Wordsworth, William. "Essay, Supplementary to the Preface." In *The Prose Works of William Wordsworth*, 3 volumes, edited by W. J. B. Owen and Jane Worthington Smyser, 3:62–84. Oxford: Oxford University Press, 1974.
Wordsworth, William. Preface to *Lyrical Ballads* (1800). In *The Prose Works of William Wordsworth*, 3 volumes, edited by W. J. B. Owen and Jane Worthington Smyser, 1:118–59. Oxford: Oxford University Press, 1974.
Yonge, Charlotte Mary. *The Clever Woman of the Family*. Edited and introduction by Clare A. Simmons. Peterborough: Broadview, 2001.
Zlotnick, Susan. "'The Law's a Bachelor': Oliver Twist, Bastardy, and the New Poor Law." *Victorian Literature and Culture* 34, no. 1 (2006): 131–46.
Zunshine, Lisa. *Bastards and Foundlings: Illegitimacy in Eighteenth-Century England*. Columbus: The Ohio State University Press, 2005.

Index

Anderson, Amanda, 58n57, 198n4
Arnold, Matthew, 212
Auerbach, Nina, 28, 52n17, 53n23, 56n45

Bank Act, 65
bastard/bastardy, 17, 26–30, 52n14, 57n50, 175
Bedford College for Women, 176
Birmingham Political Union, 103
Bodichon, Barbara Leigh Smith, 177, 205n63
Bourdieu, Pierre, 8, 9, 10–12, 13, 14, 23n38, 24n55, 24n58, 24n60, 132n64, 136
Briggs, Asa, 2, 4, 20n7, 21n21
Brontë, Charlotte, 53n23, 192
  Jane Eyre, 17, 31–2, 34, 53n23, 53n25, 54n30, 178, 179–80, 182, 201n26
  Shirley, 18, 105, 108–9, 113, 178, 180, 200n23, 201n25
  Villette, 19, 142–4, 146, 166n32, 178, 180–1, 201n27, 201n29
Brontë, Emily, 26
Browning, Elizabeth Barrett, 17
  Aurora Leigh, 17, 19, 142, 144–6, 147
  "The Cry of the Children," 145
Browning, Robert, 16–17, 167n45
Bubble Act, 63
Cabet, Étienne, 79, 146,

Cannadine, David, 4, 20n2, 21n18
Carlyle, Thomas, 78, 79, 89, 91n2, 96n64, 212
Catholic Emancipation Act, 102, 106
Chartism, 76, 78, 81, 91n2, 100, 103–4, 105, 106, 109, 110, 111, 124, 128n12, 128n13, 130n21, 131n45, 131n47
Collins, Wilkie, 55n39, 57n47, 58n54, 192, 202n39, 203n46, 203n53
  No Name, 17, 30, 35–51, 54n37, 55n39, 55n40, 55n42, 57n48, 58n56, 178, 182, 183–4
  The Woman in White, 17, 33–5, 36, 54n31, 178, 182–3
colonialism, 25n83, 53n25, 127n1, 133n75, 164n19, 206n69, 211
  see Indian Mutiny
Combination Acts, 102
Companies Act, 65
Company Act, 63, 64
Contagious Diseases Acts, 19, 178
Corfield, Penelope, 4, 20n7, 21n16
Corn Laws, 6, 65
Custody of Infants Act, 176, 199n11

days of May riots, 103
Defoe, Daniel, 27, 62
Dickens, Charles, 15, 16, 25n76, 30, 52n17, 57n47, 66, 69, 85, 100, 198n3, 211

Barnaby Rudge, 18, 105, 106–8, 113, 129n19
Bleak House, 26
Dombey and Son, 18, 69, 70, 72, 94n31, 95n48
Great Expectations, 35
Hard Times, 19, 142, 148–62, 173–5, 210
Little Dorrit, 69
Martin Chuzzlewit, 25n76, 69
Oliver Twist, 17, 30–1, 33, 52n18, 53n19
Pickwick Papers, 172n95
A Tale of Two Cities, 34
Disraeli, Benjamin, 75, 88, 100, 105, 151
Divorce and Matrimonial Causes Bill, 174

Education Act, 178
Eliot, George, 100, 116, 132n68, 132n69, 133n70, 133n73, 163n3, 192, 203n53
Adam Bede, 26
"Address to Working Men, by Felix Holt," 18, 136–7, 163n2, 212
Felix Holt: The Radical, 18, 106, 113–27, 131n61, 132n65, 132n67, 136, 162n1, 178, 184–5
Romola, 113
English Woman's Journal, 177, 205n63
European revolutions of 1848, 76, 84, 96n61, 110

Factory Acts, 176
First Reform Act, 5, 22n23, 99, 101, 127n4, 175, 198n6 *see* First Reform Bill
First Reform Bill, 1, 5, 6, 22n25, 100, 124 *see* First Reform Act

Forster, John, 14–16, 25n70, 25n76, 148, 168n67, 212
Fourier, Charles, 79, 145, 146

Gaskell, Elizabeth, 100, 148, 192
North and South, 18, 105, 111–13, 178, 181–2, 185, 201n31, 202n35
Ruth, 26
Gilmour, Robin, 7–8, 41
Girton College Cambridge, 178
Gladstone, William Ewart, 64, 105, 146
Glasgow Spinners Union, 103, 106, 128n11
Goodlad, Lauren, 7–8, 23n38, 41
Griswold, Rufus, 14–15, 25n76, 212
Gunn, Simon, 5, 20n10, 21n20, 22n30, 22n33, 23n34, 23n36, 23n38

Hegel, Georg Wilhelm Friedrich, 75, 77, 78, 79
Hobsbawm, Eric, 4, 21n17, 128n10
Hudson, George, 65, 69, 80, 92n12, 212
Hunt, Aeron, 23n37, 24n65
Hyde Park demonstration, 105, 124, 212

Indian Mutiny, 94n42, 188, 206n69

Joint Stock Companies Act, 65
Joint Stock Companies Amendment Act, 65

Kingsley, Charles, 100, 113
Alton Locke, 18, 105, 109–11, 113, 130n38, 131n45, 131n47, 132n64

Lady Margaret Hall Oxford, 178
Langham Place Group, 177, 189, 205n63, 205n66
Lesjak, Carolyn, 131n61, 131n63, 134n81, 203n49
Levine, Caroline, 20n1, 22n25
Limited Liability Act, 65, 73, 93n15
Luddism, 102, 108, 109, 128n9, 130n31, 201n26

McKeon, Michael, 3, 41, 91, 209
Married Women's Property Act, 19, 177, 178, 200n16
Martineau, Harriet, 137, 141, 169n73, 169n77
Marx, Karl, 75, 78, 79
Matrimonial Causes Act, 177, 200n15
Mill, John Stuart, 178, 212
Mines and Collieries Act, 176
Mississippi Bubble, 62, 69, 71, 92n3 *see* South Sea Bubble
Municipal Corporations Act, 199n8
Murdoch, Lydia, 28, 29, 52n16, 52n18

Napoleonic wars, 5, 21n21, 63, 102, 119, 201n26
National Reform League, 105, 124
National Society for Women's Suffrage, 19
negative assertion of value, 4, 12–17, 19, 25n83, 30, 41, 50, 93n27, 175, 179, 209, 212
New Model unions, 104, 105, 112
New Poor Law *see* Poor Law Amendment Act
Nightingale, Florence, 177
North, William, 75, 97n80, 98n83
  The City of the Jugglers, 18, 67, 74–91, 99–100, 151, 210
Northcote-Trevelyan Report, 146

Norton, Caroline, 176, 178, 199n9, 199n10, 200n15

orphans/orphanhood, 17, 26–30, 51n1, 52n7, 52n8, 52n16, 67, 102, 175

Peters, Laura, 28, 29, 31
Plotz, John, 130n29, 130n34, 200n22
political economy, 137, 138, 140, 141, 142, 149, 151, 164n10, 165n22, 165n24, 165n28, 166n30
Poor Law Amendment Act, 29, 30, 31, 52n14, 90, 101, 102, 140, 159, 175, 199n8
Poovey, Mary, 19, 80, 91n1, 92n9, 92n11, 92n14, 96n60, 137, 158, 163n8, 164n14, 164n17, 165n24, 198n4, 200n15
positivism, 116, 132n68, 137
Preston strike, 104–5, 112, 129n15, 148, 149, 157, 158
Pykett, Lyn, 55n39, 57n48, 59n59, 59n63

Quételet, Adolphe, 138, 140, 142, 143, 164n21, 165n23
Queen's College London, 176

Railway Act, 64
Railway Mania, 64–5, 69, 72, 73, 80, 92n10, 92n13
Reade, Charles, 203n53
  Hard Cash, 18, 70–3, 94n42, 95n47
Report of the Select Committee on Combinations, 103, 106
Ruskin, John, 89, 148, 212

Sadleir, John, 66, 69, 93n17, 168n65
Seacole, Mary, 199n14

Second Reform Act, 18, 105, 129n17, 136, 178, 185, 212 *see* Second Reform Bill
Second Reform Bill, 124 *see* Second Reform Act
Shelley, Percy, 18, 76, 83, 87
slavery, 51n2, 77, 93n22, 96n64, 122, 133n75
Somerville College Oxford, 178
South American bubble, 63–4, 67, 71
South Sea Bubble, 62–3, 69, 71, 92n4, 92n5 *see* Mississippi Bubble
statistics, 19, 137–8, 139, 140, 141, 144, 146, 160, 164n21, 165n26, 211
"surplus" women, 19, 174, 192, 197n1
Sussman, Herbert, 54n33, 128n7

Taylor, Jenny Bourne, 27, 28, 29, 53n19
Test and Corporations Act, 102
Thackeray, William Makepeace, 66, 150
  The History of Samuel Titmarsh and the Great Hoggarty Diamond, 18, 67–9, 71, 93n24
Third Reform Act, 178, 210
Trollope, Anthony, 66
  The Bertrams, 168n59
  Doctor Thorne, 17, 32–3, 34, 53n28, 54n29, 54n30
  The Three Clerks, 19, 142, 146–8, 167n58, 168n61, 168n62, 168n65
  The Way We Live Now, 18, 73–74, 95n54

Utilitarianism, 3, 19, 21n21, 137–8, 140, 141, 144, 165n28

Vanden Bossche, Chris, 22n23, 100, 124, 128n12, 130n21, 131n53, 131n61, 198n6
Vestries Act, 199n7

Wagner, Tamara, 56n42, 59n63, 74, 91n1, 92n3, 92n4, 92n14, 94n39, 97n81, 185, 202n39, 204n54, 204n55
Wahrman, Dror, 5–6, 22n30
Weber, Max, 8–10, 11, 12, 13, 14, 18, 23n38, 23n41, 24n46, 75, 79, 83, 90, 96n66
Webster, Augusta, 212, 213
Welsh, Alexander, 138–9, 148, 149, 164n13, 164n18, 165n27
West Middlesex Life and Fire Assurance Company, 64, 68, 69, 93n24
Wordsworth, William, 16, 17, 165n28
"Woman Question," 174, 177, 179, 212 *see* "surplus" women

Yonge, Charlotte, 186, 193, 203n53, 204n55, 204n57, 205n64, 206n72, 207n77, 207n79
  The Clever Woman of the Family, 19, 179, 185–97, 204n54, 205n63, 209, 211

Zlotnick, Susan, 31, 52n18
Zunshine, Lisa, 27, 51n6

EU representative:
Easy Access System Europe
Mustamäe tee 50, 10621 Tallinn, Estonia
Gpsr.requests@easproject.com

www.ingramcontent.com/pod-product-compliance
Lightning Source LLC
Chambersburg PA
CBHW070346240426
43671CB00013BA/2418